THE CULMINATION OF PICKETT'S CHARGE ON THE THIRD DAY OF THE BATTLE OF GETTYSBURG

From a painting by Gayle Hoskins, adapted from the Cyclorama at Gettysburg, painted by Paul Philippoteaux, of France.

THEY MET AT GETTYSBURG

by

EDWARD J. STACKPOLE

STACKPOLE BOOKS

Harrisburg, Pennsylvania

THEY MET AT GETTYSBURG

First Printing, September 1956
Second Printing, October 1956
Third Printing, November 1956
Fourth Printing, October 1959
Fifth Printing, June 1966
Sixth Printing, October 1969
Second Edition (*paperback*), October 1978
Third Edition (*paperback*), February 1982
Third Edition (*paperback*), second printing, October 1982
Third Edition (*paperback*), third printing, April 1984
Third Edition (*paperback*), fourth printing, April 1986

Published by
STACKPOLE BOOKS
Cameron and Kelker Streets
P.O. Box 1831
Harrisburg, Pa. 17105

ISBN: 0-8117-2089-6
Library of Congress Catalog Card Number: 56-13070

Printed in the U.S.A.

ACKNOWLEDGMENTS

Grateful acknowledgment for encouragement and assistance in the task of putting this book together is made to those friends and associates who have so patiently fanned the spark of effort until it broke into steady flame:

Meade D. Detweiler, III, who originated the idea and was steadfast in his support throughout all phases of preparation and execution.

Edgar Z. Wallower, a perceptive student of the Battle of Gettysburg, who made many constructive suggestions, eliminated split-infinitives and other oddities, and was generally most helpful in critiquing the manuscript.

Henry M. Scharf, who lives in, "presides over," and with one notable recent exception is perhaps the best known citizen of Gettysburg, Pennsylvania, for many helpful assists in checking the work and bringing incidents into focus.

Dr. Frederick Tilberg, National Park Service Historian, and J. Melchoir Sheads, Ranger-Historian, both Gettysburg National Military Park, for careful reviews of the manuscript and invaluable help in correcting errors of fact. Dr. Tilberg also made available rare photographs from originals by Brady and Tipton, and Bachelder maps used in locating units during the battle. His assistance in correctly spotting terrain features and troop dispositions was invaluable.

Miss Nellie B. Stevens, The General Librarian, Pennsylvania State Library, Harrisburg, for her valuable assistance in locating and making available official War Department and Confederate maps which were developed for and used in the Gettysburg campaign. These maps have been employed in this book as a basis for several of the situation maps and the endpapers.

Colonel Wilbur S. Nye, U.S.A. (Ret.), an editorial associate, for smoothing out many rough edges in the manuscript, and for his thorough, time-consuming research in accomplishing the laborious task of spotting troop positions on the illustrative tactical maps, in successfully prospecting for suitable illustrations, and in preparing the index.

Ray D. Snow, a life-long friend and business associate, for his effective work in drawing the tactical maps and creating the dust jacket.

Appleton-Century-Crofts, Inc., New York publishers, for their gracious permission to reproduce at will selected subjects from among the many superb illustrations used in the classic *Battles and Leaders of the Civil War,* originally published in 1884 by the Century Company, and revived in an abridged one-volume edition in the fall of 1956.

William Sloane Associates, New York; Charles Scribner's Sons, New York; and Yale University Press, New Haven, for their courteous permission to use certain direct quotes from copyrighted material appearing in their published works.

Finally, to Cora Martin Weeber, my long-suffering and extremely capable secretary of more years than either of us will admit to, for her painstakingly accurate conversion of dictated notes and scribbled hieroglyphics, over and over again, into a legible document for the printer.

The editors of the third edition of *They Met at Gettysburg* wish to express their thanks to Col. Jacob M. Sheads, of Gettysburg, for his generous assistance in the process of updating and correcting the original 1956 text.

TABLE OF CONTENTS

PROLOGUE TO THE
THIRD EDITION

Since Edward J. Stackpole's THEY MET AT GETTYSBURG first appeared in 1956, several notable books about the campaign and battle of Gettysburg have been published. One—a novel—won a Pulitzer Prize. Another, a scholarly study with appropriate footnotes, received critical praise from academics. For those Civil War buffs who like their history sliced very thin, there was a well-researched study of Lee's invasion of the North up to the opening of the battle and another of the interplay between Lee and James Longstreet on the field. Still another book consisted of photographs taken on the scene after the battle, plus thoughtful commentary.

Each of these books has its specialized value, but for ordinary folk who want to learn what happened at Gettysburg and why, in unadorned language, THEY MET AT GETTYSBURG remains the perfect answer. Long a student of military history, General Stackpole studied the battle carefully, walked over the terrain, consulted maps, talked to authorities, formed his own opinions and wrote his story without frills. No wonder his work has gone through so many editions.

I owe both the General and his book a special debt. Soon after moving to Pennsylvania to write editorials for the Harrisburg *Patriot News*, late in 1956, I was stricken by a virus. A fellow newspaperman and neighbor lent me his copy of THEY MET AT GETTYSBURG as I was recuperating. With my resistance already lowered by one virus, I fell easy prey to a secondary infection: Civil War mania. Captivated by the book and its excellent maps, I could hardly wait for the return of good health and warm weather so that I could tour the battlefield at Gettysburg. First the battle and then the Civil War in general became an obsession after that, leading to my joining with L. E. Smith of Gettysburg in founding CIVIL WAR TIMES as a hobby sheet for Civil War buffs.

General Stackpole wrote an article for our second issue on the subject of his third book, the battle of Chancellorsville. A year later with our little magazine getting to be too much to handle part-time, Mr. Smith and I persuaded the General to join us in forming a company, Historical Times, Inc., to publish CIVIL WAR TIMES and, eventually, three other magazines of history. Until his death in 1967, the General and I were business associates and friends. He was a remarkable man. When most men would have been in retirement, he wrote five books on the Civil War and continued to oversee the activities of his publishing, printing and broadcasting companies.

Here is a part of the tribute our AMERICAN HISTORY *Illustrated* paid him upon his death in 1967:

> To everyone except for a few of his contemporaries, he was "the General." It was unthinkable to call him anything else.
>
> His military title was well earned. Fresh out of Yale, he served in World War I as a company commander in the 110th Infantry, 28th Division. He was wounded three times, the last time so seriously that he was hospitalized for nearly two years. Among his decorations was the Distinguished Service Cross.
>
> After the war he joined the Pennsylvania National Guard and eventually became its commanding general. Although he was a genuine hero and a dedicated citizen-soldier, he was far more than just a military leader.
>
> The General was Edward J. Stackpole, publisher of this magazine, who died last month at 73. Until very near the end he was active in the affairs of Historical Times, Inc., and in a wide variety of other business and civic interests. To all of them he brought a keen, logical mind and strong common

sense. He also brought a calm presence, an indefinable spirit that inspired confidence. He was a natural leader of men.

The General's interest in Gettysburg really was life-long. A book published to commemorate the 50th anniversary of the battle, in 1913, includes a photograph of several Civil War veterans posing with two lanky youths, Edward J. Stackpole and his brother Albert H. Fifty years later, at the Centennial of the battle, the General was back as a very active member of the official commission for the observance. He, too, had the Civil War virus, and I am grateful to him for passing it on.

THEY MET AT GETTYSBURG may not affect the lives of all who read it as it did mine, but there is not a better introductory book about the greatest battle ever fought in the Western Hemisphere. I am glad it is being kept in print.

—Robert H. Fowler
Chairman of the Board
Historical Times, Inc.

PROLOGUE TO THE
FIRST EDITION

"It's all my fault, I thought my soldiers were invincible!"

It was a great general and even greater man who spoke thus feelingly from the fullness of his heart to the hurt, bewildered survivors of Pickett's Charge as they stumbled back to the protection of Seminary Ridge on that sultry afternoon of Friday, July 3, 1863.

The noble character of Robert E. Lee was never more clearly revealed than it was at Gettysburg that day. His outwardly calm, measured reaction to his first major disaster on the battlefield did more, however, than merely add luster to his already assured niche in the Hall of Fame. His words afford one very convincing explanation of the Confederate failure—a mistaken sense of invincibility. And whose evaluation merits a higher acceptance than that of the Commanding General of the invading forces, who planned and directed the campaign, held the initiative throughout, and at the end had the moral courage to take on his own broad shoulders the full responsibility for the failure?

The myth of Southern military invincibility, built up by early Confederate successes, had endured for more than two years. It was shattered at Gettysburg in three days. Psychological warfare was not known by that name during the Civil War, but something analogous to it was surely a factor during the first half of the war, when the general officers on both sides, in the eastern theater at least, became increasingly infected with the germ of Lee-Jackson infallibility. And when one recalls first Manassas, the Peninsula, the battles before Richmond, Jackson's Shenandoah Valley campaigns, second Manassas, Fredericksburg, Chancellorsville, and a host of lesser engagements, the "myth" had considerable foundation in fact.

There were numerous factors that contributed to the monotonous series of defeats chalked up against the Federal troops in the early years of the war: draft dodging, lack of united public support in the North, a business-as-usual attitude, over-confidence, to mention but a few. Topping them all, however, and of major importance was the consistently inadequate and inept generalship of the Federal army command, from McDowell and McClellan, Pope and Burnside, down to Hooker, whose euphemistic title of "Fighting Joe" ran out of justification in 1863 almost as rapidly as his organizational ability restored the morale and logistical health of the Army of the Potomac after the bungling and destructive antics of the ill-fated Ambrose Burnside.

The Civil War was half over when the Battle of Gettysburg was fought, and although nearly one hundred years have passed since that historic event, the world still beats a path to the scene of the sanguinary three-day struggle that so vitally affected the course of history.

Why is this so? Is it because approximately fifty thousand American boys, some 30 percent of the combined combat elements of the opposing armies, were listed as casualties—killed, wounded, or missing? Or because Gettysburg marked the turn of the tide which up to then had run so strongly in favor of the Confederacy? Or is it because of the intriguing and dramatic character of the battle, on the outcome of which the fate of a nation hung by such a slender thread?

Serious students of the Civil War agree that with Gettysburg, concurrently with Vicksburg, Confederate hopes of all-out intervention by Britain and France had evaporated. After more than two years of fumbling the North was given, with a double taste of ultimate victory, a lift that was badly needed to create a united front founded on tangible realities.

The War between the States was strictly a family affair, the first and only major internal passage at arms in which this country has engaged. The principal contribution of the small Regular Army was through the personnel of the professional officer corps, chiefly in the higher command positions. For this they were qualified in the main solely through the educational processes of training at West Point and a handful of excellent private military institutions, such as the Virginia Military Institute, and by limited observation of certain wars between foreign countries. The Mexican War provided a modicum of field experience for a few, but the number was negligible as a percentage of the whole.

The war that for all time cemented the bonds of America's disunited federation of separate states into a homogeneous and united nation was essentially a war between civilians in uniform, most of them without previous military training. The United States has never been a country that chose war as an instrument of national policy, or at least that is what we Americans have been taught to believe. The history of our wars testifies indisputably to the fact that they have been fought largely by citizen soldiers of varying degree of trained competence. In 1861-

1865 there was little fundamental difference between the raw soldier material of the opposing sides. The difference lay principally in the manner in which the material was moulded, conditioned, and led.

The rich industrial North from beginning to end had a decided advantage over the economically poor, predominantly agricultural South, both in resources and manpower. But the South waged a crusading all-out type of war, made the most of its inferior resources, developed military leaders who outfought the North at every turn during the first part of the war, and came dangerously close to winning it in the year 1863.

Conversion from peace to war came more naturally to the South, by temperament, outdoor living habits, the breeding and love of horses and horsemanship, individual skill with firearms—in almost every category except that of furnishing the sinews of war, in which latter the North excelled both in resources and craftsmanship. The mass of manpower in the North had become acclimated to an industrial way of life which developed a race of indoor workers, office and mechanical. Therefore it took a long, long time and a narrow escape from crushing defeat to jolt the people of the North into a realization that this was *their* fight after all.

Only then, with aggressive military leadership, disregard of excessive battle casualties, and a belated recognition and utilization of the inventive genius of the best gunsmiths in the world, did the tide turn in favor of the North. The crest was reached on Cemetery Ridge, just south of a small, otherwise unknown, Pennsylvania crossroads community named Gettysburg. Thereafter it receded slowly but inexorably until the grinding forces of attrition reached Appomattox Court House, Virginia, where General Lee surrendered to General Grant on Palm Sunday, April 9, 1865.

Gettysburg's place in the history of American arms is well established, and properly so, even though the Gettysburg fight was but one of 892 major and more than 5,000 minor battles or engagements that occurred during the four years of the Civil War. However, it is significant that almost five per cent of the Union losses in the entire war were incurred during the Gettysburg campaign. One out of every eighteen of the free male population of the United States, of an age to bear arms, fought there. Eighteen states were represented in the Union army, twelve in the Confederate. The Army of the Potomac comprised a total of 287 regiments of infantry and cavalry and 73 batteries of field artillery, for a total of 360 organizations, almost half of which were from New York and Pennsylvania; against 214 infantry and cavalry regiments and 69 artillery batteries in the Army of Northern Virginia, for a total of 283.

Whatever the reasons may be for the surprisingly wide appeal that the Gettysburg campaign continues to have for generation after generation, the fact remains that millions of words, photographs, and maps of the battle have been published about it since the little town of Gettysburg achieved immortality. That the flow still continues is impressive in face of the fact that the United States has subsequently engaged in four major wars, two of them on a global scale, since the Civil War passed into history.

For those who would take Gettysburg apart, piece by piece, the source records are adequate, with the possible exception of Confederate strength and casualty reports. Firsthand accounts of the various phases of the battle, written by the leading participants who were not killed or did not die of wounds, have long been available to the historian. Military experts, observers, reporters, and writers have had their say. Novelists have dramatized, and occasionally exaggerated, the impact on history of their respective heroes.

The following account of Lee's invasion of Pennsylvania in June and the culminating battles of Gettysburg during the first three days of July 1863, has been written from a sense of quasi-frustration on the part of the author. For many years he has lived in the vain hope that some-one, better qualified than himself, would take the time and trouble to harvest the rich fields of Gettysburgiana, sift the chaff from the wheat, and assemble the kernels.

To achieve the result of a continuous panorama, un-cluttered by the minutiae of organizational detail, has been the objective to which this writer has addressed him-self. Disclaiming any attempt at originality, his project has been simply to read extensively, assemble the major facts, analyze them carefully, and put them in consecutive order on a time and space background. He has had the added advantage of having always lived near the site of the battle, and has spent much time on the ground, mentally placing each unit in its proper place on the ter-rain, and recreating in his mind the flow and ebb of the opposing forces. He trusts the resulting picture will be reasonably clear to the reader.

—E.J.S.
1956

THE GETTYSBURG BATTLEFIELD, LOOKING NORTH

Had General Lee or General Meade been able to make an aerial reconnaissance on the morning of July 3, 1863, this is generally the way Gettysburg and the surrounding country-side would have appeared to them. However, this is a photograph of an accurate relief map in the office of the National Military Park, Gettysburg, the map having been made in 1903 from a 1901 survey.

The strip of round cord laid along the "fishhook" position of the Federals, from Culp's Hill on the north to the Round Tops on the south, is not the exact trace of Meade's posi-tion; it is the location of the present National Park avenues (Slocum, Hancock, Sedgwick, and Sykes) which closely follow that position. The next line to the left, covering generally the Peach Orchard and the Devil's Den area, indicates Sickles' advance position on the afternoon of July 2. The line running from the south to the north along Seminary Ridge, then curving around to the east through the town, is the line of the Confederate battle positions on both July 2 and 3, 1863. To the northwest and north of Gettysburg are, respectively, Buford's position and Howard's position on July 1 before he was driven back towards Cemetery Hill. The line farthest to the northwest is that on which Hill's first units deployed for their advance on the morning of July 1.

Other key localities are identified by numbers, as follows:

1. Chambersburg Pike bridge over Willoughby Run, where the initial clash occurred on July 1. 2. McPherson's farm and woods. 3. Railway cuts. 4. Seminary. 5. Oak Hill. 6. Carlisle Road. 7. Harrisburg Road bridge over Rock Creek. 8. Hanover Road. 9. Culp's Hill. 10. Cemetery Hill. 11. Bloody Angle. 12. Codori's house on Emmitsburg Road. 13. Peach Orchard. 14. Wheatfield. 15. Trostle's. 16. Devil's Den. 17. Big Round Top. 18. Little Round Top. 19. Point on Seminary Ridge from which Lee watched Pickett's Charge. 20. Meade's headquarters on Taneytown Road. 21. Baltimore Pike. 22. Spangler's farm. 23. Spangler Wood.

CONFEDERATE INFANTRY ON THE MARCH

CHAPTER 1

LEE TAKES THE OFFENSIVE

THE STORY of the Battle of Gettysburg actually begins in Virginia, after Lee's defeat of Hooker at Chancellorsville, when the hopes of the Confederacy were high and the morale of the North correspondingly low.

The brief interval between the battles of Chancellorsville and Gettysburg was destined for the Confederacy to be in retrospect the brightest period of the war. Victory after victory had been won in the first two years, with Chancellorsville the crowning touch, and with such regularity that the Southern troops had come to hold the Federals in utter contempt.

As of early June 1863 the Confederate rank and file had reached the zenith of military self-assurance. This in turn led quite naturally to a state of overconfidence, despite Lee's own appraisal of Chancellorsville as a battle in which his army lost thirteen thousand men, failed to gain any

1

ground, and was unable to pursue the enemy. Just the same, the South was riding the crest, while Lincoln was still hopefully changing generals in the search for one who could and would "go forward and give us victories"; but the future of the Union was indeed dark.

Strategic Background of the Campaign

In Lee's opinion the time was opportune for a bold stroke which might win the war for the South in a few short weeks. The general, an engineer and skilled tactician but an indifferent quartermaster, was painfully aware of the logistical shortcomings and the shrinking manpower of the Confederacy. The distinguished British General Fuller has called him one of the worst quartermasters in history, and it is an historical fact that the Confederate troops were notoriously badly served logistically. Food and clothing were always in short supply and it was common saying among the soldiers that "one of the principal objects in killing a Yankee was to get his boots."

There was a dearth of cavalry and artillery horse replacements; other requirements were difficult to fulfill because the Southern railroads were neither efficient nor strategically located; the Southern economy was wavering; and Confederate affairs in the west were in serious shape, with Grant besieging Pemberton in Vicksburg and Bragg in trouble keeping Rosecrans from advancing further in eastern Tennessee.

The campaigns of the first two years in the east had been fought mostly on Virginia soil and the strain was beginning to tell. But recognition by England and France was still a definite possibility, with all the advantages such backing would entail.

All these factors pointed to the advisability of carrying the fight to the North with the added advantage of relieving the pressure on Richmond and imposing it on Washington, Baltimore, and Philadelphia. The Army of the Potomac had understandingly become somewhat demoralized after Fredericksburg and Chancellorsville. It was no secret that there was a growing division of Northern sentiment with respect to the conduct and continuance of the war.

Collaterally, and not the least of the advantages to be gained by a successful invasion of Maryland and Pennsylvania was the serious threat to Washington, about which the Lincoln Administration was perennially jittery. Such a campaign could well have the effect of recalling not only the Army of the Potomac from Virginia soil, but also some of the troops from the west, with resultant lifting of the pressure on Vicksburg and Chattanooga.

Everything added up to the desirability of taking the calculated risk of a full-scale invasion. And so it was decided. Plans were laid, directives issued, and the Army reorganized from two to three corps, following Stonewall Jackson's accidental wounding and subsequent death at the hands of a reconnaissance party of his own troops as he was returning in the darkness to his own lines west of Chancellorsville. The Southern papers rejoiced audibly over the coming shift to the offensive. No apparent effort was made to keep the campaign a secret, possibly because the high command was so supremely confident of success. In any event, the Richmond and other newspapers advertised the forthcoming invasion weeks in advance, boasting of the manner in which they would fatten on the spoils to be taken from the prosperous farmers and full storehouses of the North.

Stuart's cavalry corps was accordingly assembled in the Culpeper-Brandy Station area to cover the shift of Lee's main body from Fredericksburg to Culpeper in prepara-

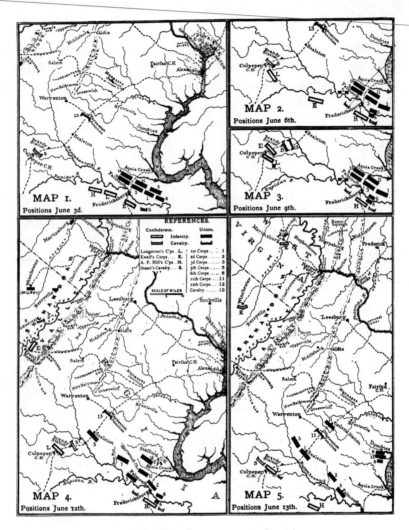

Maps 1-5. THE START OF THE CAMPAIGN

Map 1 shows the Union and Confederate corps facing each other across the Rappahannock subsequent to the Chancellorsville campaign. Map 2 shows the beginning of the Confederate concentration at Culpeper C.H., covered by Stuart's cavalry. Map 3 illustrates Pleasonton's advance toward Brandy Station, endeavoring to penetrate Stuart's screen. Meanwhile Sedgwick has thrown a force across the river at Fredericksburg in an unsuccessful reconnaissance. On Map 4 Ewell has moved north as far as Front Royal, while Hooker, apprehensive over Lee's movements, has commenced to stir. By June 13 (Map 5) Ewell has reached the northern end of the Shenandoah, Longstreet is preparing to follow, and the Union corps are starting to move north. The general map shown in the endpapers continues the development of the situation thereafter, to June 30.

tion for the invasion of Maryland and Pennsylvania. The infantry movement had begun June 3, when two divisions of Longstreet's corps, McLaws' at Fredericksburg and Hood's on the Rapidan, pulled out from their respective positions and headed for Culpeper Court House. The fol-

MAJOR GENERAL JOSEPH HOOKER
Commanding the Army of the Potomac at the start of the Gettysburg campaign.

lowing day Ewell's corps started for the concentration area, while the corps of A. P. Hill, in conformity with Lee's plan, remained at Fredericksburg to keep Hooker occupied and the Army of the Potomac under observation while the other two corps advanced into Pennsylvania.

The Hooker Balance Sheet

General Joe Hooker, Commanding the Army of the Potomac, was riding for a fall after Chancellorsville, where by all the rules of the military books he should have given Lee a resounding licking, after initially outflanking him in a beautiful maneuver. But at Chancellorsville Lee still had Stonewall Jackson to outflank the outflanker, with the result that Hooker tamely sneaked back across the Rappahannock, although he had a troop strength of 130,000 against Lee's 60,000.

Despite the implied connotation of the nickname "Fighting Joe," Hooker was something of a flash in the pan. Like McClellan, he fought amazing campaigns on the map and well deserved his reputation as an excellent organizer and logistician. As division and corps commander under the direction of others he did reasonably well, but as a field general commanding an army he lacked the moral stamina to win victories. After Chancellorsville he patently had little stomach for a fight, appearing content to lick his wounds where he was, back in the Fredericksburg area. Even after Lee had started north, Hooker acted like a man paralyzed while Lincoln kept burning up the telegraph wires urging him to bestir himself.

The sobriquet "Fighting Joe" was achieved as the result of a carelessly transcribed notice on a newspaper correspondents' dispatch from the Peninsula in 1862. The story told of severe fighting in which Hooker's corps had been heavily engaged. The dispatch was captioned "Fighting—Joe Hooker," which a thoughtless typesetter translated into "Fighting Joe Hooker." Fighting Joe it was from then on, to Hooker's perennial discomfiture.*

Although the records show that, like his predecessors, Hooker failed to win battles, he must be given credit for restoring the morale of the Army of the Potomac after Fredericksburg. He reorganized it into seven corps, abolished the cumbersome Grand Divisions, instituted an efficient supply system, and put the Federal cavalry in fighting trim after several years of fruitless effort under infantry generals who seemed to regard cavalry only as useful appendages for the work of mounted messengers, outposts, and small, detached reconnoitering parties. Hooker gave the mounted arm a comprehensive combat role by establishing a cavalry corps of three divisions, under the command of General Stoneman. This meant that for the first time since the war started the Federal cavalry was to receive appropriate missions, with the resultant effect of putting it in position to meet the Southern horsemen on more equal terms.

Hooker presumably accepted at face value the Confederate announcements of their intention to invade Pennsylvania, although in early June, after Longstreet and Ewell had started for Culpeper, he had only the vaguest knowledge of the enemy dispositions and movements. He did know that Lee was being screened by Stuart's cavalry, but just how and where was another question. He decided that a reconnaissance in force was indicated, and figured that a surprise cavalry attack by the Federals might upset Lee's timetable.

---

* Major John Bigelow, Jr., *The Campaign of Chancellorsville,* New Haven, Yale University Press, 1910.

Jeb Stuart Stages a Review

Confident in its proven superiority over the heretofore indifferently led and unaggressive Federal cavalry, the Confederate cavalry corps, ten thousand strong, was bivouacked in early June, 1863 between Culpeper, Virginia and the Rappahannock. The camps were in the vicinity of Brandy Station, a whistle-stop which lies five miles west of the river that runs through historic Fredericksburg and across which George Washington is reputed to have shied his silver dollar.

In command was General J. E. B. Stuart, the *beau sabreur* of Southern chivalry, whose exploits had become legend and whose appearance in a cavalry fight was synonymous with victory. Not one to hide his light under a bushel, or to disappoint the Southern belles, Stuart decided that a massive review of his mounted legions, to be followed by a gay dance for the officers, would be an appropriate prelude to the forthcoming long march through Maryland into Pennsylvania.

The rolling meadows of lovely Virginia furnished the perfect stage for the magnificent spectacle. The Confederate squadrons swept by at the walk, trot, and gallop, while Southern feminine hearts swelled with pride. General

An Affair of Outposts

Stuart himself was a bit unhappy because General Lee had failed to show up as promised to take the review. Several days later, however, on June 8, the Commanding General did appear and the ceremony was repeated, to the annoyance of the rank and file. This time the troops passed in review only at the walk, since Lee prohibited the faster gaits in order to conserve horse flesh for the coming invasion.

Federal Cavalry Springs a Surprise

Stuart had planned to move on June 9, the day following Lee's review of his troops. On that day his brigades were somewhat scattered, although within supporting distance of one another, and he had patrols on the Rappahannock at Beverly Ford and Kelly's Ford, separated by about six miles.

General Pleasonton had now superseded Stoneman in command of the Federal cavalry corps. He had been a West Point classmate of General Stuart; the double promise of crossing sabers with an old friend and affording his troops the opportunity of demonstrating their newly-developed combat efficiency in a test of strength presented an exciting prospect.

On Hookers' orders, and with a combined force of about ten thousand mounted and dismounted men—three divisions and one brigade of cavalry, five batteries of horse artillery, and two brigades of infantry—Pleasonton crossed the Rappahannock at the two fords before daylight June 9, drove in the Confederate pickets, completely surprised Stuart, and gave him the hardest cavalry battle he had yet fought.

At Brandy Station the Federal cavalry had the gratifying experience of assuming the offensive. Stuart was caught in a pincers movement, suffered over five hundred casual-

UNION CAVALRY CHARGE AT BRANDY STATION

ties, and was fortunate to come off without a severe defeat. With a little luck, and somewhat better coordination, Pleasonton could have won a resounding victory. One of Stuart's subordinates, who was captured, had in his possession papers which included Lee's order for an immediate advance into Pennsylvania. Which was solid confirmation with a vengeance.

After the fight at Brandy Station numerous skirmishes occurred between the opposing cavalry, in which the Confederates were invariably driven back by the Union horsemen of Pleasonton, Gregg, and Buford. The northern cavalry had at last come into its own! Brandy Station was no accident. The day of easy Confederate triumphs was gone, never to return.

The long-range results of the cavalry fight at Brandy Station had favorable implications for the Federals in neutralizing the superiority of the Southern cavalry and in toning down the hell-for-leather cockiness and dash of

Stuart's cavaliers. But it failed to deter or even delay the execution of Lee's plans for the invasion of the North, which started on schedule as Pleasonton re-crossed the Rappahannock after completing his reconnaissance in force.

CITIZENS OF PENNSYLVANIA BUILDING BREASTWORKS NEAR THE SUSQUEHANNA
TO REPEL LEE'S INVASION

CHAPTER 2

THE INVASION OF PENNSYLVANIA

THERE is no evidence to indicate that the Federal cavalry surprise at Brandy Station made any particular impression on Lee's mind. It was indeed too early to evaluate the effects of the battle and even though Lee may have taken the time to study the reports, he would in all probability have rated it a stand-off and put it out of his thoughts so far as having any strategic significance was concerned. It was the first time in two years that the Northern horsemen had demonstrated large-scale cavalry combat capabilities; and understandably Lee might have considered the affair to be merely an exception to the established rule of Confederate supremacy in the saddle.

Furthermore, his thoughts were centered on the invasion of Northern territory, his plans had matured, and his corps commanders had their orders.

Lee's Directive to his Corps

Lee's broad directive to his corps commanders for the invasion was essentially as follows:

The Second Corps under Ewell, with Jenkins' cavalry brigade attached, would lead the advance through the Shenandoah Valley, crossing the Potomac in three columns along routes touching Hagerstown, Greencastle, Chambersburg, Shippensburg, and Carlisle on the west; and Frederick, Emmitsburg, Gettysburg, and York on the east. The troops were ordered to collect horses, cattle, and flour. The First Corps, under Longstreet, was directed to follow Ewell's troops, but east of the Blue Ridge, and to cross at Williamsport, Maryland. The Third Corps, under A. P. Hill, was told to watch the Army of the Potomac on the Rappahannock and to keep it occupied while the other two corps advanced into Pennsylvania; if Hooker should pull out, Hill was to cross the Potomac at Shepherdstown and follow the western line of advance through Greencastle and Chambersburg.

General Stuart, on whom Lee had come to rely as "the eyes of the Army," was given the important dual mission of right flank guard of the Army on its march into Pennsylvania and constant reconnaissance to keep Lee informed of the movements of the Army of the Potomac.

In issuing his march orders to Ewell, Lee commented: "Your progress and direction will of course depend upon the development of circumstances. If Harrisburg comes within your means, capture it." The suggestion that he might be able to capture Harrisburg became in Ewell's mind virtual orders to do so, in the opinion of the late Douglas Southall Freeman. Ewell was instructed to keep òne division east of the mountains to deter the Federal Army, if it should cross the Potomac, from moving west-

CONFEDERATES CROSSING THE POTOMAC JUNE 11, 1863

ward before Lee could concentrate. And it was decided, probably by Ewell, that it would be appropriate to destroy the bridge across the Susquehanna at Wrightsville, a short distance northeast of York, in Pennsylvania.

Ewell's Rapid Advance Stirs the South

Covered by Jenkins' cavalry brigade, Ewell set out from the Culpeper concentration area on June 10 for the Cumberland Valley, with orders to clear the Valley in Virginia of Federal troops, some thirteen thousand of whom were stationed at Berryville, Winchester, Martinsburg, and Harper's Ferry; then cross the Potomac, move through Maryland, and carry the war into Pennsylvania.

General Ewell, successor to Stonewall Jackson, emulated that fast-moving soldier by executing so rapid and effective an advance, in his first big opportunity as a corps commander, that in less than three weeks his force had travelled over two hundred miles, driven the Federals out of Virginia, spread confusion and alarm throughout the north, and was knocking at the front door of Harrisburg,

Pennsylvania's capital on the Susquehanna River.

With some 23,000 officers and men in his three-division corps, plus Jenkins' cavalry, "Baldy" Ewell, wooden leg and all, snaked rapidly north, reached Winchester, Virginia on the third day, June 13; crossed the Potomac and seized Hagerstown and Sharpsburg in Maryland; and two days later, on June 15, his cavalry were collecting horses and cattle in Chambersburg, Pennsylvania.

The Winchester Sideshow

The opposition of the Federal General Milroy, in command at Winchester, was rather sketchy in the face of the aggressive attack of the Confederates. At Cedarville on the evening of June 12 Ewell had detached Jenkins' cavalry and Rodes' infantry division to seize McReynolds' Federal brigade at Berryville, but the latter withdrew to Winchester, in time to be routed with Milroy's main body. Unobserved by the Federal commander, Early's divisions were disposed during the 14th on three sides of the town and at 6 P. M., in a sudden attack from the west, Early seized the outworks and drove the garrisons into the main fort, leading Milroy to decide on an immediate retreat to the north. A few miles above Winchester Milroy ran into a skilfully placed brigade of Johnson's division. Following a sharp engagement the Federals, who had lost heavily, scattered and continued the retreat in the darkness.

In the Winchester affair the Confederates took 3,300 prisoners and pursued the remainder of Milroy's force in the direction of Harper's Ferry until the Southerners tired of the foot race. Meantime Jenkins' troopers, about 1,500 strong, chased Milroy's wagon train all the way to Chambersburg and, after successfully appropriating all available livestock in the vicinity, returned to Hagerstown to await the arrival of the supporting infantry.

On June 17 the Federal garrison at Harper's Ferry was

removed to Maryland Heights across the river, completely clearing the Valley of the Shenandoah of Union troops. The unhappy Milroy kept right on going until he reached Baltimore, where he faded into a more or less painless anonymity for the rest of the war.

LIEUTENANT GENERAL RICHARD S. EWELL, C.S.A.
Commander of Lee's Second Army Corps.

Ewell Advances on Harrisburg and York

Continuing the march, Ewell sent one of his divisions under Early to take the easterly road by way of Chambersburg and Cashtown ,to Gettysburg en route to York. Near Greenwood the Confederates destroyed Thaddeus Stevens' iron works at Caledonia, but the Southerners probably paid heavily for this act when Stevens rode herd on them during reconstruction days.

General Ewell was evidently quite a man. He is described by Colonel Fremantle, a young British officer who spent three months with the Confederate forces while on leave of absence from his British regiment, as "a rather remarkable looking old soldier, with a bald head, prominent nose, and rather a haggard sickly face." The loss of one leg earlier in the war evidently failed to dampen his aggressive fighting spirit, for some accounts insist that Stonewall Jackson had been particularly indebted to Ewell for a number of his earlier victories in the Shenandoah Valley.

Hoke, in his interesting account* of the invasion, gives an illuminating picture of this one-legged general:

> About 10:30 on the morning of June 24 a carriage, escorted by several horsemen, stopped in front of the Franklin Hotel in Chambersburg. One of the occupants of this carriage was a thin, sallow-faced man, with strongly marked Southern features, and a head and physiognomy which strongly indicated culture, refinement and genius. When he emerged from the carriage, which he did only by the assistance of others, it was discovered that he had an artificial limb and used a crutch. After making his way into the hotel, he at once took possession of a large front parlor, and, surrounded by six or eight gentlemanly-looking men, he

---

* Jacob Hoke, *Gettysburg, the Great Invasion of 1863*, Dayton, 1887.

was prepared for business. A flag was run out of a window and headquarters established. This intellectual and crippled man was Lieutenant General R. S. Ewell, the Commander of the Second Corps, Army of Northern Virginia.

General Ewell, a graduate of West Point, had been a civil engineer on the Columbia Railroad in Pennsylvania. At one time he was stationed at Carlisle in charge of the United States Barracks. He lost his leg in the second Battle of Bull Run, and when he rode on horseback, which he seldom did except in battle, he was invariably strapped to his horse. It is likely that he was placed in the advance because of his familiarity with the country, especially about York, Columbia, and Harrisburg, where important events were expected to take place.

When Ewell took possession of Chambersburg on the 24th, and set up headquarters in the court-house, he issued three separate requisitions demanding "5,000 suits of clothing, including hats, boots and shoes; 5,000 bushels of grain (corn or oats), 10,000 pounds of sole leather and an equal quantity of horseshoes, 6,000 pounds of lead, 10,000 pounds of harness leather, 400 pistols, 'all the caps and powder in town, also all the Neat's Foot Oil', 50,000 pounds of bread, 500 barrels of flour, 11,000 pounds of coffee, 100,000 pounds of hard bread, 25 barrels of vinegar, 25 barrels of sour kraut," and a scattering of other supplies. Judge Kimmell, appointed as a general superintendent of affairs during the war for the Chambersburg area, is reported to have replied to the demands: "Why, gentlemen, you must suppose that we are made of these things—10,000 pounds of sole leather, 10,000 pounds of harness leather, 100,000 pounds of bread, 25 barrels of sour kraut—it is utterly out of our power to furnish these things, and now, if you are going to burn us out, you will only have to do it.

That's all I have to say about it." As a result of this inter-change, the people of Chambersburg furnished what they could, but the results fell far short of Ewell's expectations.*

General Early, one of Ewell's division commanders, reached Gettysburg June 26, on his way east. Overnight he demanded of the Gettysburg citizens certain specified

MAJOR GENERAL JUBAL A. EARLY, C.S.A.
Division commander in Ewell's corps.

supplies, including ten barrels of whiskey, the value of the total requisition being set at $6,000 in goods, or $5,000 in cash. The citizens, however, professed poverty, having taken time by the forelock and shipped most of their valuable property to several spots in Philadelphia and elsewhere. Early made no effort to enforce his demands.

On June 27 York surrendered to Early and, unlike Gettysburg, paid him $28,000. Early then moved on to-

---

* *History of Franklin County, Pennsylvania,* Chicago, 1887.

EARLY'S TROOPS IN WRIGHTSVILLE, PENNSYLVANIA ON JUNE 28, 1863
In the distance is the railway bridge set on fire by the Federal militia.

wards the Wrightsville bridge, with the full intention of crossing the Susquehanna to cut the Pennsylvania Central Railroad and to attack Harrisburg from the rear. Before he could carry out his plan the local troops burned the bridge and narrowly escaped destroying the town along with it.

While Early was striking for Harrisburg by way of Wrightsville, Ewell entered Carlisle and sent the Cavalry General Jenkins and his Corps Engineer to reconnoiter the defenses of the capital, at the same time raising the Confederate flag over the famous Carlisle Barracks, later burned by Stuart.

State Capital is Threatened

At 9 o'clock on Sunday morning, June 28, the advance guard of Jenkins' cavalry reached Mechanicsburg, eight miles southwest of Harrisburg. Shortly thereafter Jenkins' entire Confederate force of cavalry and mounted infantry, with four pieces of field artillery, passed through the town and encamped about a mile outside, while Jenkins himself returned to take up his headquarters at the Ashland House. The next day, Monday, Jenkins moved on toward Shiremanstown and a village called Bridgeport, on the bank of the Susquehanna by the Harrisburg Pike (now Lemoyne). At Oyster's Point, on the turnpike about an equal distance between Mechanicsburg and Bridgeport, the Confederate cavalry ran into a force of Blue infantry sent forward by General Couch. A brief skirmish ended in an artillery duel between the Union guns planted at Oyster's Point and Jenkins' guns at the Stone Church about a half-mile north of Shiremanstown. There were no casualties on either side in this exchange of pleasantries at the northernmost point reached by any *major* Confederate force during the Civil War.*

When Jenkins reported back, on June 29, Lee ordered Hill and Longstreet to join Ewell at Harrisburg, believing that Hooker was still south of the Potomac. Thus Harris-

* Confederates from Canada raided St. Albans, Vermont, with inconsequential results and some of Ewell's men reached the foot of the mountain below Sterrett's Gap, north of Carlisle; but these were detached elements.

A SUTLER'S TENT
Predecessor of the regimental canteen, now Post Exchange.

burg became the objective of the entire Army of Northern Virginia. The movement was well under way in the early afternoon hours of June 29, just two days before the initial clash of the two forces at Gettysburg.

There is little doubt that Harrisburg could easily have been taken on Sunday, June 28, when elements of Ewell's corps reached the heights overlooking the city on the west bank of the mile-wide Susquehanna. The South having fully advertised its forthcoming punch, the North was alerted. On June 12 Pennsylvania's war Governor Curtin had issued a proclamation calling on the people of Pennsylvania to hasten to the defense of the State. This proclamation had little effect in strengthening the State's posture of defense.

President Lincoln on June 15 specifically called upon Pennsylvania and contiguous States to raise a total of 120,-000 new troops, the response to which was relatively sketchy. Possibly 50,000 militia in all responded to the call, but New York was the only State which sent a number of uniformed regiments from New York City to Harrisburg. Those which reported were organized into two divisions.

A few rifle pits were dug and breastworks thrown up here and there on both sides of the Susquehanna, but no plans seem to have been made to destroy the river bridges or set up effective blockades.

Major General Darius N. Couch, who had led the Second Corps at Chancellorsville and was senior corps commander of the Army of the Potomac, had completely lost confidence in General Hooker, in common with practically all the other general officers, but he was the only one who felt strongly enough about the matter to refuse to serve further under him. He had therefore asked to be relieved after Chancellorsville and in early June was assigned by the War Department to the Department of the Susquehanna, with headquarters at Harrisburg. Without any regular troops to form the core of an adequate defense, there was little Couch could do but make plans on paper. Fortunately for Harrisburg any further advance was halted when Lee recalled his army to Cashtown.

MAJOR GENERAL DARIUS N. COUCH
Commander of the Department of the Susquehanna,
at Harrisburg, Pennsylvania.

Lee Reverses Direction

Rodes' infantry led the march and the column was on the way to the Pennsylvania capital when the news reached Lee that Hooker's army had crossed the Potomac and was at that moment concentrated in the vicinity of Frederick, Maryland. Lee reacted quickly, sending word to Ewell to reverse his direction of march, move south, and join the other corps west of the mountains, at Chambersburg. However, those orders were quickly superseded by new instructions to the Corps Commanders to concentrate in the area of Cashtown, a few miles west of Gettysburg at the eastern exit from the South Mountains.

The information that Hooker had crossed the Potomac several days before, many hours before Stuart's cavalry had crossed, failed to reach Lee until late on June 28 or early the following morning, and the news did not come from Stuart. The longheaded Longstreet had engaged a spy by the name of Harrison, without Lee's knowledge, but with instructions to pass through the Federal army and pick up all the information possible. Harrison travelled to Washington, thence north through Maryland and Pennsylvania, gathering valuable information. On June 28 he reported to Longstreet's headquarters that at least two Federal corps had reached Frederick and that General Meade had succeeded Hooker. Although Lee was startled at the news and a bit dubious as to its accuracy, he immediately recalled Ewell from the Susquehanna and directed Hill and Longstreet, in that order, to move east of the mountain, leaving Pickett's division as train guard at Chambersburg.

Ewell's trip through Pennsylvania had been a rewarding one. Between June 10 and 29 his corps had captured 28 guns, almost 4,000 prisoners, 5,000 barrels of flour, 3,000 head of cattle, and a trainload of ordnance and medical stores at Chambersburg, in addition to food, horses, and quartermaster supplies which were seized and issued to his own men. One of Lee's objectives, the procurement of much needed supplies, was thus achieved, at least in part. All this with losses on his part of only three hundred men. Ewell's star was riding high and the South figured that a second Stonewall Jackson had emerged.

CARLISLE BARRACKS AFTER BEING BURNED BY THE CONFEDERATE CAVALRY

CHAPTER 3

HOW THE CONFEDERATES BEHAVED

THE FULLEST and possibly the most absorbing accounts of Lee's 1863 invasion of the North were those
composed from notes taken at the time by persons who observed with their own eyes most of the incidents which they
recorded. With due allowance for possible bias on the part
of the authors, three books, all published within months
or a few years at the most of the Battle of Gettysburg, in
particular afford an interesting insight into the attitudes of
the Confederate high command and the men in the ranks,
as they moved rapidly forward in hostile territory.

Lieut. Col. Arthur J. L. Fremantle, an officer of the
Coldstream Guards of the British Army, on leave of absence from his own army, spent three months with the
Confederates and wound up his tour in close and intimate
contact with Generals Lee and Longstreet just preceding
and throughout the course of the Gettysburg campaign.
Fremantle's diary, published in Great Britain several
months after the battle, created quite a stir and has been
freely quoted by many writers.

The Great Invasion of 1863, an extensive but highly illuminating document by Jacob Hoke, a citizen of Chambersburg, published in 1887, is a valuable source record that bears revealing testimony to the reportorial instinct of the Cumberland Valley resident. Mr. Hoke meticulously researched in person, and through extensive correspondence with Federals and Confederates alike, every conceivable phase of the Gettysburg campaign from the time Lee's forces crossed into Pennsylvania until they returned to Virginia.

The third of the trio of books, titled *The Rebel Invasion of Maryland and Pennsylvania,* was written and published in 1864 by Professor M. Jacobs of Gettysburg College. This account presents a penetrating close-up of the exciting ex-

CONFEDERATES AT A FORD

periences through which the citizens of Gettysburg passed during the few weeks that the Confederates spent on Pennsylvania soil.

Confederate Conduct is Generally Good

From the standpoint of the civilians whose country or state is being overrun, invasion by hostile forces can by no stretch of the imagination be considered a desirable experience. The history of warfare furnishes few examples of forbearance by the invading troops, while the extent and character of the depredations committed have usually reflected the attitude of the commanding general and the discipline, or lack of it, in the enlisted ranks.

Lee's invasion of the North was one of the better examples, despite the fact that his own State of Virginia had suffered severely in bearing the brunt of the fighting during the early years of the war, and Northern troops had not always been considerate of the feelings and property of the people of the South whose lands were being fought over.

Lee may well have been influenced, in his decision to respect the persons and homes of the Pennsylvanians whose communities were engulfed by the Confederate army, by the belief that Great Britain and France, as well as the northern Peace Party, would be favorably impressed by a restrained treatment of civilians; or it may have been strictly in character, with no ulterior motive, for him to take the attitude that he did. Whatever the reasons, the orders which he issued to the army on the subject set a high standard of performance by the Southern ranks, particularly among the infantry.

There were exceptions, of course, a notable one being the treatment accorded the home of Dr. Schmucker which stood on Seminary Ridge a short distance west of Gettysburg's historic Lutheran Theological Seminary, of which he was the head. The good Doctor was a prolific writer and a confirmed Abolitionist, whose home was one of the stations of the "underground railroad" by which Southern slaves were wont to find their way safely to Canada. It appears that he was a marked man, and when Lee's troops took permanent possession of Seminary Ridge the afternoon of July 1, Dr. Schmucker's valuable books and papers were scattered, torn, and defaced, while his furniture and and other household appurtenances suffered the roughest kind of vandalism.

Lee Restrains His Army

On Sunday, June 21, General Lee, then at Berryville, south of the Potomac, issued the following general order:

Head-Quarters Army of Northern Virginia,
June 21st, 1863.

General Orders No. 72.

While in the enemy's country, the following regulations for procuring supplies will be strictly observed, and any violation of them promptly and vigorously punished:

I.   No private property shall be injured or destroyed by any person belonging to or connected with the army, or taken, except by the officers hereinafter designated.

II.   The chiefs of the commissary, quartermaster, ordnance and medical departments of the army will make requisitions upon the local authorities or inhabitants for the necessary supplies for their respective departments, designating the places and times of delivery. All persons complying with such requisitions shall be paid the market price for the articles furnished, if they so desire, and the officer making such payment shall make duplicate receipts for the same, specifying the name of the person paid, and the quantity, kind, and price of the property, one of which receipts shall be at once forwarded to the chief of the department to which such officer is attached.

III. Should the authorities or inhabitants neglect or refuse to comply with such requisition, the supplies required shall be taken from the nearest inhabitants so refusing, by the orders and under the directions of the respective chiefs of the departments named.

IV. When any command is detached from the main body, the chiefs of the several departments of such command will procure supplies for the same, and such other stores as they may be ordered to provide, in the manner and subject to the provisions herein prescribed, reporting their action to the heads of their respective departments, to which they will forward duplicates of all vouchers given or received.

V. All persons who shall decline to receive payment for property furnished on requisitions, and all from whom it shall be necessary to take stores or supplies, shall be furnished by the officers receiving or taking the same with a receipt specifying the kind and quantity of the property received or taken, as the case may be, the name of the person from whom it was received or taken, the command for the use of which it is intended, and the market price. A duplicate of said receipt shall be at once forwarded to the chief of the department to which the officer by whom it is executed is attached.

VI. If any person shall remove or conceal property necessary for the use of the army, or attempt so to do, the officers hereinbefore mentioned will cause such property and all other property belonging to such persons that may be required by the army, to be seized, and the officer seizing the same will forthwith report to the chief of his department the kind, quantity and market price of the property so seized, and the name of the owner.

By command of GENERAL R. E. LEE,
R. H. CHILTON, A.A. and I.G.

JENKINS' CONFEDERATE CAVALRY RIDING INTO CHAMBERSBURG

A few days later, at Chambersburg, Lee commended his troops for their generally exemplary conduct, in the following published order:

Head-Quarters Army Northern Virginia,
Chambersburg, Pa., June 27th, 1863.

General Order No. 73.

The commanding general has observed with marked satisfaction the conduct of the troops on the march, and confidently anticipates results commensurate with the high spirit they have manifested.

No troops could have displayed greater fortitude, or better performed their arduous marches of the past ten days.

Their conduct in other respects has, with few exceptions, been in keeping with their character as soldiers, and entitles them to approbation and praise.

There have, however, been instances of forgetfulness on the part of some that they have in keeping the yet unsullied reputation of this army, and that the duties exacted of us by civilization and Christianity are not less obligatory in the country of the enemy than in our own.

The commanding general considers that no greater disgrace could befall the army, and through it, our whole people, than the perpetration of the barbarous outrages upon the unarmed and defenseless, and the wanton destruction of private property, that have marked the course of the enemy in our own country. Such proceedings not only degrade the perpetrators and all connected with them, but are subversive of the discipline and efficiency of the army, and destructive of the ends of our present movement.

It must be remembered that we make war only upon armed men, and that we can not take vengeance for the wrongs our people have suffered without lowering ourselves in the eyes of all whose abhorrence has been excited by the atrocities of our enemies, and offending against Him to whom vengeance belongeth, without whose favor and support our efforts must all prove in vain.

The commanding general, therefore, earnestly exhorts the troops to abstain, with most scrupulous care, from unnecessary or wanton injury to private property, and he enjoins upon all officers to arrest and bring to summary punishment all who shall in any way offend against orders on this subject.

R. E. LEE, General.

Confirming the general's own approval of the discipline of his army, Colonel Fremantle in his diary spoke highly of that same discipline, emphasizing the absence of straggling or entering private homes on any pretext, and remarking that in towns that the troops passed through, sentries were placed outside many of the more pretentious houses to enforce the general's edict.

Confederate Cavalry Criticized

On the other hand, Jenkins' cavalry evidently failed to earn the clean bill of health given to the infantry, if Professor Jacobs' account was accurate. A Professor of Mathematics at Pennsylvania College in Gettysburg, the Rev. Dr. Jacobs reports:

> Previous to Saturday, the 20th of June, portions of Jenkins' party had advanced as far as Waynesboro, Franklin County, Pennsylvania, robbing the inhabitants of horses and of whatsoever else they saw fit to take or to destroy. These and other acts, some of which consisted of a most wanton destruction of articles of no value whatsoever to them, they perpetrated in the face of their oft-repeated assurance that private property would be respected, that private citizens should not be molested, and that *they* would show themselves not to be such barbarians as the Yankees had been whilst in their country. After they had overrun and robbed the country west of the South Mountain and thoroughly searched its numerous valleys for horses, which, they had been informed by disloyal citizens, had been secreted there, they came down the southeastern flanks of the mountains in search of booty.
>
> Friday, June 26. The advance guard of the enemy, consisting of 180 to 200 Cavalry, rode into Gettysburg at 3¼ P. M., shouting and yelling like so many savages from the wilds of the Rocky Mountains, firing their pistols, not caring whether they killed or maimed man, woman, or child; and rushing from stable to stable in search of horses, the most of which, however, had fortunately a few hours before been sent forward to Hanover and York.
>
> This advance party was soon followed by 5000 infantry, being General Gordon's brigade of Early's division of Ewell's corps. Most of the men were exceed-

ingly dirty, some ragged, some without shoes, and some surrounded by the skeleton of what was once an entire hat, affording unmistakable evidence that they stood in great need of having their scanty wardrobe replenished; and hence the eagerness with which they inquired after shoes, hat and clothing stores, and their disappointment when they were informed that goods of that description were not to be had in town; and it ought not to have surprised us that they actually took shoes and hats from the persons of some of our Franklin County cousins, whom they considered more able to endure the loss than we, whilst they permitted us to escape that infliction.

Citizen Reactions

Quite naturally the communities in the path of Lee's invading army were thrown into a state of intense excitement as the rumors of the approaching Confederates flew thick and fast. Hoke's book quotes Dr. Philip Schaff of Mercersburg, in a letter dated June 18, as saying:

> The present state of things in this community is certainly worse than the rebel raid of General Stuart's cavalry in October last, when they suddenly at Mercersburg, at noon-day, seized a large number of horses, shoes and store goods, and twelve innocent citizens as candidates for Libby Prison, but did no further harm and left after a few hours for Chambersburg.
>
> But now the whole veteran army of Lee, the military strength and flower of the southern rebellion, is said to be crossing the Potomac and marching into Pennsylvania. We are cut off from all mail communication and dependent on the flying and contradictory rumors of passengers, straggling soldiers, runaway negroes and spies. All the schools and stores are closed; goods are being hid or removed to the country, valuables buried in cellars or gardens and other places of concealment; the poor negroes, the innocent cause of the

war, are trembling like leaves and flying with their little bundles 'to the mountains,' especially the numerous runaway slaves from Virginia, from fear of being captured as contrabands and sold to the South. This is a most intolerable state of things, and it would be a positive relief of the most painful suspense if the rebel army would march into town.

Shortly after the above was written, various detachments of Lee's Army took and kept possession of Mercersburg until the terrible battles at Gettysburg, and although public and private houses were ransacked, horses, cows, sheep and provisions stolen day after day without mercy, negroes captured and carried back into slavery, and many other outrages committed by the lawless guerilla bands of McNeil, Imboden, Mosby, etc., yet the actual reign of terror, bad as it was, did not after all come up to the previous apprehensions created by the 'wars and rumors of wars,' and the community became more calm and composed, brave and unmindful of danger.

Hoke also reports a conversation between a number of Confederate officers and citizens in Chambersburg while Ewell's troops were in the vicinity. Upon being questioned by one of the officers as to how long the war would continue, one of the citizens replied:

This war will continue as long as you Southern people are able to fight. If you can stand it twenty years more, then the war will last twenty years yet. You gentlemen must have seen for yourselves since you came north that there are any number of able-bodied men yet to draw upon, and the people here have scarcely yet awakened to the fact that there is a war upon their hands; but this invasion will open their eyes to the fact, and if it were possible for you to annihilate the whole of our armies now in the field, that would only bring out another and larger one to take you some morning before breakfast.

The comment by the Confederate officer to the effect that "there is more truth than fun in what he says" suggests an interesting speculation as to the possible effect on Southern morale of their invasion of the rich North. It is not surprising that there were numerous deserters from the Confederate army while it was in Chambersburg.

News of the advance of the Confederates towards Chambersburg resulted in the hasty departure of most of the colored folk and the removal insofar as possible of everything of value that could be transported. Stocks of dry goods were boxed and shipped to Philadelphia and elsewhere, bank officers removed their valuables, court house records were packed and sent away, and much other material of value was buried in beer vaults underground and in whatever secret hideouts were immediately available.

Early on the morning of June 15, the farmers residing in the southern portion of Franklin County began to pass through Chambersburg and on down the Harrisburg Pike with their livestock and other possessions. The road was crowded with wagons, horses and cattle, followed by large numbers of colored men, women and children, bearing with them huge bundles of clothing, bedding, and articles of housekeeping. During the morning, to add to the excitement, 40 or 50 wagons, escorted by a handful of cavalrymen, dashed down Chambersburg's main street shouting that the enemy were in close pursuit, that a large part of the train had been captured, and that the Confederates were about to enter the town.

As it turned out, the wagons which caused the ensuing panic were in reality a part of General Milroy's train which Jenkins' cavalry had pursued from Berryville, Virginia. Actually the Confederate invaders were more than 20 miles away, but the effect was to cause a further exodus on the part of the citizens of Chambersburg.

UNION TROOPS ON THE MARCH NORTH FROM VIRGINIA

CHAPTER 4

LINCOLN SWAPS HORSES

E WELL was moving rapidly through Maryland and Pennsylvania in the two-week period between June 10 and 29, without opposition worthy of the name except the natural hostility that could be expected from the townspeople and farmers who were forced to exchange their goods for worthless Confederate money or the equally doubtful I.O.U.'s of the Confederate government. Meantime what was the Army of the Potomac doing down in Virginia?

It will be recalled that Hooker sent Pleasonton June 9 on a reconnaissance in force to tangle with the Confederate cavalry south of the Rappahannock in the Culpeper area and to bring back information of the whereabouts and, if possible, the probable intentions of the Army of Northern Virginia.

Pleasonton executed his mission admirably. Hooker therefore knew by June 10, at the latest, that Lee was on the move for Pennsylvania. But it was not until June 25, more than two weeks later, that the head of Hooker's Army crossed the Potomac at Edward's Ferry, by which time Lincoln had made up his mind that Hooker must never be permitted to fight another battle as army commander.

Lincoln's Famous Letter of Appraisal

The now famous letter which Lincoln wrote when he placed him in command of the Army of the Potomac prophetically foreshadowed the event. Much has been written about the political implications of his selection—the battle for power among the members of Lincoln's cabi-

PRESIDENT LINCOLN VISITING TROOPS IN THE FIELD

net—which is a story in itself. Briefly stated, the President, Secretary of War Stanton, and General-in-Chief Halleck all had doubts about Hooker when the choice of Burnside's successor had narrowed down to Reynolds, Hooker, and Meade. The post was confidentially offered to General Reynolds, who indicated that he would expect a liberty of action that probably would not be forthcoming, and under the circumstances he would not volunteer to take on the job. So General Halleck dropped him from consideration. Stanton was definitely against the selection of Hooker, but a powerful political faction, scheming to have Treasury Secretary Chase succeed Lincoln as President, recognized the importance of a military alliance with whatever general would crush the rebellion. Hooker's friends and supporters in Washington gave the Chase clique assurance that Hooker would under no circumstances aspire to the Presidency, whereupon he became their candidate. Lincoln was persuaded, over Stanton's forceful opposition, to appoint him. In the last analysis, however, Hooker failed because he just didn't possess the necessary ability.

This is what the President had written:

Executive Mansion,
Washington, January 26, 1863.

Major General Hooker:
General:
I have placed you at the head of the Army of the Potomac. Of course I have done this upon what appear to me to be sufficient reasons. And yet I think it best for you to know that there are some things, in regard to which, I am not quite satisfied with you. I believe you to be a brave and a skilful soldier, which, of course, I like. I also believe you do not mix politics with your profession, in which you are right. You have confidence in yourself, which is a valuable, if not an indispensable

quality. You are ambitious, which, within reasonable bounds, does good rather than harm. But I think that during Gen. Burnside's command of the Army you have taken counsel of your ambition, and thwarted him as much as you could, in which you did a great wrong to the country, and to a most meritorious and honorable brother officer. I have heard, in such way as to believe it, of your recently saying that both the Army and the Government needed a Dictator. Of course it was not for this, but in spite of it, that I have given you command. Only those generals who gain successes can set up dictators. What I now ask of you is military success, and I will risk the dictatorship. The government will support you to the utmost of its ability, which is neither more nor less than it has done and will do for all commanders. I much fear that the spirit which you have aided to infuse into the Army, of criticising their Commander, and withholding confidence from him, will now turn upon you. I shall assist you as far as I can, to put it down. Neither you, nor Napoleon, if he were alive again, could get any good out of an army, while such a spirit prevails in it.

And now, beware of rashness—Beware of rashness, but with energy, and sleepless vigilance, go forward, and give us victories.

Yours very truly

A. Lincoln

Hooker's Removal Foreshadowed

In Steele's *American Campaigns** it is stated that Hooker started on the night of June 13 toward Manassas Junction, expecting to cross the Potomac near Leesburg. But he did not attempt to move across until June 25-26. During this long time lapse Hooker was apparently trying to make up his mind. Unbelievable as it may sound, on

---

* Matthew Forney Steele, *American Campaigns* (War Department Document No. 324), Harrisburg, 1945.

June 13 Lee's army was stretched out for a length of at least 75 miles, with the head at Martinsburg and the tail at Chancellorsville, yet Hooker did little but write letters to Lincoln. He made no effort to seize the passes over the Blue Ridge, or to comply with Lincoln's frantic urging that he grasp the golden opportunity to break Lee's back at any one of a number of places. Instead Hooker actually ordered four infantry corps and his cavalry to fall back on Manassas Junction from Thoroughfare Gap and Leesburg, while three other corps were instructed to withdraw to Dumfries and await orders.

On June 22 Hooker sent Lincoln his opinion "that Ewell had moved up country for purposes of plunder, and if the enemy should conclude not to throw new additional force over the river, I desire to make Washington secure and, with all the force I can muster, strike for his line of retreat in the direction of Richmond."

These were hardly the words of a general anxious to come to grips with an enemy who had invaded his own territory. In any event his proposed action would hardly have brought Lee back, since Lee had voluntarily left Virginia soil and taken the calculated risk of leaving the way to Richmond open for Hooker. Lee, shrewd at estimating situations, doubtless was satisfied in his own mind that Lincoln would never permit Washington to be exposed in the manner suggested by Hooker.

At last, however, on June 26, after repeated urgings, Hooker put his army into motion. Once started he advanced rapidly by hard marches on Frederick, so maneuvering his columns as to keep between Lee and Washington and Baltimore, and to that extent frustrating one of Lee's major objectives. One report credits Hooker's march from Fairfax to Frederick as one of the most rapid of the war, the Eleventh Corps having covered 54 miles in two days.

WARTIME VIEW OF HARPER'S FERRY

According to General Henry J. Hunt, Chief of Artillery of the Army of the Potomac, Hooker ordered the Twelfth Corps to march on June 28 to Harper's Ferry, cut Lee's communications and, in conjunction with Reynolds who was occupying Middletown and the South Mountain passes with three corps, to operate on Lee's rear. Washington through General Halleck countermanded Hooker's order, whereupon the latter sought permission to abandon Harper's Ferry. This too was refused, at which Hooker huffily asked to be relieved of command. Apparently Washington was just waiting for this opportunity. The request was granted so promptly that it must have made Hooker's head swim.

Hooker is Replaced by Meade

There is no doubt that the Army of the Potomac, officers and men alike, in company with Secretary Stanton and

President Lincoln, had utterly lost confidence in Joe Hooker. The President's patience was exhausted. On June 28, one day after York had surrendered to Early; when Gordon was approaching the Wrightsville bridge; Ewell had entered Carlisle; Jenkins' cavalry was reconnoitering the defenses of Harrisburg; and Jeb Stuart was far away

MAJOR GENERAL HENRY W. HALLECK
General in Chief of the Federal Armies.

to the south at Rockville, frittering away valuable time— while these interesting events were transpiring, Lincoln appointed George Gordon Meade as Commander of the Army of the Potomac.

The transfer of command, with the invading enemy roaming at will and now deep in Union territory, was risky business in spite of its dramatic aspect. The Chief of Staff to Secretary Stanton, General Hardie, a friend of both Meade and Hooker, was entrusted by Lincoln with the mission of delivering the Presidential order to both commanders and making it effective. Hardie changed to civilian clothes to afford him a better chance of evading Stuart's troopers. He then made his way to Frederick and about 4 o'clock on the morning of June 28 located Meade's headquarters tent, several miles outside the town, after being repeatedly accosted and delayed en route by drunken Federal soldiers making the most of the Maryland whiskey.

Awakened from a sound sleep, Meade's first groggy reaction was that he was under arrest; the Federal high commanders must have been a bit on the nervous side about that time. When Hardie broke the news, Meade protested that the army expected Reynolds to succeed to the command, and offered all the arguments he could think of in opposition to the order. But Hardie had been well briefed, so finally off the two generals went on horseback to see Hooker and effect the transfer of command. Shortly thereafter Hooker and Hardie departed for Baltimore and Washington respectively, while Meade walked alone into the army commander's tent to face his destiny.

Meade's promotion from command of the Fifth Corps to army commander was a surprise, and not too welcome a one at that. His son and aide has written that Hooker had made no future plans whatsoever with respect to the army. General Meade was therefore forced to start from scratch, not only to ascertain the whereabouts of Lee, but to learn just how the other corps of the Army of the Potomac were disposed. Under the circumstances one cannot envy General Meade the timing of his assignment to command.

STUART CAPTURES A WAGONTRAIN AT ROCKVILLE, MARYLAND

CHAPTER 5

JEB STUART SLIPS HIS HALTER

IT IS A popular belief that General J. E. B. Stuart disregarded Lee's orders for the invasion of Pennsylvania and, instead of paralleling Ewell's route and protecting his right, rode around the Army of the Potomac, engaged in fruitless side-enterprises, and ended up by failing to rejoin his own army until the last stage of the Battle of Gettysburg. In the meantime Lee knew nothing of Stuart's whereabouts, received no information of Hooker's movements, and presumably was obliged to carry out his risky major foray deep in enemy country without benefit of cavalry reconnaissance or flank security.

The controversy has never been satisfactorily resolved. One widely accepted version, that Gettysburg might have resulted in a Confederate victory and thus altered the course of history, had Lee's cavalry functioned as he intended it should, and had Stuart suppressed his undoubted flair for glamorous exploits, fails to take into account a number of factors which had a decided influence on the event and which place a goodly portion of the responsibility on General Lee himself.

Lee's Instructions to Stuart

There was no misunderstanding as to what Stuart was to do, only how he should do it. The instructions given him were twofold: first, to screen the advance of the two corps, A. P. Hill's and Longstreet's, as they followed Ewell across the Potomac and into Maryland; for the second phase, to cross the Potomac with his own cavalry brigades, serve as right flank guard of the army as it moved north into Pennsylvania, and at the same time keep Lee informed of the movements and actions of the Army of the Potomac.

By June 22 the Federal cavalry had withdrawn to the north, although Lee didn't know it. That evening Stuart received written instructions from Lee, which read in part as follows:

> If you find that he (Hooker) is moving northward, and that two Brigades can guard the Blue Ridge and take care of your rear, you can move with the other three into Maryland, and take positions on General Ewell's right, place yourself in communication with him, guard his flank and keep him informed of the enemy's movements, and collect all the supplies you can for the use of the Army. You will, of course, take charge of Jenkins' brigade and give him necessary instructions.

The letter then went on to give information on Ewell's line of advance and explicit orders against plundering in the enemy's country.

MAJOR GENERAL J.E.B. STUART, C.S.A.
Commander of Lee's cavalry.

On the night of June 23, at Stuart's headquarters near Middleburg, Virginia, another dispatch from Lee came in:

> If General Hooker's Army remains inactive, you can leave two Brigades to watch him, and withdraw with the three others, but should he not appear to be moving northward, I think you had better withdraw this (west) side of the mountains tomorrow night, cross at Shepherdstown next day, and move over to Fredericktown. You will, however, be able to judge whether you can pass around their Army without hindrance, doing them all the damage you can, and cross the river east of the mountains. In either case, after crossing the river, you must move on and feel the right of Ewell's troops, collecting information, provisions, etc. Give instructions to the commander of the brigades left behind to watch the flank and rear of the army and (in event of the enemy leaving their front) retire from the mountains west of the Shenandoah, leaving sufficient pickets to guard the passes, and bringing everything clean along the valley, closing upon the rear of the army. ** I think the sooner you cross into Maryland, after tomorrow, the better.

Lee's orders of June 22 and 23, while anything but concise, were clear enough when read together. If the Federal army stayed on the Rappahannock, Stuart was to keep it under observation with a part of his force. The instructions were concise with respect to Robertson's cavalry, which was to move from the mountains west of the Shenandoah, then north to close upon the rear of the army, and protect Lee's line of communication. If and when Hooker moved, Stuart was to move north to the east of Blue Ridge Mountains, cross the Potomac at Shepherdstown and continue on to Fredericktown, covering the flank of Lee's army in close contact with Ewell, the advance corps. Thus Lee believed he would be adequately served by his cavalry, as he should have been.

Stuart Uses His Own Discretion

In studying those instructions it is clear that Lee allowed Stuart too much discretion and that the latter interpreted his orders as sanction for another grandiose raid such as he had staged in 1862. It is equally clear that if explicitly followed the orders would have robbed Stuart of the chance for the independent adventure that his spirit seemed to crave. For him the choice was easy. In his own words he decided "to move entirely in the enemy's rear, intercepting his communications with his base (Washington) and, inflicting damage upon his rear, to rejoin the army in Pennsylvania in time to participate in its actual conflicts."

Stuart had the choice of two possible routes: the one through the Shenandoah Valley; the other to sweep around the rear of Hooker's army, pass between him and Washington, cut communications, do all the damage possible, and then join Ewell in Pennsylvania. Like Custer the dashing Stuart selected the dramatic and exciting alternative, leaving two of his brigades, about 3,000 men, to hold the Blue Ridge passes in Virginia until the army had cleared and then to revert to General Lee for such further missions as the latter might assign.

Lee Had Plenty of Cavalry

It is generally believed that because Stuart was in the wrong place at the wrong time, and Lee was therefore deprived of vital information at a critical period, the Army of Northern Virginia had no cavalry operating directly with it as it advanced into Pennsylvania. That was not true. Even before June 10 Lee had detached Imboden's cavalry brigade of 2,000 men from the cavalry corps and had sent them into Maryland to destroy the railway from Cumberland to Martinsburg, and the Chesapeake and Ohio canal. Imboden certainly must have been included in Lee's plans for further cavalry missions after completing the task of destruction. There was also Jenkins' cavalry brigade of 3,800 officers and men, likewise detached from Stuart's command after the review on June

BRIGADIER GENERAL WADE HAMPTON, C.S.A.
Commander of a brigade under Stuart. He became Stuart's successor when the latter was killed at Yellow Tavern.

5. A brigade of that size, preceding the army in its northward trek, was certainly adequate, coupled with Imboden's brigade, the aggregate exceeding 5,000 soldiers, for rather widespread reconnaissance in addition to its covering mission.

Stuart took with him on his historic ride around Hooker the three brigades of Wade Hampton, Fitzhugh Lee, and W. H. F. Lee. This force totalled less than 5,000 troopers, but they were a compact, experienced body of hard riding cavalrymen under commanders in whom Stuart had full confidence, and with whom he had worked closely in many previous battles. Therefore there appears to have remained available to Lee, and under his direct command, a cavalry force of some 8,000, viz: Jenkins' brigade (with Ewell), Imboden's brigade, and the brigades of Robertson and Jones, under the command of Robertson.

Colonel John S. Mosby, after scouting Hooker's positions on the Rappahannock with his rangers, had informed Stuart that the Army of the Potomac was widely scattered and that Stuart, if he moved promptly, should have little difficulty in passing through or around them. We shall see, however, that Stuart missed that opportunity when he moved out with his three brigades on June 24. On the 25th he found that all the roads he had planned to use were occupied by the Army of the Potomac moving north, so that he was forced to take a long detour to the southeast, which in fact did put him in Hooker's rear and within a few miles of Washington.

Stuart had left General Robertson with his two brigades of cavalry and two batteries of field artillery in the vicinity of Middleburg to cover Ashby's and Snicker's Gaps, watch the enemy, and harass his rear if he should withdraw. In the latter event (as actually happened), Robertson was instructed by Stuart to withdraw to the west side of the Shenandoah, cross the Potomac, and follow the Army of Virginia, keeping on its right and rear. He was further directed to report "anything of importance" to General Longstreet, by communicating with him "by relays through Charlestown."

Mosby was not backward in criticizing Robertson for being dilatory, to say the least, in following his instructions. He has written that instead of keeping on the right of the army and in close contact with the enemy Robertson dallied in the mountain gaps June 26 to 29, when he received orders from Lee to rejoin the army. He states that the rear guard of the Federal army crossed the Potomac on June 26, east of the Blue Ridge, while Robertson crossed at Williamsport, about 25 miles west of the Blue Ridge, five days later, on July 1, the day the fighting began at Gettysburg.

Be that as it may, Robertson's 3,000 troopers were of no perceptible use to Lee during the invasion, any more than were Stuart's 5,000. On the other hand there is no evidence that Lee himself or his staff made any subsequent effort to recover these two powerful reconnaissance tools when it became evident that his basic plan for their utilization had gone awry.

Major Henry B. McClellan, Chief of Staff of the Cavalry Corps, Army of Northern Virginia, in his *Life of Stuart* says: "It was not the want of cavalry that General Lee bewailed, for he had enough of it had it been properly used. It was the absence of Stuart himself that he felt so keenly; for on him he had learned to rely to such an extent that it seemed as if his cavalry were concentrated in his person, and from him alone could information be expected."

Stuart Rides off into the Blue

Stuart of course knew perfectly well that he was not to delay in joining Ewell, already well on his way. But he was still smarting over Brandy Station and the resulting public indignation which the leading Southern newspapers took no pains to conceal. Like Custer at the Little Big Horn thirteen years later, Stuart needed renewed public acclaim to replace him on his pedestal. It was high time to get going.

Lee's orders had been to cross the Potomac as soon after June 24 as practicable. The cavalry assembly point was fixed at Salem, on the Manassas Gap railroad 8 miles west of Thoroughfare Gap. The columns were directed by Stuart to move shortly after midnight, June 24. The march was planned through Glasscock's Gap of Bull Run Mountain (about 7 miles northeast of Warrenton), thence to Haymarket and turn northward, the shortest road to Ewell's flank in Pennsylvania.

However on the Warrenton-Centreville Turnpike Stuart encountered Hancock's Federal Second Corps moving north towards Gum Spring and Edward's Ferry—almost the same route Stuart had intended to follow. So he changed course to the southeastward on June 26, from Buckland to Bristoe Station (close to Manassas Junction), to Brentsville, thence north to a bivouac near Wolf Run Shoals on Occoquan Creek. Here he paused to rest and graze his horses, some of which were worn out by hard campaigning earlier in the month.

It was now the morning of June 27. Stuart had been on the march for fifty hours, yet had covered only 34 miles and was still 25 miles from the nearest fords of the Potomac, which he was to cross "as soon after June 24 as practicable." Rather a dismal showing for the supposedly mobile cavalry. Without further contact with Federal troops the column crossed the Occoquan at Wolf Run Shoals and moved northward through Fairfax Station to Fairfax Court House, where a halt of several hours was called. While there Stuart received a message that the Army of the Potomac was converging on Leesburg. This information decided his further course, so on he moved to the Leesburg-Alexandria Turnpike, turned west and then north through Dranesville to the Potomac, which was reached at 3 A.M. June 28. During the night all troopers and guns crossed without mishap at the deep but passable Rowser's Ford.

Stuart was now across the Potomac. He had been on the road 72 hours, yet had reached only the southern fringe of Maryland soil, within 20 miles of Washington, and had no idea where Lee might be at the moment. His orders

BRIGADIER GENERAL FITZHUGH LEE, C.S.A.
Commander of a brigade under Stuart.

required him to join Ewell and cover his right, but his horses were tired, his men and animals were living off the country (he had left his own trains in Virginia in order not to slow him down), and he wasn't sure just where Ewell was to be found. According to the local residents, the Army of the Potomac was en route to Frederick and only the day before Hooker had been at Poolesville, to the west. Well, at least he had circled the enemy's rear as planned!

Should he take the road through Frederick, which was probably in the hands of the Federals, or the one through Hanover, keeping to the east of Hooker's army, and heading towards York or Carlisle? Naturally the road to Hanover was selected; by noon of Sunday, the 28th, the column reached Rockville, 12 miles from Washington, where Fortune either smiled or frowned on Jeb Stuart, depending on the point of view.

Stuart Captures a Wagontrain

Rockville was on the direct supply line between Washington and Hooker's army. While Stuart paused there, word came in that a Federal wagontrain was approaching. Soon the mounted Federal guards moved into the town, entirely unaware of the presence of the enemy. Suddenly they spotted the gray-clad horsemen and turned to spread the alarm to the one hundred and fifty wagons stretched out on the highway. Brand new, with shining harness, fat mules, and loaded with oats, corn, bacon, sugar, hams, and considerable bottled whiskey, the prize was too rich a one for Stuart's men to lose.

It was a mad chase, down the road towards the Capital. as the wagons turned and started back at a fast trot. But it was a hopeless attempt, 125 of them being captured. Stuart couldn't bear to give them up. Valuable time was lost writing out paroles for the 400 prisoners who had been taken and, since the vehicles couldn't be paroled along with the men, they were taken along. A worse millstone could hardly be imagined.

Early in the morning of June 29, after a night march of about 20 miles through Maryland, the advance guard ran into a small Federal command at Cooksville, took prisoners, and moved on to Hood's Mill where more delay was caused in tearing up the track of the B & O Railroad.

UNION CAVALRY SKIRMISHING WITH STUART NEAR HANOVER, PENNSYLVANIA

Shortly after noon the march was resumed to Westminster where a small body of Union cavalry charged them bravely but ineffectually. There forage was found for the horses —the distribution and feeding depriving the troops of rest or sleep for most of the night.

Affair at Hanover

Groggily the column moved on toward Hanover on June 30. Reaching the high ground overlooking the town from the south, Stuart, riding up front, spotted an advancing squadron of blue cavalry, a part of Jud Kilpatrick's cavalry division. A swift Confederate charge drove the Federals back into Hanover, but they were promptly reorganized and launched a countercharge during which Stuart came very close to being captured. With an aide at his side, the general left the road in a wild gallop through tall timothy grass, culminating in a magnificent leap across a wide and deep gully, to clear which his thoroughbred must have covered a distance of not less than twenty-five feet in the air. At that point the pursuing cavalry lost interest in the chase.

Stuart's weary troopers were in no condition to contest the right of way with the Federal cavalry, whose new lease on life and improved morale had recently been given a special fillip with the issue of the new Spencer rifle, a seven-shot repeating arm that was the equivalent of at least quadrupled manpower for dismounted fighting.

The 6th Michigan and 1st West Virginia Cavalry regiments, of Custer's and Farnsworth's brigades respectively, are known to have been recently armed with the Spencer repeater, and both were engaged with Stuart's troopers in the Hanover skirmish. Whether they used their Spencers effectively from horseback is questionable, but the fact remains that Kilpatrick definitely blocked Stuart from the two roads leading north from Hanover to Carlisle. The Southerners were forced to bypass Hanover and take the round-about route through Jefferson to Dover, a few miles northwest of York, which they reached on the morning of July 1, after marching all night. In Stuart's official report he admits that his captured train was a serious embarrassment and that he thought he might save it by the detour to the east. It is a certainty he would have lost the train had he tried to force his way through Kilpatrick's division, but conversely he might have rewritten the Battle of Gettysburg.

So Near, yet so Far

The Hanover affair occurred June 30 just 14 miles east of Gettysburg, where on the following morning other Federal cavalry was destined to open the Battle of Gettysburg. Although Stuart didn't know it, he was but a short march away from a junction with Lee's main body, if only he could have turned west and shaken off Kilpatrick.

Meade himself was at Taneytown that day, where he had set up army headquarters. On all the roads west of Stuart's chosen line of march the blue hosts were marching northward, while the cavalry divisions of Kilpatrick and Gregg, two-thirds of Pleasonton's Federal corps, had fanned out to the east to screen the Army of the Potomac and intercept Stuart, whose general whereabouts were no longer a secret.

The Confederates had picked up several hundred prisoners on the 29th and 30th, which added that much more weight to the pace-slowing impedimenta that had

BRIGADIER GENERAL HUGH JUDSON KILPATRICK
Federal cavalry division commander opposing Stuart near Hanover.

already put Stuart at least two days behind even his retarded march schedule. Had he known what was transpiring a few miles away in the direction of Gettysburg there is no doubt that he would have jettisoned his captured wagons, paroled his prisoners, and taken off at a smart clip across country, despite the jaded condition of his men and horses. As a possible result the Battle of Gettysburg might not have been fought at that place.

After another night march from Hanover, Stuart reached Dover on the morning of July 1 but found no

Confederates there. After a few hours' rest he started for Carlisle via Dillsburg, reaching the former town in the late afternoon. All rations had been consumed, the men and horses were practically exhausted, and the troops were beginning to wonder how they might escape from their predicament. Brig. Gen. W. F. "Baldy" Smith was in command at Carlisle, but Stuart didn't know that and, thinking the garrison was made up of home-guard troops, sent in a flag of truce calling for surrender on pain of having the town put to the torch.

About this time one of Stuart's messengers returned with the news that he had found the army and that Lee wished him to move to Gettysburg. Before leaving, Stuart directed that the cavalry barracks at Carlisle be burned, but nothing else was disturbed.

It was the afternoon of July 2, the second day of the Gettysburg battle, before Stuart, riding ahead of his men, joined Lee on Seminary Ridge. Tradition has it that Lee's only comment was: "Well, General Stuart, you are here at last." Whether true or not, Lee's written reactions are officially recorded in his report on the battle, in which he confined himself to the mild statement that "the movements of the army preceding the Battle of Gettysburg had been much embarrassed by the absence of the Cavalry."

Stuart's Adventure Appraised

Despite Jeb Stuart's flamboyant love of finery, pomp and ceremony, he was a man of strong character, beloved of his troopers, an astute tactician, an aggressive leader, a stern disciplinarian with high standards of performance, and an indomitable fighting man. Of medium height, he was broad-shouldered and powerfully built, with a ruddy complexion and flashing blue-gray eyes.

It could be that his military showmanship was of the

calculated type similar to that of a later great Captain—
General George S. Patton, Jr.—a modern-day cavalryman
who recognized and employed to the hilt the psychological
impact, on the minds and hearts of soldiers, of a leader
who knew how to put on a show.

Not much over thirty years of age when he died of a
bullet wound received at Yellow Tavern in 1864, Stuart
neither smoked nor drank—he was in fact a deeply religious man, another Stonewall Jackson in that respect.
It is told of him that when he was offered a drink of brandy
to deaden the pain of dying moments, he refused—saying
he had promised his mother he would never take a drink
and saw no reason to break his promise.

And so we come to the question—was Stuart a major
cause of Lee's failure to win the Battle of Gettysburg?
There is no clean-cut answer nor unanimity of opinion
among historians. The controversy still rages, although not
so caustically as between the critics and defenders of
Custer, who are still writing books and digging into the
unyielding Montana soil in which the remnants of the
Battle of the Little Big Horn lie buried eighty years after
the event.*

In defense of Stuart, the fact must be recognized that
Brandy Station and subsequent skirmishes in northern
Virginia had a notable effect in taking the starch out of
the Confederate cavalry. It wore them down in hard riding and fighting when they needed to conserve their
strength and that of their irreplaceable horses for the long
march into Pennsylvania, and it convinced them that they
were up against a vastly improved Federal cavalry corps
which had recently demonstrated its fighting capabilities.

It seems just as clear that Lee's orders to Stuart allowed
entirely too much discretion, at a critical juncture, to the

---

*Now one-hundred-and-six years after the event. *Editor.*

man who was smarting under public disapproval and who must, like Custer, have pictured the chance to restore by a bold stroke the prestige which he had so greatly enjoyed before Brandy Station. In this case Lee would have been well advised to issue more precise orders to insure strict conformity by his subordinate with his overall plan. So far as Stuart had been informed, Lee's strategic plans were rather vague and incomplete, with no specific geographic objective to tie Stuart to a fixed course or deadline date. Beside which Lee had at his disposal plenty of cavalry in addition to Stuart's brigades, had he properly employed them.

On the other hand, those who place the blame on Stuart maintain that he lagged badly in following Lee's time schedule and, either through misadventure or faulty judgment, failed miserably both in catching up to and covering Ewell's right and in keeping his commanding general informed, through Ewell, of the movements and actions of the Army of the Potomac.

He was certainly guilty of poor judgment in further delaying his own already retarded advance by burdening his column and slowing his pace through Maryland and Pennsylvania to that of the slow-moving Federal wagon train which he captured in his unprofitable side-adventure at Rockville and carried with him to Gettysburg.

Finally, his decision to move around Hooker's rear rather than cross the Potomac at Shepherdstown, as Lee had strongly suggested, had the effect of interposing Hooker between Lee's main body and himself, thus making it a practical impossibility for him to carry out either one of his two major missions.

The conclusion must therefore be that it is a fielder's choice as to whether Stuart was the villain of the piece.

LEE   MEADE

CHAPTER 6

LEE versus MEADE—A STUDY IN LEADERSHIP

THE history of warfare through the ages has demonstrated that the field commander is a major influence
in campaigns and battles. It is equally true that the political and economic war aims of the opposing governments;
the quality of the military and civil leadership; the
spiritual and allied factors which influence the minds and
hearts of the people of the fighting nations; and the industrial and financial capacities and capabilities of the
warring countries all play a part in winning or losing a
war. Nevertheless the fact remains that it is the field commander whose final responsibility it is to utilize the means
at his command to defeat the enemy on the battlefield and
ultimately destroy him or cause his surrender.

To understand fully and evaluate the Battle of Gettysburg, or any major battle for that matter, it is helpful if
not absolutely essential for the reader to have at least a
working knowledge of the timeless principles of war, and

61

to comprehend the influence of terrain features and characteristics on military operations. He should also know something about the type of military organization, troop composition and strength, battlefield experience, supply and morale of the opposing forces, and the relative capabilities of the army, corps, and division commanders on each side.

At the risk of oversimplification it could be said that the Battle of Gettysburg was a contest-at-arms between Robert Edward Lee of Virginia, aged 56, and George Gordon Meade of Pennsylvania, (born in Cadiz, Spain), aged 47, commanding generals respectively of the Army of Northern Virginia and the Army of the Potomac. Meade and Lee, beyond reach of the direct influence of their civilian bosses in Washington and Richmond, held between them the immediate destinies of approximately 170,000 American soldiers, almost one-third of whom were killed or suffered wounds at Gettysburg; and of even greater historical significance, the determination of ultimate victory for the North or the South, with all that victory implied in its impact on the future of America and the world.

They were the generals whose word was law to their subordinates, who were responsible for planning the strategy and moving the players into position, and who made the major decisions that sent tens of thousands of men into action and death.

It would therefore seem to be in order at this point to take a quick look at the background of the two principals, to gain a better appreciation of the manner in which they conducted themselves during the supreme test.

Meade and Lee Compared

Both were professional soldiers and graduates of West Point, Lee in 1829 and Meade in 1835. Both were Engineers, which in the tradition of the Military Academy means that they ranked relatively high in scholarship during their undergraduate days. Both were deeply religious men, if we may judge from their orders and letters, which almost invariably reflect a reliance on the Almighty for military successes. But that is about as far as one can go in discovering parallels in their respective characters and careers.

Meade suffers by comparison with Lee from the fact that so little has been written about him, which of course could mean that poetic justice has been done. What we know about Meade is extracted chiefly from his military orders and letters to his wife, published by his son who as a Captain served as the General's aide at Gettysburg. Meade's profile reveals a brave, conscientious, self-reliant, and skilful commander upon whom his superiors could always depend to carry out orders in strict conformance with convention. Thoroughly respected by his fellow generals, he had fought well as a brigade commander in the Peninsular campaign and at the second Battle of Bull Run; as a division commander at South Mountain and Antietam, where he was assigned to temporary corps command in the midst of the battle, and at Fredericksburg; and finally as a full-fledged corps commander at Chancellorsville.

The records show that he was irascible, perhaps dyspeptic, and spent much of his time poring over books. His training gave him little experience in public relations, if we may judge from his attitude toward army reporters, who at one time entered into an agreement to give him the silent treatment because he once called a reporter a liar. He was outspoken in his lack of confidence in the volunteers in his army, and was not backward about expressing himself on that point. This may well have had some influence, in conjunction with the hostility of the press, in removing him from what otherwise might later have been serious consideration for the Presidency.

Meade's was an uninspiring personality, which lacked the sparkle and dash that usually marks the great Captain. He was stern, gaunt and taciturn, subject to frequent outbursts of temper, and by no stretch of the imagination

GEORGE G. MEADE

Bookish, uninspired, unimaginative, irascible, lacking in the offensive spirit; an "average" general who, nevertheless, made few serious mistakes and maneuvered his troops admirably at Gettysburg.

could be called a lovable character. He apparently believed in playing it safe, in taking no chances, and in making the fewest possible mistakes. Nevertheless his make-up had some iron in it, as evidenced by his circular of June 30 to his army, which closed with the chilling sentence: "Corps and other commanders are authorized to order the instant death of any soldier who fails in his duty at this hour."

On balance, Meade appears to have been an average general, without originality or imagination, but with sufficient ability to handle his troops well. He performed acceptably although not brilliantly at Gettysburg. Lacking the aggressive spirit, he was content to leave the initiative

Courtesy of Washington and Lee University
ROBERT E. LEE

One of the great "Captains," a man of character and perceptiveness, a keen strategist and tactician but an indifferent quartermaster. Master of offensive warfare. Ever mindful of the welfare and feelings of his officers and men, he enjoyed their loyalty and affection to a man, in defeat as in victory.

entirely to invader Lee. After winning the Battle of Gettysburg, Meade did not worry overly much about destroying the Confederate army, but was satisfied to see it depart from Pennsylvania's soil.

Robert E. Lee entered West Point in 1825 with 87 other hopeful cadets as members of a class which by graduation time had shrunk to 46, among whom he stood second on the list. Among the cadets at the Point were a handful of youngsters destined for later fame—Jefferson Davis, Albert Sidney Johnston, Joseph E. Johnston, Leonidas Polk.

The Playing Fields of Eton
The Cloisters of West Point

It has been said of England's illustrious past that many of her battles were won on the playing fields of Eton. Perhaps it could equally be said, without straining credulity too far, that many of Robert E. Lee's early victories were won in the austere cloisters of West Point. For it was there, in the fall of 1852, that he assumed his duties as the ninth Superintendent of the U. S. Military Academy; and where, during the succeeding three years that he served as Superintendent, many cadets who became brigade, division, and corps commanders a few short years later, in the Army of Northern Virginia on the one side, and the Army of the Potomac on the other, were instructed in the art of war under the benign but firm direction of Colonel Lee, already a veteran of the Mexican War. These included such names as John B. McPherson, Phil Sheridan, John B. Hood, Fitzhugh Lee (a nephew), John Pegram, W. D. Pender, O. O. Howard, and J. E. B. Stuart. The last named, a frequent visitor at the Superintendent's home, appears to have completely won Lee's heart. Lee's confidence in Stuart increased to such an extent that it reached a state of semi-dependence in the early war years, when Jeb Stuart became the symbol of the Southern Cavalry and in Lee's eyes his principal reliance in the field of intelligence and counterintelligence.

Other famous names can be found on the roster of the instructors who served under Lee at West Point and who were later opponents on the Northern side—Major George H. Thomas, Instructor in Artillery and Cavalry; Fitz John Porter, the Academy Adjutant, and John F. Reynolds, Assistant Professor of Philosophy. In all at least two dozen instructors and cadets during Lee's superintendency at the Point became general officers in the Federal forces and were directly opposed to Lee on the battlefield.

At the start of the Civil War Lee had been in the Army for 32 years, 26 of them on staff duty and only 6 in the line. Of the latter, but 3 years had been spent with troops and at no time had he commanded more than 300 men in the field and on that occasion merely on a brief scout through a desert. His only service with infantry or artillery was with a battery at Vera Cruz.

In Mexico he had had considerable experience in reconnaissance, in which he developed great proficiency. He was an excellent topographer and his engineering training and practical experience in engineering projects after his graduation provided a strong foundation. His education had however been sadly neglected on the subject of supply, he never having been engaged on quartermaster or commissary duties. Contributory, possibly, was the fact that he had been reared in a society where the business of supply was handled by plantation overseers.

In the history of warfare the great Captains have chiefly been those who in appraising enemy capabilities have weighted the scales with keen perceptiveness in their knowledge of the capacities and estimate of the probable actions of opposing commanders. At West Point as a cadet, later as Superintendent, and during the Mexican War under Scott, Lee acquired a background knowledge of the characters and capabilities of many of those young officers who were later to become Northern generals. He was well qualified mentally and professionally to anticipate, almost uncannily, what his adversaries would be likely to think and do in any given set of circumstances.

It cannot be doubted that division and corps commanders in both armies had developed a profound respect for their old classmate and teacher, even to the extent of acquiring inferiority complexes in many instances. That fact might explain the consistency with which Northern generals overestimated the strength of their opponents on the Southern side, through a subconscious process of crediting to the person of General Lee himself a combat strength of one or more divisions or corps, depending on the state of mind of the Federal commander at the time. For McClellan of course this was standing operating procedure,

BALDY, GENERAL MEADE'S MOUNT

From a photo taken three months after Gettysburg. This horse, though wounded numerous times, survived Meade by a decade.

and the records show that Meade himself was not immune in his substantial overestimate of Lee's strength at Gettysburg.

The judgment of history, and the record supports it, is that Lee was a great general. A remarkable fact about his military stature is that he seems to have had no detractors and very few critics, either during or after the war.

In weighing all the evidence one may marvel at his successes in the field considering the lack of industrial capacity and the manpower handicaps of the Confederacy and its short supply of the sinews of war. Lee made up for these deficiencies by superior military leadership, together with repeated victories on the battlefield resulting in the capture of almost enough small arms and artillery to equip his own army. Furthermore, his diplomatic achievements in the handling of Confederate politicians and government officials, although not so well known as his military campaigns, were considerable and of vital significance to the war effort of the Southern States.

Lee's Attitude Towards Subordinates

An abiding patience and an overly-generous readiness to excuse sins of omission and commission on the part of his subordinates were outstanding characteristics. He spent far more time in listening to others than he did in expressing his own opinions, to such a degree in fact that on more than one occasion his calm reticence was mistaken for acquiescence in the views put forth by the other party to the conversation.

He was distinctly a gentleman of the old school, and the truth unfortunately is that his ever-present amiability resulted in allowing far too much leeway to his corps commanders, as exemplified in Longstreet's case at Gettysburg and Stuart's elsewhere.

His readiness to excuse the failures of his subordinates and to take full responsibility for their mistakes was one of the characteristics that endeared him to his men. But the paternal attitude, which worked so effectively among the enlisted men from one so high in the hierarchy of command, could be carried to extremes where summary or at least disciplinary action was indicated. The end result of Lee's considerate and understanding treatment of enlisted men was that the soldiers of the Army of Northern Virginia gave him a fierce loyalty and respectful affection, in defeat no less than in victory. "His consideration for others, the virtue of the gentleman, had been his vice as a soldier."*

Lee's conception of the function of the army commander, a deep-seated conviction that lasted throughout the war, was to put his troops in the right place at the right time, assign them missions and objectives, and then leave the conduct of the battle to his corps and division commanders, interposing only when necessary to lend assistance.

Ewell's ineptness and Longstreet's consciously dilatory tactics at Gettysburg well illustrate the point. In neither case did Lee either criticize or take over, and his forbearance in those two historic instances has been a cause of wonder to military men ever since. Lee's attitude toward his corps commanders was a fruitful one in the case of Stonewall Jackson and Jeb Stuart (barring only the invasion of Pennsylvania), which very fact may have convinced Lee as to the soundness of the policy. But there was only one Stonewall Jackson!

Lee was a man of powerful intellect, extremely keen in the evaluation of intelligence, and a consistent advocate

---

* Douglas Southall Freeman, *R. E. Lee,* Charles Scribner's Sons, New York, 1935, Vol. IV, page 168.

Courtesy of Washington and Lee University
GENERAL LEE ON TRAVELER

of the offensive, both strategic and tactical. His campaigns show that he was a daring, even audacious commander, but the daring was calculated and intelligent, never reckless.

The high morale of his army was due to Lee's attitude towards the men in the ranks more than to any other single cause. Their welfare was constantly in his thoughts and they knew it. His bearing and obviously sincere interest when talking to an enlisted man, multiplied a thousandfold, created in the minds of the troops such a feeling of confidence and affection that everything he did was right in their eyes. It gave them tremendous confidence in themselves as soldiers and was an important factor in developing their traditional sense of invincibility.

Particularly apropos is the statement by Major General Baron von Freytag-Loringhoven, in his book *The Power of Personality in War:**

The methods we use to accomplish our great goal will be as different as the methods by which this conviction is established in different persons. Men like Scharnhorst, Gneisenau, Lee, Moltke, acquired the ability to inspire great effort and self-sacrifice in others by strict self-discipline and strong religious faith. The purity of their characters was so evident that they seemed to be the incarnation of the ideal leader formulated by Clausewitz. The religion of these men was the truest Christianity; and from this they drew that humility which made them strong against all difficulties.

---

* Military Service Publishing Co., Harrisburg, Pa., 1955.

LONGSTREET'S PASSAGE OF A GAP IN THE BLUE RIDGE

CHAPTER 7

CONFEDERATE STRATEGY IN JUNE 1863

MILITARY strategy, inadequately defined in most dictionaries, is generally regarded among professional army officers as the science of implementing national war plans by disposing major forces of all arms and services in such a way as to impose one's own will upon the enemy. The manner in which the troops are employed, after contact is established between the opposing forces, brings into play what is called military tactics.

Applied to the Battle of Gettysburg, Lee's strategy was conceived along the Rappahannock in late May of 1863, activated in the invasion of Pennsylvania, dissolved into the tactical slugging match of July 1-3, and reached its anticlimactic conclusion with the virtually unhindered recrossing of the Potomac into Virginia on the night of July 13.

Lee's Flexible Plans

Simply stated, Lee figured that he had everything to gain and little to lose by going over to the strategic offensive, shifting the theater of operations to northern soil for a welcome change, improving the faltering source of food and supply for his army, and collaterally keeping the Federals off balance and the Lincoln administration in continued mortal terror of losing Washington or at least Baltimore or Philadelphia.

The history of warfare might have been more carefully studied by the top echelons at both capitals, Washington and Richmond. Had they done so, and profited by their researches, neither Lincoln nor Jefferson Davis would have been so likely to permit their political preoccupation to becloud the fact that wars are won by destroying the armies of the enemy or at least their will to continue the fight, rather than by seizing cities and temporarily occupying hostile real estate, however sacred.

It does appear that Lincoln was less afflicted with that type of myopia than Davis, despite the Federal high command's insistence on always keeping large military forces on Washington's doorstep. An excellent example was the President's clearheadedness in rejecting Hooker's proposal to march on Richmond with the Army of the Potomac after Lee had moved into Pennsylvania, on the premise that Lee's army and not Richmond was Hooker's true objective. On the other hand, Lee was confident that Richmond would not be threatened and was willing to take the calculated risk.

There is no evidence that Lee's invasion timetable was anything but a flexible one. He knew exactly what he wanted to accomplish, but not precisely how. And that was typical

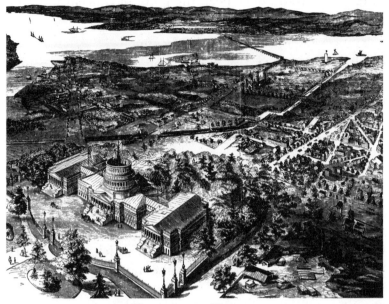

WASHINGTON IN WARTIME

of Lee, whose confidence in his heretofore victorious troops was unlimited; who invariably outlined military objectives and then left it to his corps commanders to achieve those objectives in their own way; and who was quite willing to "play by ear" within reasonable limits. Depending on how the situation should develop, he might shoot for Washington, Baltimore, Philadelphia, Harrisburg or with luck even New York.

Although scarcely conclusive, a letter from Colonel W. H. Swallow, General Rodes' Adjutant General, to author Hoke in 1886, stated that "General Ewell and Colonel Turner, of his staff, both told me in confidence at Berryville, before crossing the Potomac, that York, Pennsylvania or that vicinity was to be the ground where General Lee expected to concentrate his army. I believe that if Longstreet had not tarried so long at Chambersburg, York would have been the point of concentration on the 30th instead of Gettysburg."

Lee Misses Jackson

Although neither Lee nor anyone else could have foreseen the effect, the death of Stonewall Jackson at Chancellorsville created a void which was never filled, either by Longstreet, upon whom Lee subsequently relied as his "old war horse," or by Ewell, who for a few short weeks gave a flashy but unsustained preview of a worthy successor to Jackson.

Longstreet was an extremely able general and a courageous leader in the field. But he proved himself to be the tortoise to the Jackson hare when it came time to duplicate the fantastic bursts of speed which characterized Jackson's "foot cavalry" under the rapid-fire movements which the latter was wont to execute with such startling success on so many fields. Whether Lee was justified in expecting Longstreet or Ewell to emulate the Jackson techniques or not, Gettysburg proved that if Lee had counted on another Jackson in the execution of his plans, he was sadly disillusioned.

Longstreet is Obstinate

The conclusion is likewise inescapable that Longstreet suffered from delusions of grandeur in the belief that his strategic sense was so highly developed as to qualify him to offer advice to Lee with confidence that it would be accepted per se. In expounding his theories, before the march into Pennsylvania, to the patient, gentlemanly Lee, Longstreet opposed the invasion on the premise that the Army of Northern Virginia should take strong defensive positions and force the enemy to attack. His self-assurance as to the soundness of his own strategic thinking, and because he evidently mistook Lee's courteous attention for acquiescence, resulted at Gettysburg in effectively disrupting Lee's attack plans and in allowing the Federals sufficient time to stabilize their position on Cemetery Ridge.

After the war Longstreet admitted that he had failed to win Lee over to his own conception of the strategic de-

LIEUTENANT GENERAL JAMES LONGSTREET, C.S.A.
Commander of the First Army Corps, Army of Northern Virginia.

fensive, but maintained doggedly that in then pressing his case for the tactical defensive, in conjunction with Lee's preference for the strategic offensive, the latter had tacitly concurred. This was obviously not the case, in view of Lee's directives and orders on every one of the three days at Gettysburg.

Interestingly enough it turned out to be Meade, not Lee, who embraced the Longstreet theory, seized and held a strong position on Cemetery Ridge, and permitted Lee to shatter his forces against the Federal position. Thus it might be argued that events at Gettysburg vindicated Longstreet's theory, were it not for the fact that his execution of Lee's orders on the battlefield left much to be desired. In dragging his heels on July 2 and 3, Longstreet demonstrated fairly conclusively, in retrospect at least, that Stonewall Jackson's loss to the Confederacy had been, from Lee's standpoint, an irreparable one.

LIEUTENANT GENERAL AMBROSE P. HILL, C.S.A.
Commander of the Third Army Corps, Army of Northern Virginia.

Lack of Enemy Information

Lee's strategic plans for the invasion of Maryland and Pennsylvania were militarily well conceived and sound in principle. The disposition and movements of his three infantry corps were executed in conformity with the overall plan to march into Pennsylvania through the Shenandoah and Cumberland Valleys under the protection of the high mountain range to the south. The mission of the three brigades of cavalry under the immediate command of General J. E. B. Stuart was to parallel, east of the Blue Ridge Mountains, the northerly march of the infantry in combined screening and reconnaissance operations. Stuart's slowness in getting under way and his failure to regain touch with Ewell or to send any information whatsoever to Lee on the location and movements of the Army of the Potomac kept Lee in the dark as to Hooker's and later Meade's whereabouts or intentions. As the situation developed, this failure played a large part in causing the inevitable meeting of the two armies to take place at Gettysburg rather than in the York area, at Chambersburg, Emmitsburg, or elsewhere.

Lee was handicapped not only by the loss of Jackson but also by the fact that he had just reorganized his two corps into three, of which only one, Longstreet's, was under the command of an experienced corps commander. Ewell and A. P. Hill, newly promoted from command of divisions, both showed promise based on experience, but were untried in the employment of larger bodies of troops. Longstreet, who was born in South Carolina and spent his early life in Georgia, concurred in the choice of Ewell for one of the corps on the basis of lineal rank, ability, and services, but felt that D. H. Hill, of North Carolina, who he maintained was A. P. Hill's superior in rank, skill, judgment, and distinguished services, should have been appointed. Next in rank was Lafayette McLaws, of Georgia, one of Longstreet's own division commanders. McLaws had a distinguished battle record, but he was not in the best of health, nor was he a Virginian. Longstreet implied that the latter was a strong influence against Lee's selection of D. H. Hill or McLaws for corps leadership, and in failing to select either one Lee had impaired somewhat the morale of his troops. Granting Lee's right to make his own selection, the probability exists that cooperation between the corps commanders at Gettysburg would have been more effective if Longstreet's recommendations had been accepted. A study of the history of the battle discloses much evidence of a lack of harmony and necessary team spirit between Longstreet, Ewell, and A. P. Hill.

Lee's Army is Overextended

The Army of Northern Virginia flowed northward in the latter days of June, strung out along the Cumberland Valley and spreading ever more widely into the triangular area Chambersburg—Harrisburg—York, with Ewell pointed for Harrisburg via Carlisle from the west and Columbia from the south. These scattered forces, infantry and cavalry alike, offered a rare opportunity for an enterprising opponent, offensively-minded and with his army well concentrated, to break up the invasion and inflict severe punishment if not destruction on the invaders. By direct routes Harrisburg and York are each more than fifty miles distant from Chambersburg, Lee's command post for almost a week. But that didn't worry Lee, who as late as June 28 thought the Army of the Potomac was still in Virginia, with Hooker still in command.

Lee had every reason to feel that his line of communications and supply all the way back to Virginia by way of the Cumberland and Shenandoah Valleys was reasonably secure. All Federal forces had been forced to evacuate the valley of Virginia by Ewell's advance corps. Two divisions of cavalry left behind by Stuart were presumably protecting his rear and the important passes through the mountains to the east; and Stuart himself with three divisions of cavalry had been told to operate on Ewell's right, east of the mountains and paralleling the latter's march into Pennsylvania.

From the start of the invasion, it will be noted, Lee himself rode with Longstreet's corps, which he apparently regarded as the temporary army reserve and his major reliance in case of unexpected developments requiring speedy action. Or, as believed by some, he may have ridden there to keep Longstreet on his toes. In effect, then, it was chiefly Ewell's corps which had fanned out widely, with A. P. Hill close enough to give Lee on short notice at least two-thirds of his main army for the initial stages of a general engagement.

HEADQUARTERS IN THE FIELD

CHAPTER 8

MEADE TAKES COMMAND

THERE does not appear to have been any strategic planning worthy of the name to meet Lee's threat, so far as the employment of the Army of the Potomac was concerned. Washington was concerned primarily with its own security, although Lincoln saw clearly the importance of going after Lee. Even after the President had pushed Hooker into moving, and the Army of the Potomac had reached the Frederick area, Lincoln had no intention of permitting Hooker to fight another battle. He waited only for a valid excuse to remove him. It seems clear that Hooker, forced to move in a direction at variance with his own undigested plans, was thinking only from hour to hour. And Meade, when he took over at Frederick, failed to find any estimates of the situation, possible plans, contingent orders, or anything else that he could put into operation, modify, or improve upon. He did not know the exact location and disposition of the elements of Hooker's army other than his own corps, and he was forced by necessity, with the Confederates ranging widely to the north, to take prompt and effective action with inadequate information to guide him. Necessarily then his first day of command was spent in familiarizing himself with the strength and dispositions of his army and in considering possible plans.

Halleck's Initial Instructions to Meade

On the day he took command, June 28, his instructions from Washington were as follows:

> Headquarters of the Army,
> Washington, D. C., June 27, 1863.

Major General G. G. Meade,
Army of the Potomac.

General:

You will receive with this the order of the President placing you in command of the Army of the Potomac. Considering the circumstances, no one ever received a more important command; and I cannot doubt that you will fully justify the confidence which the Government has reposed in you.

You will not be hampered by any minute instructions from these headquarters. Your army is free to act as you may deem proper under the circumstances as they arise. You will, however, keep in view the important fact that the Army of the Potomac is the covering army of Washington, as well as the army of operation against the invading forces of the rebels. You will therefore maneuver and fight in such a manner as to cover the Capital and also Baltimore, as far as circumstances will admit. Should General Lee move upon either of these places, it is expected that you will either anticipate him or arrive with him, so as to give him battle.

All forces within the sphere of your operations will be held subject to your orders.

Harper's Ferry and its garrison are under your direct orders.

You are authorized to remove from command and send from your army any officer or other person you may deem proper; and to appoint to command as you may deem expedient.

In fine, General, you are intrusted with all the power and authority which the President, the Secretary of War, or the General-in-Chief can confer on you, and you may rely on our full support.

You will keep me fully informed of all your movements and the positions of your own troops and those of the enemy, so far as known.

I shall always be ready to advise and assist you to the utmost of my ability.

Very respectfully,
Your obedient servant,
H. W. Halleck,
General-in-Chief.

The security complex was still controlling in Washington, and Meade was consequently restricted to that extent in evolving whatever plans he might otherwise have conceived for an aggressively strategic offensive. He wired Halleck as follows:

Frederick, Md., 7 a. m., June 28, 1863.

H. W. Halleck,
  General-in-Chief:

The order placing me in command of this army is received. As a soldier I obey it, and to the utmost of my ability will execute it. Totally unexpected as it has been, and in ignorance of the exact condition of the troops and position of the enemy, I can only now say that it appears to me I must move towards the Susquehanna, keeping Washington and Baltimore well covered, and if the enemy is checked in his attempt to cross the Susquehanna, or if he turns towards Baltimore, to give him battle. I would say that I trust that every available man that can be spared will be sent to me, as, from all accounts, the enemy is in strong force. So soon as I can post myself up I will communicate more in detail.

George G. Meade,
Major General.

Meade's Timid Attitude

The extent to which Halleck's directive influenced Meade's subsequent actions can only be imagined. Like many of the Federal generals Meade was apparently obsessed with the myth of Lee's invincibility, because he greatly overestimated the Confederate invasion strength and from the time he took command of the army seemed strangely timid about crossing swords with Lee. It had not been noticeable in his previous service as brigade and division commander, but his actions from Frederick on reveal a defensive psychology, as will presently appear. From time to time Lincoln almost despaired of him as he had of previous army commanders; first when Meade mentioned that he had forced Lee "to fall back from the Susquehanna"; and again when, after the Battle of Gettysburg, Meade congratulated his army on "freeing Northern soil of the invader," as though that were all that was expected.

At the time he took command, Meade's army was concentrated in the Frederick area, while the Confederates were scattered all over the landscape to the north. This would seem to have offered a splendid opportunity for Meade, keeping his army together, to defeat Lee's separate corps by instalments. However, his telegram to Halleck, dispatched within a few hours of the time when he was officially notified of his appointment, could not at such an early stage represent the result of any considered strategic planning.

Recalling Hooker's plan to have Slocum's Twelfth Corps move from the Frederick area towards Harper's Ferry and, reinforced by the large garrison at that important crossing of the Potomac, to operate on Lee's line of communication and supply down the valley, it would be interesting to speculate on subsequent developments had Meade adopted Hooker's plan. Washington didn't like the idea, however, and when Halleck refused to permit the Harper's Ferry garrison to come under Hooker's control, Slocum was recalled and Hooker submitted his resignation. Whereupon, with Meade in command, Halleck immediately reversed himself and assigned the Harper's Ferry garrison to him, thus tacitly agreeing to the Hooker project under his successor.

A heavily reinforced army corps on Lee's tail, with a moderate sized cavalry contingent as covering force (which was entirely practicable), was an intriguing possibility. If, keeping his main body intact, Meade had moved energetically northward, it is conceivable that he might have bottled Lee in the mountains west of Cashtown with a pivot of maneuver and overwhelmed Ewell's divisions piecemeal as they came hurrying back, under Lee's concentration orders, from the York and Carlisle area.

Such an exciting prospect was apparently not within the scope of Meade's imaginative processes. He seems merely to have offered lip service to the very practicable idea of moving rapidly north to attack and defeat Lee's forces in detail. So Slocum's Twelfth Corps retraced its steps from South Mountain and joined the main body in its measured and cautious march in the general direction of the Confederate army and the Susquehanna river.

Meade evidently reasoned that Lee must scatter in order

to subsist and, while he talked about possibly defeating his enemy in detail, his orders for the advance of his army on June 28 and 29 were not such as to realize that prospect. A study of the map, the road net, and the terrain indicates that Meade's logistics were based primarily on a program: first, to cover Baltimore and Washington; second, to indicate a defensive line, in keeping with the security of the Capital, upon which to meet Lee's attack, if made; and third, to attack Lee if, after finding him, he could do so with impunity. The important supply point and communication center at Frederick was taken care of by Meade's order to General French to move the 7,000 men of the Harper's Ferry garrison to Frederick, which nicely covered Meade's rear in the direction of the Potomac.

Meade Plays It Safe

It is not surprising under the circumstances that Meade played it safe in deciding to adhere strictly to Halleck's admonition so to maneuver as to assure the security of Baltimore and Washington. The Army of the Potomac had been under a cloud for a long time, and the impression prevailed strongly among some of its high ranking officers that to put it mildly it was not exactly in favor at the War Department. Major General Henry J. Hunt wrote bitterly that "rarely, if ever, had it heard a word of official commendation after a success, or of sympathy or encouragement after a defeat." At the very least the frequent changes in army commanders presupposed a lack of confidence on the part of the administration in the ability of the generals commanding, which seems to have been warranted by the facts. There was certainly no indication, however, that Washington had lost confidence in the army itself.

One can imagine the overwhelming procession of thoughts that must have crowded Meade's mind as the

newly appointed army commander walked alone into his
tent on the outskirts of Frederick after bidding Generals
Hooker and Hardie goodbye on the afternoon of June 28.
All he had to do was to halt Lee's march on Harrisburg,
bring him to battle, preferably on a field that offered
superior advantages to his own army, be certain that in so
doing he would protect the Capital, and then defeat Lee
and wind up the business by sending him on his way back
to Virginia!

But first Meade must find out what he had to fight with
and just where the troops were.

An Unwanted Chief of Staff

One would have thought that the Army Chief of Staff,
on the arrival of a new Army Commander, would have
immediately briefed the General on that most vital information, the location and disposition of his troops, The
fact remains that he did not, possibly because considerable
coldness existed between Major General Dan Butterfield,
who had been Hooker's Chief of Staff, and General Meade.
Clearly the circumstances called for a waiver by both parties of any personal differences or lack of harmony that
may have existed. Close cooperation was essential to the
welfare of the Army of the Potomac at a critical moment.

The fact was that Meade did not want to keep Butterfield as his Chief of Staff, and that he offered the position
both to General Seth Williams, his Adjutant General, and
to General Warren, his Chief of Engineers, as a temporary
assignment in addition to their other duties. General Humphreys, a division commander in Sickles' corps, was the
man Meade really wanted for the job, but he was reluctant
to transfer him away from Sickles at that stage. Under the
circumstances, Meade asked Butterfield to remain temporarily as Chief of Staff, which he did until wounded

slightly on the third day of Gettysburg, at which time Humphreys was appointed to the post.

So Meade pores over his maps, which were none too good, and then sends his engineers to reconnoiter the ground to the north. The line of Big Pipe Creek, a well-defined landmark that the troops could easily identify,

BRIGADIER GENERAL A. A. HUMPHREYS
Division commander under Sickles at Gettysburg. Later Meade's Chief of Staff.

seems to run in the right direction and to be appropriately located to meet all the requirements of a defensive line. Big Pipe Creek it is, then, and it was a sound appraisal as things looked to Meade at the time.

The Pipe Creek Plan

The "Pipe Creek circular," written late on the night of June 30 and based on the report of his engineers, directed that, if and when the circular was made effective, the Army would form line of battle along the general line

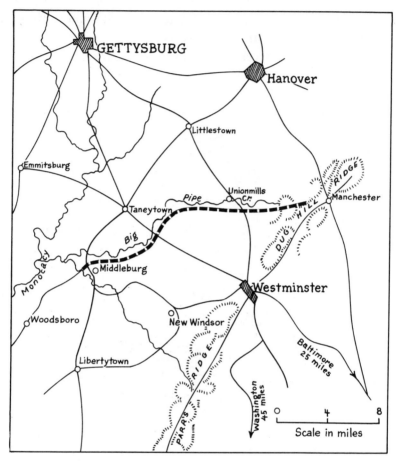

Map 6. MEADE'S PROPOSED POSITION ON PIPE CREEK

On June 30, Gen. Meade, the new commander of the Army of the Potomac, still regarded his mission as being to protect Washington and Baltimore. He had a defensive line reconnoitered along Pipe Creek from Manchester to Middleburg, shown on this map as a heavy broken line. In notifying Halleck of this plan, Meade pointed out that the position afforded a good reserve line along Parr's Ridge—Dug Hill Ridge, and that it was oriented to protect not only Baltimore but also his base of supplies at Westminster. Halleck in his reply generally approved Meade's plan, but suggested that perhaps Meade was too far east. He said that vast quantities of supplies along the Potomac canal were being captured by the Confederates, and that Meade ought to give thought to protecting that area rather than Westminster.

of the creek with the left at Middleburg and the right at Manchester. The map shows that this position would cover the main routes to Baltimore and Washington, and the important railroads running to the same cities, with the added advantage that Parr's Ridge—Dug Hill Ridge would furnish an excellent reserve line to fall back on in case of need.

Meade was strongly criticized for the Pipe Creek circular, although the circular itself explained what he had in mind, in the following words:

> This order is communicated that a general plan, perfectly understood by all, may be had for receiving attack, as made in strong force upon any portion of our present position. Developments may cause the Commanding General to assume the offensive from his present positions.

At the same time Meade made it plain to his corps commanders that he had no intention of assuming the offensive "until Lee's movements or positions should render such an operation certain of success." He even went so far as to inform them that, if the enemy should attack, he would hold them in check long enough to remove his trains and baggage and then withdraw to the defensive position generally along Pipe Creek.

The famous Pipe Creek order has been the subject of endless controversy. Writers favorable to Meade defend the order as a legitimate document which any thoughtful army commander would distribute to his high ranking subordinates as precautionary instructions in the event of a contingency requiring a retrograde movement. His detractors, on the other hand, maintain that the Pipe Creek order was simply further evidence of Meade's defensive psychology and unwillingness to take the risk of attacking Lee, no matter how favorable the situation.

Another factor that should not be overlooked was that Meade could not be sure, at that stage, that Lee would come through the Cashtown Pass. Lee could perfectly well have moved south under cover of the Blue Ridge and turned east on the Waynesboro-Westminster road, in an effort to turn Meade's left flank and interpose himself between the Army of the Potomac and Washington. This was the possibility which Halleck feared when he implied that Meade was moving too far east, uncovering Frederick and the area immediately east of the Blue Ridge. Seen in this light, the Pipe Creek circular was about as good a hedge as could be devised at the moment, pending more detailed information on Lee's position and movements.

In any event, there can be no blinking the fact that the initiative was left largely to Lee. Meade's every thought seemed to be based on the desire to get Lee back to Virginia, without a fight if possible, and this theme continued to dominate as Lee retreated southward after the battle, Meade's slowness in pursuit furnishing the final evidence.

FEDERAL ARTILLERY ADVANCING OVER DIFFICULT ROADS

CHAPTER 9

THE UNION ARMY ADVANCES ON A BROAD FRONT

ON THE night of June 28, Meade's first day of command, his army had reached the line Emmitsburg-New Windsor, on a front of over 20 miles, with Buford's cavalry covering the left at Fairfield, Gregg's the right at Westminster, and Kilpatrick's in front near Hanover. On that day Ewell was at Carlisle and York, Longstreet at Chambersburg, and Hill between Fayetteville and Cashtown.

Meade's Orders and Movements

To understand fully Meade's plans for the movement of his army for the next three days, June 29, 30 and July 1, an examination of the map in conjunction with the timetable for the successive march objectives will be enlightening:

93

Corps	Commander	June 29	June 30	July 1
First	Reynolds	Emmitsburg	Marsh Creek	Gettysburg
Eleventh	Howard	Emmitsburg	Emmitsburg	Gettysburg (or supporting distance)
Third	Sickles	Taneytown	Bridgeport	Emmitsburg
Twelfth	Slocum	Taneytown	Littlestown	Two Taverns
Second	Hancock	Frizzleburg	Uniontown	Taneytown
Fifth	Sykes	Uniontown	Union Mills	Hanover
Sixth	Sedgwick	New Windsor	Manchester	Manchester
Army Command Post		Middleburg	Taneytown	Taneytown

Meade's selection of the small village of Taneytown for his headquarters during the advance was a logical one, because it was the ideal point from which to keep in touch with the chessboard movements of his seven corps. Conversely, incoming mounted couriers and foot messengers would have no difficulty in locating the command post. Situated on the Frederick branch of the Northern Central Railroad, the town was an important crossroad on high ground which commanded an exceptionally good view of the countryside in all directions. Taneytown in 1863 had attained the ripe age of 109 years, but according to local historians the story that it was named after Chief Justice Taney of the U. S. Supreme Court is incorrect, since that distinguished gentleman happened to have been born in 1777. The town is a part of Carroll County, Maryland, reputed to be the fourth richest agricultural county in the United States.

The advance for June 30 was in reality a continuation of the previous day's march. It will be noted that three corps are pointed towards Gettysburg; on June 30 Meade formed these three, the First, Third and Eleventh, into a provisional left wing, in view of probable early contact with the enemy, and placed General Reynolds in command.

General Buford, whose cavalry division was now operat-

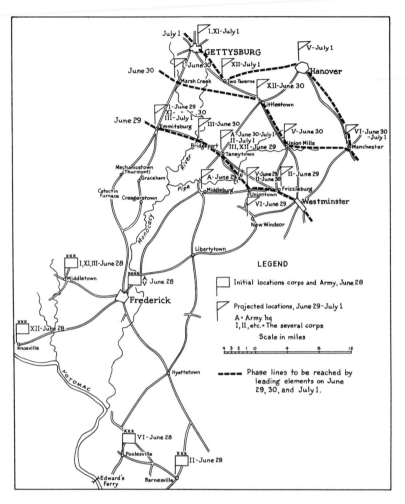

Map 7. MEADE'S PLAN OF ADVANCE FOR JUNE 29—JULY 1

This map shows the various localities which Meade directed his corps to reach on successive days. The heavy broken lines show the phases of this planned advance.

ing in the vicinity of Gettysburg, kept sending back information of the enemy from that vicinity. On June 30 Meade issued the following precautionary and informative circulars:

> Headquarters Army of the Potomac,
> June 30, 1863.

Circular:

The Commanding General has received information that the enemy are advancing, probably in strong force, on Gettysburg. It is the intention to hold this army pretty nearly in the position it now occupies, until the plans of the enemy have been more fully developed.

Three corps, 1st, 3d and 11th, are under the command of Major General Reynolds, in the vicinity of Emmettsburg, the 3d Corps being ordered up to that point. The 12th Corps is at Littlestown. Gregg's division of cavalry is believed to be now engaged with the cavalry of the enemy, near Hanover Junction.

CAVALRY SCOUTS NEAR GETTYSBURG

Corps commanders will hold their commands in readiness at a moment's notice, and upon receiving orders, to march against the enemy. Their trains (ammunition trains excepted) must be parked in the rear of the place of concentration. Ammunition wagons and ambulances will alone be permitted to accompany the troops. The men must be provided with three days' rations in haversacks, and with sixty rounds of ammunition in the boxes and upon the person.

Corps commanders will avail themselves of all the time at their disposal to familiarize themselves with the roads communicating with the different corps.

By command of Major General Meade.

S. Williams,
Asst. Adjt. Gen'l.

Headquarters Army of the Potomac,
June 30, 1863.

Circular:

The Commanding General requests that, previous to the engagement soon expected with the enemy, corps and all other commanding officers address their troops, explaining to them briefly the immense issues involved in the struggle. The enemy are on our soil; the whole country now looks anxiously to this army to deliver it from the presence of the foe. Our failure to do so will leave us no such welcome as the swelling of millions of hearts with pride and joy, as our success would give to every soldier of this army. Homes, firesides and domestic altars are involved. The army has fought well heretofore; it is believed that it will fight more desperately and bravely than ever, if it is addressed in fitting terms.

Corps and other commanders are authorized to

order the instant death of any soldier who fails in his duty at this hour.

By command of Major General Meade.

S. Williams,
Asst. Adjt. Gen'l.

The above circulars were followed shortly thereafter by orders for the march of July 1, which were directed to be executed immediately upon their receipt. Since the battle was joined on the morning of July 1, the order for the final march is of sufficient interest to be reprinted in full:

Headquarters Army of the Potomac,
June 30, 1863.

Orders:

Headquarters at Taneytown:

3d Corps to Emmettsburg.	1st Corps to Gettysburg.
2d Corps to Taneytown.	11th Corps to Gettysburg. (or supporting distance).
5th Corps to Hanover.	12th Corps to Two Taverns.

Cavalry to front and flanks, well out in all directions, giving timely notice of operations and movements of the enemy. All empty wagons, surplus baggage, useless animals, and impedimenta of every sort, to Union Bridge, three miles from Middleburg; a proper officer from each corps with them; supplies will be brought up there as soon as practicable.

The General relies upon every commander to put his column in the lightest possible order. The Telegraph Corps to work east from Hanover, repairing the line, and all commanders to work repairing the line in their vicinity between Gettysburg and Hanover.

Staff officers to report daily from each corps, and with orderlies to leave for orders. Prompt information to be sent into headquarters at all times. All ready to move to the attack at any moment.

The Commanding General desires you to be informed that, from present information, Longstreet and Hill are at Chambersburg, partly towards Gettysburg; Ewell, at Carlisle and York; movements indicate a disposition to advance from Chambersburg to Gettysburg. General Couch telegraphs, 29th, his opinion that enemy's operations on Susquehanna are more to prevent cooperation with this army than offensive.

The General believes he has relieved Harrisburg and Philadelphia, and now desires to look to his own army and assume position for offensive or defensive, as occasion requires, or rest to the troops. It is not his desire to wear the troops out by excessive fatigue and marches, and thus unfit them for the work they will be called upon to perform.

TELEGRAPH STATION WITH THE FEDERAL ARMY

Vigilance, energy and prompt response to the orders from headquarters are necessary, and the personal attention of corps commanders must be given to reduction of impedimenta. The orders and movements from these headquarters must be carefully and confidentially preserved, that they do not fall into the enemy's hands.

By command of Major General Meade.
                                        S. Williams,
                                   Asst. Adjt. Gen'l.

It is pertinent to note that, in Meade's orders for June 29 and 30, the army was disposed in two north-south columns within supporting distance of one another. The order for July 1, after later information had been received as to Lee's movements, had four of the seven corps converging on Gettysburg, while the Second, Fifth, and Sixth Corps were moved to within a short distance of the possible defense line of Big Pipe Creek. Sedgwick's Sixth Corps of over 15,000 men was in army reserve at Manchester, on the direct road to Baltimore, but over 35 miles distant from Gettysburg.

Lee Reacts Promptly to Meade's Threat

Meade's threat to Lee's flank and rear confronted the latter with an entirely new problem requiring prompt decision and action, as the Army of the Potomac fanned out from Frederick along the roads to the north. On arrival of the main body of his army in the Chambersburg area on Friday, June 26, Lee had established his headquarters in a grove which at that time stood along the pike leading to Gettysburg, near the eastern edge of Chambersburg. It was once known as Shetter's Woods, later as Messersmith's Woods, and was for years a popular place for local picnics and celebrations. Lee remained there until Tuesday morning June 30, received reports from his troops, held councils of war, planned the attack on Harrisburg, and finally issued the orders to cross South Mountain to seek out the Union army.

It was on the night of June 28 that Longstreet's scout had brought the first news of the presence of Meade's army and it was there, at Shetter's Woods, that Lee learned his old opponent, the Army of the Potomac, was not only un-expectedly alive and kicking under a more worthy com-mander, but was actually moving rapidly forward in such a way as to constitute an acute danger to the widely dis-persed Army of Northern Virginia

Lee was quick to react. The first and most important job was to effect a rapid concentration of his army, pre-ferably east of the Blue Ridge where he would have room for maneuver and could deny the vital pass at Cashtown to the Federals. The showdown battle was near at hand. He must have his troops assembled where he could employ them to advantage in whatever manner the next few days might indicate.

Stuart was still far to the south, with the Federals crowd-ing the roads between Lee and himself. Although little has been written on the subject, the Confederate cavalry brigades under Lee's immediate command were all seem-ingly too far north or too far in Lee's rear in the valley to perform the reconnaissance missions necessary to deter-mine the dispositions and movements of the Union forces, which were then only a few miles away on the other side of the mountains.

On the 29th Ewell was recalled from the Susquehanna and told to rejoin the other corps at Chambersburg. Then, on second thought, Lee directed all three of his corps to concentrate in the Cashtown area, east of the mountains.

FEDERAL COLUMNS MOVING NORTH THROUGH MARYLAND

These orders of course took some time to reach Ewell, but he was no laggard when explicit instructions were given. His retrograde movement was initiated and executed with commendable dispatch.

Situation on the Eve of Battle

On the night of Tuesday, June 30-July 1, the eve of the battle, this was the situation: more than 70,000 troops were in camp within a few miles of Gettysburg—27,000 Union infantry and cavalry and about 43,000 Confederate infantry, with a small scattering of cavalry.

On the Union side, Reynold's First and Howard's Eleventh Corps, totalling over 22,000 men, were bivouacked four to eight miles southwest of Gettysburg along Marsh Creek, with two-thirds of Buford's overstrength cavalry division, some 4,000 men, on the Chambersburg turnpike about a mile and a half northwest of Gettysburg.

With the exception of the aforementioned units, the Army of the Potomac was poised at varying distances south and southeast of Gettysburg: Sickles' corps a few miles east of Emmitsburg, eight miles south; Slocum's at Littlestown, and Sykes' at Union Mills, both within fifteen miles of Gettysburg on the Gettysburg-Westminster road; Hancock's Second Corps at Uniontown, about twenty-four road miles from Gettysburg; while Sedgwick was out of immediate circulation at Manchester, on the direct road between Baltimore and Hanover. The Federal cavalry was tactically well disposed and active to the front and flanks, serving Meade far more effectively than was the case with Stuart and his detached brigades.

On the Confederate side, A. P. Hill's corps of 23,000 and Longstreet's 14,000 (excluding Pickett's division of 5,000 which was left to protect the rear and the trains at Chambersburg), an aggregate of approximately 37,000 men, were stretched out on the road between Chambersburg and Gettysburg or in bivouac on both sides of that pike. Hill's Corps was in the lead, with Heth's division east of South Mountain, having cleared the Cashtown pass. The other two divisions of Hill's corps, Pender's and Anderson's, joined Heth at Cashtown over night, with Anderson going into bivouac at Cashtown and Pender joining Heth a few miles further east along Marsh Creek, about four miles from Gettysburg.

Ewell's corps of 23,000 was moving in from the north, with advance elements of Rodes' division bivouacking near Heidlersburg on the Harrisburg road, less than ten miles from Gettysburg, while Ewell's other divisions were on the march to Cashtown by all available roads from Harrisburg, Carlisle and York. Johnson's division of this corps spent the night at Greenwood, coming by way of Shippensburg, through Scotland.

The Confederate cavalry was still widely scattered, Stuart near Hanover and Jenkins covering Ewell's flank and rear to the north. Imboden's cavalry, twenty miles southwest of Chambersburg in the valley, was keeping the way open for the troopers of the two cavalry brigades commanded by Generals Jones and Robertson, who were coming up from the Potomac with instructions to protect the rear of Ewell's trains on arrival and then to follow the army towards Gettysburg.

The Gettysburg Area

There have been many discussions over the years as to whether Gettysburg was consciously selected by either or both of the opposing commanders as the focal point for the inevitable showdown battle. Persuasive arguments can be advanced for either premise, but it is difficult to believe that the meeting at that place was entirely accidental. No military man trained in the study of terrain and its influence on tactics could fail to appreciate the tremendous importance of the road net of which Gettysburg was the center. Not only that, the entire countryside to the southeast of Gettysburg, including the area of Meade's concentration, was virtually a troop commander's tactical dream. It was and is ideal country for maneuvering, no matter which way one happens to face. The terrain is rolling, with innumerable low ridges, streams, woods, and hedge rows, with plenty of defiladed space and protected areas for military operations.

From Lee's point of view, concentration and battle at Gettysburg would have the effect of keeping Meade east of the mountains and away from his own line of communications down the Cumberland Valley. In case of victory in the vicinity of Gettysburg, Lee would have a choice of advancing via Harrisburg and Philadelphia, or Baltimore and Washington; if defeated his line of retreat would be protected through the vital mountain passes, the easiest kind of a line to defend.

The strategic and tactical advantages of Gettysburg with its remarkable road net must surely have been known to Meade, a Pennsylvanian. Yet there is strong evidence that in the disposition of his army on June 28-30 the impelling factors were Washington's insistence on covering Baltimore and Washington and his own conviction that he would be fulfilling his mission if, in selecting a line

MAJOR GENERAL DAVID BIRNEY

Commander of a division under Sickles. Temporarily in command of Sixth Corps.

of defense not too far north, he could force Lee to reverse his direction and bring on the fight well south of the Susquehanna.

It seems logical that the Gettysburg area as a battlefield was in the minds of both commanding generals, although the precise terrain upon which the battle was fought was purely accidental. Both Lee and Meade initiated the development of their armies late on June 28, and in the natural course of events the movement of each was in the direction of the other. As recounted in Chapter 11, the actual spark was ignited when Pettigrew's brigade of Heth's Confederate division, marching into Gettysburg to pick up some badly needed shoes, collided with Buford's Federal cavalry on the Chambersburg road, a short distance west of Gettysburg. From then on the development of both armies progressed in a hectic race "to get there fustest."

The theater of operations which served as the backdrop for the climactic battle of Gettysburg was a vast area that included portions of four states, Virginia, Maryland, West Virginia and Pennsylvania. The main battle area, except for the initial clash at Winchester and sporadic cavalry skirmishes on the fringes, covered a few square miles of country in a lush Pennsylvania valley, 70 miles northwest of Washington, 38 miles south of Harrisburg, and 8 miles east of the vital Cashtown pass in the Blue Ridge Mountains through which the Confederate forces were debouching from their concentration area in the vicinity of Chambersburg to meet the Army of the Potomac coming up from the south.

In 1863 Gettysburg, the county seat of Adams County, was a small borough of some two thousand people, but important even in those days as the hub of a network of 12 (10 main and 2 branch) roads which angled out in every direction, a strategic factor that played a not inconsiderable part in the drama about to unfold. These roads, radiating from the town square, passed through a rich agricultural country of well-tilled fields and big red barns belonging to the hard working, thrifty farmers of predominantly German or Dutch extraction, and ultimately reached the cities or towns of Washington, Frederick, Hagerstown, Chambersburg, Carlisle, Harrisburg, York, and Baltimore. All were dirt country roads except the Chambersburg, York and Baltimore Pikes, which according to the best information available were hard-surfaced with a mixture of stone and gravel.

A newspaper reporter with the Union forces, as the two armies approached one another, sent off to his paper a dispatch which in a few paragraphs painted a typical picture of the character of the countryside forming the stage for the impending battle.

Describing the trip from Taneytown to the front, he* wrote:

> Riding through the marching columns became more and more difficult as we advanced, and finally to avoid it we turned off into a by-way leading to the right. We were told that our by-path would bring us into the Baltimore pike, certain to be less obstructed. Across the hills to the left we could see the white covered wagons slowly winding in and out through the trees and the blue-coated masses toiling forward. The shades of the evening dimmed and magnified the scene until one might have thought the hosts of Xerxes in all the glory of modern armor were pressing on to Gettysburg.
>
> Selecting a promising looking farm-house, with a more than usually impressive barn in the rear, we stopped for supper. Great cherry trees bent before the door under their weight of fruit; the kitchen garden was crowded with vegetables; contented cattle stood about the barn; sleek horses filled the stables; fat geese gave a doubtful hiss of welcome as we came too near, and the very farm yard laughed with plenty. To add to our comfort the farmer's hearty welcome was supplemented by a well-spread table.
>
> It was dark when we resumed our journey, but our by-path had now become a road with a full moon

---

* Jacob Hoke, *Gettysburg, the Great Invasion of 1863*, Dayton, 1887.

casting occasional glances at us from behind the clouds. At last camp-fires gleamed through the woods ahead and we caught the hum of the camps. We passed in front of a house where all the lights were out, but the family had gathered on the door-step too much interested in the, to them, unfamiliar sounds and sights to go to bed. 'If you want to stop for the night,' they said, pointing off the road to the right, 'turn up by the school-house. Squire Durburrow is such a nice man!'

Squire Durburrow is a very nice man. We roused him out of bed where he must have been for two or three hours. 'Can you take care of us until morning?' we asked. 'I will do it with pleasure,' he replied. The horses are housed in one of those great horse-palaces these people build for barns; we are comfortably and even luxuriously quartered.

The reporter who sent the above dispatch was later to become the Ambassador representing the United States at the Court of St. James, the Hon. Whitelaw Reid.

GETTYSBURG FROM OAK HILL, LOOKING SOUTH

CHAPTER 10

THE STAGE IS SET

IT IS a truism that the influence of terrain features and characteristics on military operations is all-important; and the fact is confirmed by the frequency with which battles are identified as a result of the decisive part played by rivers, mountains, hills, roads, and towns in the drama of warfare.

Gettysburg Amphitheater a Tactical Paradise

Gettysburg was no exception. On the contrary, it is one of the foremost examples in American military history of the extent to which the topographical features of the countryside mark the course of battles. The Blue Ridge Mountains, the Cashtown pass, Oak Ridge, Seminary Ridge, Cemetery Ridge, the Emmitsburg road, Culp's Hill, the Round Tops, Willoughby Run, Marsh Creek, Devil's Den—all afford eloquent testimony of the impelling significance of terrain features in determining the what, where, why, and how of a battle which has few counterparts in American history from the viewpoint of tactical possibilities.

The town of Gettysburg nestles in a small valley surrounded by low ridges and hills, with the South Moun-

109

tain range looming on the horizon 10 miles to the west. About a half mile west of the town square is a moderate elevation called Seminary Ridge, running north and south, named from the Lutheran Theological Seminary that stands on its crest, midway between the Cashtown and Fairfield roads and about 300 yards from each. The ridge is covered throughout its entire length with open woods. The ground slopes away to the west and then rises to form McPherson's Ridge about 500 yards from the first. Both ridges start at Oak Hill, 1,200 yards north of the Chambersburg pike.

Willoughby Run crosses the Chambersburg pike in a north-south direction between McPherson's and still a third short, unnamed ridge to the west, and empties into Marsh Creek a few miles southwest of Gettysburg. Still further west is the last of the four parallel ridges, known as Herr Ridge, each of them several hundred yards apart and all forming natural successive positions, plentifully covered with open woods. These ridges, small valleys, and streams, coupled with an unfinished railway, just north of and paralleling the Cashtown pike, which crossed them all through cuts and fills, formed the stage upon which occurred the first skirmishes of the battle of Gettysburg.

While Seminary Ridge and its angled prolongation through Gettysburg itself subsequently constituted the main Confederate position, an even more important key position was Cemetery Ridge, extending more than two miles directly south from the town. The ridge is flanked at its northern end by Cemetery Hill at the southeastern fringe of Gettysburg, and at its southern extremity by Big Round Top which is connected by a saddle to Little Round Top, several hundred yards to its north. Cemetery Ridge generally parallels the Emmitsburg road, with Big Round Top, the highest point in the area, towering per-

LUTHERAN THEOLOGICAL SEMINARY
This shows the face of the seminary facing east. Both Buford and Reynolds
used the cupola as an observation post.

haps a hundred feet above Little Round Top. Both hills
are boulder-studded—glacial deposits—terminating at the
western base in a skirmisher's nightmare called Devil's
Den.

East and southeast of Cemetery Hill rises wooded Culp's
Hill, of almost equal importance with Round Top, since
possession of Culp's Hill was vital to the troops occupying
Cemetery Hill and Ridge, for flank protection and to pre-
clude the devastating enfilade artillery fire of an opponent
who could otherwise make Cemetery Hill untenable. The
troops who control the Round Tops, Cemetery Ridge,
Cemetery Hill, and Culp's Hill come pretty close to
dominating the battlefield for defensive operations.

When the concentration of the opposing armies was
complete, they faced one another on parallel ridges
separated by approximately 1,200 yards of apple orchards
and cultivated fields of wheat and grass, with the Emmitsburg Road bisecting them down a shallow valley, the
whole adding up to a unique amphitheater upon which
the major scenes of the drama were destined to be played
out.

It may be interesting to note that in and around the
town of Gettysburg is the greatest concentration of trap

ridges in the southern part of Pennsylvania. Originally identified as such by Pennsylvania's first geologist, and shown on a geological map published in 1858, the possibility exists that General Meade and the geologist, Henry D. Rodgers, were acquainted before the war. Both were residents of Philadelphia, and it is an intriguing speculation that Meade may have been subconsciously aware of the solid strength of the Gettysburg hills.

Lee in the Saddle Early; Meade Stays at Command Post

General Lee was in the saddle early on July 1, accompanying the rather slow movement of Longstreet's corps, which had been held up to allow one of Ewell's divisions, returning by the Carlisle-Chambersburg road, to pass through Longstreet's column. Having already issued the necessary orders for the concentration, Lee left the details of execution to his corps commanders, as was his custom, and consequently was free to devote his attention to consideration of possible plans for the inevitable battle, wherever it might occur.

VIEW OF CULP'S HILL FROM A POSITION NEAR THE CEMETERY

The wooden tower on the right, built by the Gettysburg Battlefield Memorial Association, no longer stands.

PENNSYLVANIA COLLEGE, GETTYSBURG
The cupola was used successively by Federals and Confederates as an observation post and signal tower.

General Meade, still playing a conservative game of chess, remained at his command post in Taneytown, estimating the situation, receiving a succession of reports from his cavalry, and conferring with his staff and the general officers whom he most trusted.

The march orders which he had sent out the night of June 30 for the next day directed Reynolds, now in command of the three-corps left wing (First, Third and Eleventh Corps), to move his own First Corps to Gettysburg early next morning, followed by Howard's Eleventh, with Sickles' Third to inch westward a few miles from Bridgeport to Emmitsburg, eight miles south of Gettysburg. Reynolds was given authority to order Sickles further forward if needed, but Meade was still apparently concerned about the mountain pass west of Emmitsburg and wanted to be sure that Lee should not catch him napping. Slocum's corps at Littlestown was to advance to Two Taverns, four miles closer and just halfway between Littlestown and Gettysburg on the Baltimore road.

Meade remained uncertain of Lee's intentions and was reluctant to pass up his Pipe Creek line of defense. So he compromised by advancing what might be called his first line of four corps to Gettysburg and vicinity, while retaining Hancock's, Sykes', and Sedgwick's corps on the arc Taneytown-Hanover-Manchester, within short marching distance of Big Pipe Creek, ready to jump either way. Sykes' projected move from Union Mills to Hanover, while the long way about to Gettysburg, had the merit of closing that very vital road net at Hanover, 14 miles east of Gettysburg, in case Stuart's cavalry should become too aggressive, or Early's corps, known to have been at York, should decide to come down that way.

Strength and Composition of the Opposing Forces

At this point a few important statistics are listed, for later reference, on the organization, strength, designation, and commanders of the major elements of the opposing armies. The data has been taken from several sources, principally *Battles and Leaders of the Civil War,* and Steele's *American Campaigns,* but for a number of reasons exact reconciliation of the figures is impossible. Those having to do with the Union army are reasonably accurate, but the breakdown of Lee's strength by corps is simply an educated guess. The names of the division commanders are included because in succeeding chapters there will be reference to at least some of the more prominent ones. Normally the units will be identified by their numerical designation or the name of its commander.

Federal and Confederate records show the organization and strength of the two armies at Gettysburg as follows:

UNION ARMY	CONFEDERATE ARMY
(Off. and Enl. Men)	(Enlisted Men)

UNION ARMY		CONFEDERATE ARMY	
Infantry	77,042	Infantry	54,356
Artillery	7,183	Artillery	4,460
Cavalry	13,144	Cavalry	9,536
Special Troops, Engrs. etc.	2,550		
Reinforcements July 1-3:		Officers (Present for duty)	6,116
To First Corps	2,500	Accessions between	
To Twelfth Corps	1,700	May 31 & July 3*	5,600
To Cavalry	110	2 Artillery Bns. est.	800
			80,868
		Less	3,350**
	104,229		77,518

* Jenkins and Imboden's cavalry brigades and Pettigrew's infantry brigade.
** Detachments left in Virginia at Hanover Court House and Winchester, and one regiment of Stuart's cavalry.

The average strength of corps and divisions of the Union army was about half that of the Confederate tables of organization. The Union organization was considered by many to have been unwieldy, with too many corps resulting in less effective control by the army commander because of an excessive number of subordinate commanders and staffs.

The figures given make no allowance for the sick, stragglers, deserters, or losses in recent skirmishes. Considering the fact that it was summertime, which normally means less sickness among the troops, an arbitrary deduction of 5% for non-effectives would reduce the combat strength to approximately 99,000 for the Union Army and 73,500 for the Confederate Army, an aggregate total of 172,500 officers and men.

Twenty-nine states in all were represented in the military forces at Gettysburg, Maryland having troops in both armies.

COMPOSITION OF THE OPPOSING FORCES
UNION ARMY
Major General George G. Meade, Com'd'g

Corps	Major General Commanding	Corps Insignia	No. of Divisions	No. of Brigades	Strength *
G. H. Q.		....	..	..	50
First	John F. Reynolds	Full Moon	3	7	12,589
	Abner Doubleday				
	John Newton				
Second	Winfield S. Hancock	Trefoil	3	10	12,996
	John Gibbon (Brig. Gen.)				
Third	Daniel E. Sickles	Diamond	2	6	11,924
Fifth	George Sykes	Maltese Cross ...	3	9	12,509
Sixth	John Sedgwick	Greek Cross	3	8	15,679
Eleventh	Oliver O. Howard	Crescent Moon ..	3	6	9,893
Twelfth	Henry W. Slocum	5-pointed Star ..	2	6	10,289
Artillery	Henry J. Hunt				
	(Brig. Gen.)		..	..	....
Art'y Res. .	Robert O. Tyler				
	(Brig. Gen.)		..	5	2,546
Cavalry	Alfred Pleasonton		3	8	13,254
Special Tr'ps			..	..	2,500
Total			22	65	104,229

* Incl. organic artillery and battle reinforcements, July 1-3.

Meade had 362 guns, 110 of them in the Artillery Reserve; 249 regiments of infantry, 38 regiments of cavalry, and 65 batteries of field artillery.

CONFEDERATE ARMY
General Robert E. Lee, Com'd'g

Corps	Lieut. General Commanding	No. of Divisions	No. of Brigades	Estimated strength (in round figures)
First ...	James Longstreet	3	11	19,000
Second .	Richard S. Ewell	3	13	23,000
Third ..	Ambrose P. Hill	3	13	23,000
Cavalry	Maj. Gen. J. E. B. Stuart		7	12,500
Total		9	44	77,500

Lee had 287 guns, each corps having its own artillery reserve; 182 regiments of infantry, 32 regiments of cavalry, and 69 batteries of field artillery.

DESIGNATION OF COMMANDERS DOWN TO DIVISIONS
BATTLE OF GETTYSBURG

			Approximate time of arrival on battlefield
ARMY OF THE POTOMAC	George G. Meade	Maj. Gen. *	Midnight, July 1
FIRST CORPS	John F. Reynolds	Maj. Gen.	10 A. M. July 1
	Abner Doubleday	Maj. Gen.	10:15 A. M. July 1
	John Newton	Maj. Gen.	4 P. M. July 2
First Division	J. S. Wadsworth	Brig. Gen.	10 A. M. July 1
Second Division	J. C. Robinson	Brig. Gen.	10:30 A. M. July 1
Third Division	T. A. Rowley	Brig. Gen.	10:15 A. M. July 1
SECOND CORPS	Winfield S. Hancock	Maj. Gen.	4 P. M. July 1
	John Gibbon		About daylight, July 2
First Division	J. C. Caldwell	Brig. Gen.	About daylight, July 2
Second Division	John Gibbon	Brig. Gen.	About daylight, July 2
Third Division	Alexander Hays	Brig. Gen.	About daylight, July 2
THIRD CORPS	Daniel E. Sickles	Maj. Gen.	7 P. M. July 1
First Division	D. B. Birney	Maj. Gen.	5:30 P. M. July 1
Second Division	A. A. Humphreys	Brig. Gen.	1 A. M. July 2
FIFTH CORPS	George Sykes	Maj. Gen.	6 A. M. July 2
First Division	James Barnes	Brig. Gen.	6-7 A. M. July 2
Second Division	R. B. Ayres	Brig. Gen.	6-7 A. M. July 2
Third Division	S. W. Crawford	Brig. Gen.	6-7 A. M. July 2
SIXTH CORPS	John Sedgwick	Maj. Gen.	4 P. M. July 2
First Division	H. G. Wright	Brig. Gen.	4 P. M. July 2
Second Division	A. P. Howe	Brig. Gen.	4 P. M. July 2
Third Division	John Newton	Maj. Gen.	4 P. M. July 2
ELEVENTH CORPS	Oliver O. Howard	Maj. Gen.	11:30 A. M. July 1
First Division	F. C. Barlow	Brig. Gen.	1 P. M. July 1
Second Division	Adolph von Steinwehr	Brig. Gen.	1:30 P. M. July 1
Third Division	Carl Schurz	Maj. Gen	1 P. M. July 1
TWELFTH CORPS	Henry W. Slocum	Maj. Gen	7 P. M. July 1
First Division	A. S. Williams	Brig. Gen.	5:30 P. M. July 1
Second Division	J. W. Geary	Brig. Gen.	5 P. M. July 1
CAVALRY CORPS	Alfred Pleasonton	Maj. Gen.	
First Division	John Buford	Brig. Gen.	June 30
Second Division	D. McM. Gregg	Brig. Gen.	July 2
Third Division	Judson Kilpatrick	Brig. Gen.	July 2
Reserve Artillery	H. J. Hunt	Brig. Gen.	About daylight, July 2

* Rank in all cases is brevet or temporary in U. S. Volunteers.

ARMY OF NORTHERN VIRGINIA	Robert E. Lee	General	1-2 P. M. July 1
FIRST CORPS	James Longstreet	Lieut. Gen.	4-5 P. M. July 1
McLaw's Division	Lafayette McLaws	Maj. Gen.	10 P. M. July 1
Pickett's Division	George E. Pickett	Maj. Gen.	4 P. M. July 2
Hood's Division	John B. Hood	Maj. Gen.	1-2 A. M. July 2
SECOND CORPS	Richard S. Ewell	Lieut. Gen.	About noon, July 1
Early's Division	Jubal A. Early	Maj. Gen.	2:30 P. M. July 1
Johnson's Division	Edward Johnson	Maj. Gen.	Dusk, July 1
Rodes' Division	Robert E. Rodes	Maj. Gen.	11-12 A. M. July 1
THIRD CORPS	Ambrose P. Hill	Lieut. Gen.	About 10 A. M. July 1
Anderson's Division	Richard H. Anderson	Maj. Gen.	4-5 P. M. July 1
Heth's Division	Henry Heth	Maj. Gen.	9 A. M. July 1
Pender's Division	William D. Pender	Maj. Gen.	11 A. M. July 1
CAVALRY CORPS	J. E. B. Stuart	Maj. Gen.	July 2
Fitzhugh Lee's Brigade	Fitzhugh Lee	Brig. Gen.	July 2
Hampton's Brigade	Wade Hampton	Brig. Gen.	July 2
W. H. F. Lee's Brigade	J. R. Chambliss	Colonel	July 2
Jenkin's Brigade	A. G. Jenkins	Brig. Gen.	July 1
Robertson's Brigade	B. H. Robertson	Brig. Gen.	—
Imboden's Brigade	J. D. Imboden	Brig. Gen.	July 3
Jones' Brigade	W. E. Jones	Brig. Gen.	—

BUFORD'S CAVALRY OPPOSING THE CONFEDERATE ADVANCE

CHAPTER 11

GETTYSBURG OPENS WITH A CAVALRY ENGAGEMENT

WEST Pointer John Buford, a major in the Inspector General's Department, was a man of ideas with a capacity to make them work. It was in 1862 that General Pope, then commanding the Army of Virginia, accepted as sound Buford's lack of confidence in the effectiveness of the current cavalry techniques practiced in the Army. Pope promoted him rapidly from major to brigadier general and placed him in command of the largest of the three cavalry brigades in the service, so that he might try out what was then a somewhat revolutionary concept.

Stuart's Southern horse outfits had set the pattern of mass charges with the saber, which was in character because the Confederate cavalry was largely made up of men who had lived their lives in the saddle, mostly owned their own mounts, and for whom mounted maneuvers and skirmishes represented more fun than work.

119

Buford's New Tactics

For his part Buford considered the saber to be of little practical value. He thought of the horse as a means of transportation, useful chiefly because of the greatly increased mobility which it gave to the mounted troops. He treated cavalry as mounted infantry, and instilled that belief in his brigade and later his division, until it became practically instinctive. The procedure was to move rapidly to a critical position and dismount the troops to quickly form

BRIGADIER GENERAL JOHN BUFORD
Commander of the 1st Cavalry Division.

an infantry skirmish line, while one out of every four men became horseholder for the group, under cover to the immediate rear, ready at all times for the set of fours to remount in an instant and gallop off to a new position. Buford knew that the inexperienced Union cavalry could never meet the Confederate cavalry on equal terms in mounted combat, so he made a winning virtue out of stark necessity.

An outstanding example of his methods had occurred just before second Manassas. Buford's brigade was at Thoroughfare Gap when Longstreet came through at the head of Lee's columns. Buford dismounted his cavalry and with 3,000 troopers held up 27,000 Confederates for six hours.* Although Pope failed to support Buford, and Longstreet finally broke through to bring on the second Battle of Manassas, Buford had so dramatically demonstrated the effectiveness of the new technique that it became virtually standing operating procedure from then on.

Buford's rise to fame as a cavalry leader stemmed logically from his success in proving the efficacy of his new methods. It was he who fought Stuart to a standstill at Aldie and Middleburg, as Lee's invasion was getting under way. So effective was the work of the Federal cavalry in Virginia during June that Stuart never did learn the significance of Hooker's movements. He was delayed to such an extent in his own timetable that he was forced to make a wide sweep around Hooker's rear by way of Rockville, a dozen miles north of Washington, with results disastrous to Lee's invasion program.

The extent to which the Spencer seven-shot repeating rifle contributed to Buford's success in Virginia is not entirely clear, but careful researching in the last few years has uncovered material which may cause historians to reappraise the relative cavalry capabilities of the opposing sides and the resulting impact on Civil War campaigns and battles following Chancellorsville.** What is certain

* Fletcher Pratt, *Eleven Generals*, New York, William Sloane Associates, 1949.
** J. O. Buckeridge, *Lincoln's Choice*, The Stackpole Company, Harrisburg, 1956.

is that Buford's cavalry division was armed in part with the repeater before leaving Virginia for the Gettysburg campaign and concurrently several regiments of Kilpatrick's division received an issue of the same new weapon prior to their fight with Stuart at Hanover on June 30. It is therefore not difficult to imagine the superior firepower that the Federal cavalry was enabled to bring to bear against the Confederates who in the main were still forced to rely on their muzzle-loading single-shot muskets both at Hanover and at Gettysburg on the morning of the first day.

Federal Cavalry Advances to Gettysburg

On June 29 Buford's cavalry division was covering the Eleventh Corps west of Emmitsburg. Buford learned that Hill and Longstreet were in the direction of Chambersburg and Ewell in the Carlisle-York area. He saw the importance of occupying Gettysburg, so he marched there on June 30. He arrived just in time to make contact with the leading scouts of Pettigrew's brigade of Heth's Confederate division. Heth had sent Pettigrew to capture some stocks of shoes thought to be at Gettysburg. Pettigrew withdrew to Cashtown, while Buford outposted the high ground west of Gettysburg.

In anticipation of the enemy's return, Buford on the night of June 30 had divided the area west and north of Gettysburg into two parts. He assigned Gamble's brigade to the western sector and Devin's to the northern, and designated the Chambersburg pike as the dividing line, with pickets extending from beyond the Fairfield road on the southwest to a hillock near Rock Creek on the northeast. Buford was spread rather thin, if indeed he had any serious idea that he could for long hold an outpost line extending for some five miles in the above described arc, against Heth's division of 7,500 men and five artillery batteries. But it was a bold calculated risk and when the payoff came between 8:00 and 10:00 o'clock the next morning he had his dismounted squadrons in position to stage a typically Bufordian delaying action.

The First Clash

The gray light of dawn was beginning to outline the trees, buildings, and other objects for the four-man Federal picket posted on the Chambersburg turnpike near Willoughby Run about a mile and a half west of Gettysburg. It was 5:20 on the morning of Wednesday, July 1. The night had proven uneventful for the lonely cavalry groups strung across country in a huge semicircle along Willoughby Run, from southwest to northeast cutting across the several roads that reached out from the town, where the pickets had been placed by Buford's cavalry commanders the preceding afternoon after driving out a scouting party of Confederates, who fled towards Cashtown.

Corporal Alphonse Hodges,* Company F, 9th New York Cavalry, Buford's Division, had very much on his mind the division commander's warning to his troopers that Confederate troops were on the move and they must be even more alert than usual. There had been no sign of the enemy, expected from the direction of Cashtown. The corporal's relief would soon take over and permit him to get back to a welcome breakfast of hard tack and bacon, with a scalding tin-cup full of fragrant coffee to wash it down.

As the darkness faded and visibility improved, the corporal observed shadowy figures moving down the road towards him, a half-mile away. Sending his men to notify

* *Battles and Leaders of Civil War*, p. 275.

VIEW OF GETTYSBURG FROM MCPHERSON'S RIDGE, LOOKING EAST

This is Gettysburg just as Heth's Confederates saw it on the morning of July 1 as they approached along the Chambersburg Pike, seen on the right. The unfinished railway grade is on the left.

the pickets to right and left and the support in rear, Hodges advanced down the road for a closer look. Just then the enemy fired on him. Jumping for cover, he sent several shots in their direction and then judiciously doubled back to McPherson's Ridge where he joined the organized skirmish line that his regimental commander, as soon as he heard the shots, had promptly built up from the pickets on duty north and south of the pike.

The Battle of Gettysburg had opened.

In a few moments the advance guard of Pettigrew's Confederate brigade, heretofore unaware of the existence of more than a reconnaissance detachment of the enemy in Gettysburg, appeared in force, deployed to right and left

of the road, and pushed forward their skirmish lines. Buford immediately dispatched couriers to Meade, Reynolds, and his own corps commander, General Pleasonton.

More Units Drawn into the Fight

During that hectic two-hour period on the morning of July 1, what started out as a dignified frontal meeting engagement with advance elements of both forces astride the Chambersburg pike soon developed into a snarling dogfight. Heth's Confederate division moved into position with two brigades in line and two in support, confronting two Federal cavalry brigades. The Federals had dismounted and consequently were able to use only 75 percent of their strength for fighting; the horse holders—one for every four men—had their hands full keeping the animals quiet in rear of the fighting line. It is likely that Buford had considerably less than 3,000 rifles on the line against Heth's strength of more than twice that number. Buford was further handicapped by a shortage of artillery. Calef's Battery A, Second U. S. Artillery alone supported the Federal cavalry with six guns. Several times, unaided by rifle fire, it disrupted violent enemy infantry rushes.

MAJOR GENERAL HENRY HETH, C.S.A.
Commanding a division in Hill's corps.

Both sides suffered heavy casualties in the early stages, particularly in and near the railroad cuts which parallel the Chambersburg Pike north of the Seminary and near McPherson's farmhouse. The cut near McPherson's was especially critical. Initially Gamble's brigade of Buford's division took position with its right resting on the cut and extending south across the road. When Wadsworth's division (First Corps) arrived and relieved the cavalry about 10 A.M. Calef withdrew, being replaced by Hall's 2d Maine Battery which in turn supported Wadsworth.

Buford had personally taken advantage of the Lutheran Seminary on the ridge and was putting it to effective use as an observation post. His message to General Reynolds reached the latter as he was leading his First Corps up

BRIGADIER GENERAL J. JOHNSON PETTIGREW, C.S.A.
Commanding the First Brigade of Heth's division, and later the division.

from its overnight bivouac on Marsh Creek. Hearing the sounds of battle, Reynolds quickly diverted the column across country and galloped to the Seminary, from which he and Buford rode on to the front on the last personal reconnaissance that Reynolds was ever to make.

The battle-experienced Reynolds lost no time in estimating the situation. He sent word back to Howard to rush the Eleventh Corps forward, and directed the divisions of Wadsworth and Robinson, now within a short distance of the field, to assume the burden of the fight by passing through and relieving the weakened lines of the hard-fighting dismounted cavalry.

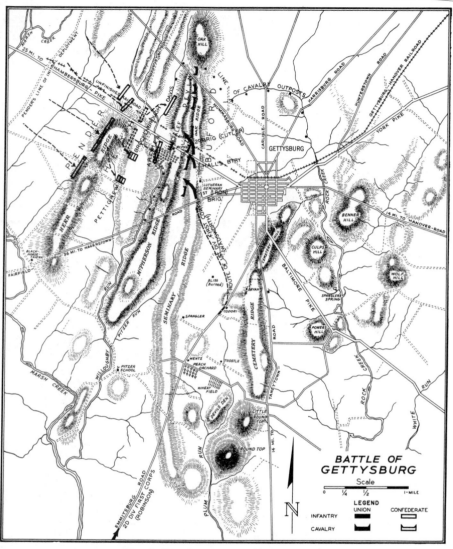

Map 8. The Situation at 10 am, July 1

This portrays the initial clash, and the relief of Buford's cavalry by the leading elements of Doubleday's First Corps who were hastening north to the sound of cannon fire in the Seminary Ridge area. Devin's brigade withdrew around the right flank, covering the deployment of the Federal divisions north of the town, while Buford's other brigade took a covering position to the west, astride the Fairfield Road. In the preparation of Maps 8-15, terrain features have been subordinated to a portrayal of troop dispositions. Wooded areas have been mostly omitted, as have all but a few significant farmhouses. The main roads are shown but not all the lanes and wagon tracks; the use of double lines to signify roads does not mean that they were improved. In 1863 even the turnpikes were mostly earth surfaced. These maps are based on contemporary surveys.

McPherson's Woods

In the course of the melee, as the lines surged back and forth on and between the ridges, Davis' Confederate brigade drove Cutler's Federal brigade back to Seminary Ridge and was in turn decimated and driven from the field by the Fourteenth New York Infantry and the Sixth Wisconsin in combination. On another part of the battlefield Archer's Confederate brigade seized McPherson's Woods where it was in turn attacked by the famous "Iron Brigade," composed of troops from Wisconsin, Michigan and Indiana. Archer's brigade was outflanked, and captured almost to a man, including General Archer himself.

McPHERSON'S WOODS

Looking eastward toward the Seminary. The point of woods is where Reynolds fell. The civilians are believed to be photographer Brady (right) and John Burns, a citizen of Gettysburg who fought in the battle.

McPherson's Woods will be remembered for two other reasons, for it was there that a sharpshooter's bullet killed John F. Reynolds, and the Confederates belatedly learned that they had tangled with a tougher foe than the local troops that had been encountered in their virtually unopposed advance through northern territory. Catching

MAJOR GENERAL JOHN REYNOLDS
Commander of the First Corps, Army of the Potomac. Killed at McPherson's Woods.

sight of the black-hatted members of the Iron Brigade, an excited Confederate soldier was heard to shout: "Hell, that ain't no milishy—that's the Army of the Potomac!"

Lee's Divisions Converge on Gettysburg

Meantime, Buford had side-slipped Devin's cavalry brigade to the vicinity of Oak Hill, northwest of the town, to dispute the advance of Ewell's troops who were approaching Gettysburg from the north by the Carlisle and Harrisburg roads. There the hard-fighting cavalrymen duplicated their stellar performance on the Chambersburg road, forced Rodes' Confederate division to deploy and slow down, and made it extremely difficult for Ewell and A. P. Hill to coordinate the advance of their respective

CONFEDERATE SHARPSHOOTER IN TREE
A marksman of this type probably picked off Gen. Reynolds.

corps from the north and west. After which, sometime in the early afternoon, the exhausted troopers of both cavalry brigades were pulled out and reassembled in the shallow valley south of Gettysburg along the Emmitsburg Road. There they caught their second wind, and undertook the mission of protecting the army's left flank in the general area south of the town.

By 11 A.M. Reynold's entire First Corps was suitably deployed on both sides of the Cashtown Pike and hotly engaged, while Devin's cavalry brigade was covering the right flank east of the Mummasburg Road in the Oak Hill area and disputing the right of way of advance elements of Ewell's threat from the north. For the time being, despite the vastly superior Confederate forces at the point of contact, the Federals had the advantage of position, the confidence that went with it, and the morale-inducing satisfaction that they had stopped Lee in his tracks for the moment at least.

Heavy fighting swirled in and about the railroad cut, occupied by Federal infantry who inflicted severe casualties on Confederates advancing from the northwest. When the Federals withdrew from the cut it was quickly occupied by a Mississippi regiment, most of whom were in turn promptly captured as the result of a sudden Union countercharge. The railroad bed came under enfilade fire from Confederate artillery, which gave Hall's Battery a bad time as it withdrew in successive stages to the east under orders from General Wadsworth, who feared the complete loss of his major artillery support.

Human flesh and blood simply cannot sustain that kind of toe-to-toe slugging without occasionally stopping for breath and realignment. By noon both contestants found it necessary to take time out to reestablish their lines and prepare for the next round. This was not long in coming.

Buford's Contribution

The significant contribution which Buford's cavalry made to the final checkmate of the Confederates at Gettyburg has never received adequate recognition. It covered the left front and effectively screened Meade's army from observation as it advanced to meet Lee. Buford, with only

RAILWAY CUT WEST OF GETTYSBURG
In 1863 this cut appeared about as it appears here except that the ties and rails had not been laid. This was the scene of heavy fighting on the first day.

two of his three brigades (Merritt's had been left at Mechanicstown to guard the trains), was first on the scene at Gettysburg's critical crossroads at the right time. Then with not over 4,000 cavalrymen he delayed the advance of Hill's corps from Cashtown and Ewell's corps from Heidlersburg, causing the leading divisions of both to effect premature deployments. At the same time he gave the Union Army the necessary breather for Reynold's First Corps and Howard's Eleventh to reach the scene, engage the Confederates in a desperate struggle and then, falling back, to solidly occupy Cemetery Ridge, which turned out to be the keystone of the Federal defense.

To sum up Buford's accomplishments in the face of overwhelming Confederate superiority; although he was finally engulfed by main force, his troops had held for over two hours and by their dogged delaying tactics had gained time for the First Corps to come up and further delay Lee's concentration, and for Meade to speed the development of the rest of his army in the direction of Gettysburg. It is not too much to say that Buford's cavalry was the major instrument that caused the battle to be fought at Gettysburg rather than elsewhere. They were successful in preventing coordinated action in the approach march by Hill and Ewell. That in turn delayed Longstreet's corps, which failed to reach the battlefield in time to exploit Hill's afternoon success in driving the First and Eleventh Federal Corps back to Cemetery Ridge. The successive chain of events contributed much to Ewell's failure to attack and seize Culp's Hill until it was too late.

HALL'S BATTERY ON CHAMBERSBURG ROAD, FIRST DAY

CHAPTER 12

TWO UNION CORPS OVERWHELMED

I AM satisfied that Longstreet and Hill have made a junction. A tremendous battle has been raging since nine and one-half a.m. with varying success. At the present moment the battle is raging on the road to Cashtown, and in short cannon range of this town (Gettysburg); the enemy's line is a semi-circle on the height from north to west. General Reynolds was killed early this morning. In my opinion there seems to be no directing person—we need help now."

Buford's well-known dispatch to cavalry commander Pleasonton, who was at Meade's headquarters in Taneytown, early on the afternoon of July 1, told the story up to then in a few brief, pithy sentences.

Howard's three-division Eleventh Corps had bivouacked the night of June 30 about eight miles south of Gettysburg along Marsh Creek, but for some unexplained reason failed to emulate the rapid movement of the First Corps to the battlefield to support Buford, and it was not until 1 P.M. that the leading elements of Howard's corps came up the Emmitsburg road. By that time Buford had informed Howard of Ewell's advance from Heidlersburg,

135

whereupon Howard promptly sent word to Sickles at Emmitsburg and Slocum at Two Taverns to send up reinforcements at once.

Seven Successive Commanders

During the early hours of the developing battle, that portion of the Union army reaching the field was successively commanded by four general officers, Brig. Gen.

MAJOR GENERAL ABNER DOUBLEDAY
Succeeded Reynolds as commander of the First Corps.

John Buford, and Major Generals John F. Reynolds, Abner Doubleday, and Oliver O. Howard. Doubleday commanded the Third Division of Reynolds' corps, and assumed overall command when he reached the field and was informed of Reynolds' death. Howard, commanding the Eleventh Corps, reached the field in person shortly before noon. As senior in command he took over from Doubleday, but his chief contribution was to place the troops of the First and Eleventh Corps as they streamed back to Cemetery Ridge in the afternoon. Two more corps commanders, Major Generals Hancock and Slocum, also became acting army commanders during the course of the day, for it was not until midnight of the first day that General Meade himself arrived on the field to personally take charge of the campaign. Rarely if ever has history

MAJOR GENERAL OLIVER O. HOWARD

recorded a single battle in which the supreme command on the field was vested in seven different generals in a period of less than sixteen hours. The confusion among the lower echelons, caused by the rapid change in command, will be readily understood by those who have had battlefield responsibility.

On taking over army command from Doubleday, Howard assigned one of his division commanders, General

Schurz, temporarily to command the Eleventh Corps, instructing him to extend Doubleday's (First Corps) defensive line in the direction of Barlow Knoll. Schurz placed Schimmelfennig's and Barlow's divisions with three batteries in support, as directed, holding Steinwehr's division and two batteries in reserve on Cemetery Hill, an extremely wise decision as it turned out.

MAJOR GENERAL CARL SCHURZ
Commanding the 3d Division of the Eleventh Corps. Also acting corps commander on the first day.

Schurz disposed his 6,000 men in the open about 800 yards north of Gettysburg, astride the Harrisburg, Carlisle, and Mummasburg Roads, but the line was terribly thin to cover such a wide frontage and failed by a considerable margin to connect with Doubleday's First Corps to the west of town.

By the middle of the afternoon two of Ewell's divisions,

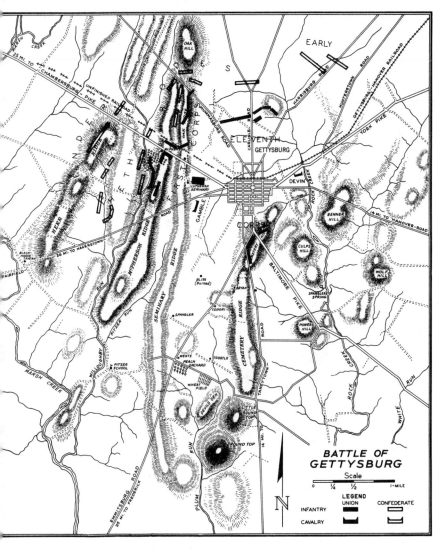

Map 9. The Situation at 2:30 pm, July 1

he situation has developed swiftly since 10 AM (Map 8). Hill's and Ewell's corps are
essing the Union First and Eleventh Corps and are overlapping their lines, particularly
the Federal right flank. The Union forces, already in trouble, are soon to collapse and
ithdraw in disorder toward Cemetery Hill. Note Buford's covering position on the
left.

Rodes' and Early's, and two of Hill's, Heth's and Pender's, were linked up in a wide semicircle north and west of Gettysburg. The Federals were now threatened on two fronts by the combined Confederate corps, which initiated a formal, coordinated attack on the Union First and Eleventh Corps. There was severe fighting for over an hour, during which Devin's dismounted Federal cavalry-

MAJOR GENERAL WINFIELD S. HANCOCK
Commanding the Second Corps.

men were driven from their position on Rock Creek. Barlow's division of the Eleventh Corps suffered the same fate after restoring the line given up by the cavalry under overwhelming pressure. By 4 P.M. the Confederates outnumbered the Federals so heavily, both west and north of Gettysburg, that a withdrawal to Cemetery Hill was ordered by Howard.

The Federals Break for Cemetery Ridge

Fighting a desperate rear guard action, and struggling to prevent outflanking maneuvers by the Confederates on both the left and right of the overextended Federal line, the First and Eleventh Federal Corps were pressed relentlessly back on Gettysburg. Doubleday's corps withdrew through the southern edge of town and across Seminary Ridge and the Emmitsburg Road south of Gettysburg, while the Eleventh Corps was forced to pass directly through the heart of the town. Buford's cavalry, after being relieved, had reassembled in the open area south of Gettysburg between Seminary and Cemetery Ridges, covering the left flank. During the withdrawal of the First Corps, the cavalrymen again went into effective action and prevented Hill from interfering with the retrograde movement of the infantry by coming around on the latter's left rear.

The retreat of the Eleventh Corps, first to break, uncovered the right flank and rear of the First Corps, which might otherwise have held for a longer period. The latter well-disciplined organization, however, effected its withdrawal in reasonably good order and what remained of it was placed on the left of Steinwehr's reserve brigade, which had been posted on its arrival on the crest of Cemetery Hill and from which it was not moved during the first day's fighting.

Steinwehr, a professional soldier who had served in the German Army, with methodical Teuton thoroughness had immediately put the men of his brigade to work digging gun emplacements and rifle pits among the tombstones of the cemetery. This salutary move served the dual purpose of strengthening the position for defense and giving a much needed lift to the morale of the surviving portions of the First and Eleventh Corps.

The retreat of the two divisions of the Eleventh Corps, in contradistinction to the action of the First Corps, unfortunately developed into what may fairly be called a rout. The men got themselves thoroughly entangled in the

MAJOR GENERAL ROBERT E. RODES, C.S.A.
Commanding a division in Ewell's corps.

streets of Gettysburg, were overrun by the pursuing Confederates, and lost several thousand effectives as prisoners. The rout would have been even worse had not Steinwehr sent forward one of his two brigades to the north side of Gettysburg to serve as a rear guard in covering the panicky withdrawal of the other two divisions of the corps.

Hancock Restores Order

As the retiring Federals streamed back from two directions toward Cemetery Hill, the presence of General

Hancock on the eminence, and his calmness in the face of the disorganized retreat had a magic effect in restoring shattered morale and in bringing some order out of chaos. The losses of the First and Eleventh Corps on the first day had exceeded 10,000 men in killed, wounded, captured, and missing, leaving less than half of their original strength for the heavy work ahead. Despite their losses, it was no time to stand on ceremony or to sympathize with their predicament. General Hancock was a determined character. He had galloped up from army headquarters at Taneytown under orders from Meade to take charge of operations, and to advise the commanding general if the Gettysburg area was the place to stand and fight. The vital importance of his recommendation, for or against, placed a heavy responsibility on Hancock, but he was equal to it. Observing Culp's Hill a few hundred yards to the east of Cemetery Hill, and immediately recognizing its tactical significance, Hancock ordered Doubleday, just arriving with the depleted First Corps, to send a division to occupy it. Doubleday was understandably upset, protesting that he had no men to spare and that they were not in condition to make any further effort right then. Hancock refused to accept his protestations, despite the circumstances, and exerting his authority as acting army commander, summarily ordered him to send Wadsworth's division to Culp's Hill. This was done, but the state of mind and strength of the occupying division was such that the Confederates could probably have pushed them over with a feather had they made the effort at any time during the afternoon.

Howard's official report, summing up with fair accuracy, as far as it went, the events of the first day, during most of which he had acted as the overall field commander, stated that "The First and Eleventh Corps, numbering less

CLOSE FIGHTING THE FIRST DAY NEAR THE SEMINARY.

than 18,000 men, nobly aided by Buford's Division of cavalry, had engaged and held in check nearly double their numbers from 10:00 o'clock in the morning until 7:00 in the evening."

Major E. P. Halstead, assistant Adjutant General in Reynolds' First Corps, has given a clear account* of the incident wherein General Howard took exception to General Hancock's assumption of command about 4:30 in the afternoon of July 1. Carrying a message from Doubleday to Howard requesting reinforcements and orders, the major found the latter in the cemetery and apparently not too happy. Halstead writes:

He looked the picture of despair. On receipt of the message he replied "Tell General Doubleday that I

---
* *Battles and Leaders of the Civil War*, p. 284.

have no reenforcements to send him. I have only one regiment in reserve." I then asked if he had any orders to give, and called his attention to the enemy then advancing in line of battle overlapping our left by nearly half a mile. He looked in that direction and replied rather sharply: "Those are nothing but rail fences, sir!" I said, "I beg your pardon, General; if you will take my glass you will see something besides rail fences." Turning to a staff-officer, he bade him take the glass and see what it was. The officer looked, and in an instant lowered the glass, saying: "General, those are long lines of the enemy!" General Howard then turned to me and said: "Go to General Buford, give him my compliments, and tell him to go to General Doubleday's support." When asked where General Buford could be found, he replied: "I don't know! I think he is over this way," pointing toward the east.

After riding in that direction as far as I deemed it wise or prudent, I returned to where General Howard sat, just as General Hancock approached at a swinging gallop. When near General Howard, who was then alone, he saluted, and with great animation, as if there was no time for ceremony, said General Meade had sent him forward to take command of the three corps. General Howard replied that he was the senior. General Hancock said: "I am aware of that, General, but I have written orders in my pocket from General Meade, which I will show you if you wish to see them." General Howard said: "No; I do not doubt your word, General Hancock, but you can give no orders here while I am here." Hancock replied: "Very well, General Howard, I will second any order that you have to give, but General Meade has also directed me to select a field on which to fight this battle in rear of Pipe Creek." Then, casting one glance from Culp's Hill to Round Top, he continued: "But I think this the strongest position by nature upon which to fight a battle that I ever saw, and if it meets your approbation I will select this as the battle-field." General Howard responded: "I think it a very strong position, General Hancock; a very strong position!" "Very well, sir, I select this as the battle-field." General Hancock immediately turned away to rectify our lines.

To the objective reader, who recalls that Howard's Eleventh Corps had been in disrepute ever since Stonewall Jackson surprised and routed them on the Union right flank at Chancellorsville, Major Halstead's account may sound slightly prejudiced. The Eleventh Corps contained many regiments composed largely of men of foreign lineage, especially Germans. A rallying cry attributed to the soldiers of the corps had been: "I fights mit Sigel," the name of the illustrious German who first led them. After a change of commanders and the disaster at Chancellorsville, some of the other corps had added the rather unkind legend: "I runs mit Howard."

Hancock's diplomatic attitude undoubtedly prevented what could easily have been a bitter difference of opinion, with resultant conflicting actions, further loss of confidence, and the probable loss of Cemetery Hill, Cemetery Ridge, and the Battle of Gettysburg. His own official report, following the battle, is concise history at its best. It will be noted that Hancock makes no reference to his altercation with Howard. This is his account:*

On the morning of July 1st the command (Second Corps) marched to Taneytown, going into bivouac about 11 A. M. I then proceeded in person to General Meade's headquarters, and, on reporting to him, was informed as to his intention with reference to giving battle to the enemy, the orders for preparatory move-

---

* *Battles and Leaders,* p, 287.

ments being then ready for issue. A few minutes before 1 P. M. I received orders to proceed in person to
the front and assume command of the First, Third,
and Eleventh Corps, in consequence of the death of
Major-General Reynolds. Having been fully informed
by the major-general commanding as to his intentions,
I was instructed by him to give the necessary directions upon my arrival at the front for the movement
of troops and trains to the rear toward the line of
battle he had selected, should I deem it expedient to
do so. If the ground was suitable, and circumstances
made it wise, I was directed to establish the line of
battle at Gettysburg. . . . At 3 P. M. I arrived at
Gettysburg and assumed the command. At this time
the First and Eleventh corps were retiring through
the town, closely pursued by the enemy. The cavalry
of General Buford was occupying a firm position on
the plain to the left of Gettysburg, covering the rear
of the retreating corps. The Third Corps had not yet
arrived from Emmitsburg. Orders were at once given
to establish a line of battle on Cemetery Hill, with
skirmishers occupying that part of the town immediately in our front. The position just on the southern
edge of Gettysburg, overlooking the town and commanding the Emmitsburg and Taneytown roads and
the Baltimore turnpike, was already partially occupied
on my arrival by direction of Major General
Howard. Some difficulty was experienced in forming
the troops of the Eleventh Corps, but by vigorous
efforts a sufficiently formidable line was established
to deter the enemy from any serious assault on the
position. They pushed forward a line of battle for a
short distance east of the Baltimore turnpike, but it
was easily checked by the fire of our artillery. In forming the lines, I received material assistance from
Major-General Howard, Brigadier-Generals Warren
and Buford, and officers of General Howard's command. . . . The trains of all the troops under my command were ordered to the rear, that they might not

interfere with any movement of troops that might be directed by the major-general commanding. My aide, Major Mitchell, was then sent to General Meade to inform him of the state of affairs, and to say that I would hold the position until night. Shortly after, I addressed a communication to the major-general commanding, sending it by Captain Parker, of my staff, giving in detail the information in my possession, and informing him that the position at Gettysburg was a very strong one, having for its disadvantage that it might be easily turned, and leaving to him the responsibility whether the battle should be fought at Gettysburg or at a place first selected by him. Between 5 and 6 o'clock, my dispositions having been completed, Major-General Slocum arrived on the field, and, considering that my function had ceased, I transferred the command to him. The head of the Third Corps appeared in sight shortly afterward, on the Emmitsburg road.

About dark I started for the headquarters of the army, still at Taneytown, thirteen miles distant, and reported in person to General Meade. I then ascertained that he had already given orders for the corps in the rear to advance at once to Gettysburg, and was about proceeding there in person.

The Confederates Miss an Opportunity

The Confederates had lost a rare opportunity to win the battle before dark the first day, and the blame must fairly be divided between Lee and Ewell. As Lee, from his position on Seminary Ridge in the early afternoon, through his field glasses watched the Federals streaming back through Gettysburg and across the fields to the protection of Cemetery Hill, he felt instinctively that victory was in his grasp. He immediately dispatched his Adjutant General, Colonel W. H. Taylor, to tell General Ewell that he, Lee, could see the enemy retreating over the hills in confusion and apparently greatly disorganized. Colonel Taylor's account quotes Lee as using these words: "It was only necessary to press 'those people' in order to secure possession of the heights; and, if possible, he wished General Ewell to do this." Taylor writes that he immediately galloped over to General Ewell and delivered Lee's order and that Ewell did not indicate any objection but left the

MAJOR GENERAL EDWARD JOHNSON, C.S.A.
Commanding a division in Ewell's corps.

impression on Taylor's mind that the order would be executed.

Lee's message to Ewell reached the latter early in the afternoon, before Hancock had come up to Cemetery Hill and was bringing order into the Union ranks. Ewell's corps had suffered heavily in the day's fighting up to that time and both he and Hill had earlier received specific orders from Lee not to bring on a general engagement, but to wait until the army was assembled. Johnson's division of Ewell's corps had not yet arrived, so in the exercise of the discretion which Lee invariably permitted to his corps commanders, and also having in mind Lee's earlier admonition, Ewell vacillated. Finally, despite vehement urging from at least two of his general officers, he put off the pursuit until evening. By this time Union reinforcements had arrived and it was too late for Ewell to make the attack with reasonable assurance of success.

General Johnson, whose division had been on the way from the Chambersburg area since early morning, was under orders on arrival to extend the Confederate line from Rock Creek to the east. But his division did not arrive until after sunset, and in the meantime the Federals occupied Culp's Hill and profitably thickened their defensive line on Cemetery Hill and the Ridge.

A letter from General Meade to G. G. Benedict, of Burlington, Vermont, dated March 16, 1870, and published in the Philadelphia Weekly Press of August 11, 1886, referred to a conversation with General Ewell after the war.

> Lieutenant-General Ewell, in a conversation held with me shortly after the war, asked what would have been the effect if, at four P. M. on the 1st, he had occupied Culp's Hill, and established batteries upon it. I told him that, in my judgment, in the then condition of the Eleventh and First corps, with their morale affected by their withdrawal to Cemetery Ridge, with the loss of over half of their numbers in killed, wounded and missing (of the six thousand prisoners we lost on the field, nearly all came from these corps on the first day), his occupation of Culp's Hill, with batteries commanding the whole of Cemetery Ridge, would have produced the evacuation of that ridge and the withdrawal of the troops there,

by the Baltimore pike and Taneytown and Emmitsburg roads. He then informed me that at four P. M.
on the 1st he had his corps, twenty thousand strong,
in column of attack, and on the point of moving on
Culp's Hill, which he saw was unoccupied and commanded Cemetery Ridge, when he received an order
from General Lee directing him to assume the defensive, and not to advance; that he sent to General Lee
urging to be permitted to advance with his reserves,
but the reply was a reiteration of the previous order.
To my inquiry why Lee had restrained him, he said
our troops (Slocum's) were visible, and Lee was under
the impression that the greater part of my army was
on the ground, and deemed it prudential to await
the rest of his.*

Either General Meade's or Ewell's memory is at fault
in the foregoing statement. Johnson's division did not
reach Gettysburg until about 8 o'clock in the evening,
and at no time previous to that, nor at any time that day,
were the two divisions on the ground—Early's and Rodes'—
in position as General Ewell stated. If they were, all the
authorities quoted are at fault.

Ewell Fails to Measure Up

Ewell's reputation suffered badly as a result of his
indecision. The hopes of the Confederacy that they had
found a worthy successor to Stonewall Jackson were rudely
shattered. Undoubtedly Lee, after the great promise which
Ewell had shown in his rapid and aggressive march
through Pennsylvania, expected him to do as Jackson
would have done. But Ewell was cast in a different mold
and had not yet learned to successfully interpret Lee's
discretionary orders in the Jacksonian manner. Ewell was
accustomed to positive and precise instructions from Jack-

---

* Jacob Hoke, *The Great Invasion*, 1887, p. 289.

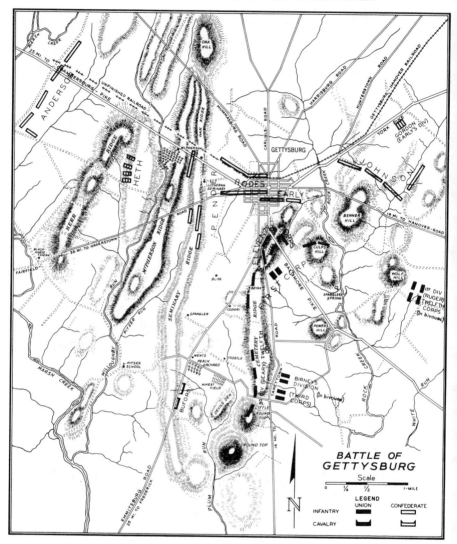

Map 10. The Situation at 6 pm, July 1

With the arrival of additional Union corps and their extension of Hancock's position on Cemetery Ridge, the Federal situation becomes less hazardous. Culp's Hill, initially unoccupied, and at 6 PM only lightly held, was the key to victory. But Ewell failed to press forward, and a golden opportunity was lost to the Confederates.

son, his former corps commander. He lacked the self-assurance and initiative, possibly even the character necessary to exercise corps command in a decisive way.

The Confederate Colonel Swallow, who was present and witnessed all that transpired, has said that he personally pointed out the opportunity to Generals Early and Hays of Ewell's corps, convinced Early that Culp's Hill could be seized, with its strategic command of the Baltimore road, and that the two generals then prepared to launch the attack on Culp's Hill as soon as they could secure positive orders from Ewell. But in that they were unsuccessful.

So depressed were Ewell's subordinates, knowing how Jackson would have acted under similar circumstances, that one of them, General Trimble, is reported to have thrown his sword aside with the statement that he would refuse further to serve under such a general. Ewell's failure to differentiate between bringing on a general engagement and aggressively exploiting such an opportunity as was presented to him to completely disrupt Meade's buildup, simply means that Ewell, in refusing to take a calculated risk, failed to demonstrate the qualities of a great general.

Even after Johnson's division arrived and took position on the left of the Confederate line, and before it had advanced any great distance, Johnson received orders to halt. Colonel Taylor* has quoted Johnson as telling him after the war that no reason was given for him to halt. But considering the timing of the message, early evening of July 1, it is apparent that Ewell was tired, confused, and unable to think constructively, hence took the easy course and marked time. By that time, however, the golden opportunity had passed. It was perhaps just as well that Ewell did not send Johnson forward.

---

* Colonel W. H. Taylor, *Annals of the War*, pp. 308-309.

In Ewell's official report he gave as his reasons for not ordering the attack the fact that he could not bring artillery to bear on Cemetery Hill; that all his troops on the field were worn out by twelve hours of marching and fighting; that Cemetery Hill was not assailable from the town; that when Johnson's division arrived it was his intention to take possession of Culp's Hill, which in turn would command Cemetery Hill. Before Johnson's arrival, Federals had been reported moving in the direction of Ewell's left flank and by the time their movement had been reconnoitered and Johnson had arrived, "the night was far advanced," in Ewell's words.

VIEW FROM THE SEMINARY, LOOKING SOUTHEAST. CEMETERY RIDGE IN THE BACKGROUND

CHAPTER 13

LEE MOVES IN AS MEADE HESITATES

THE road from Chambersburg to Gettysburg must have been a frustrating stretch of real estate during June 30 and July 1, not only to Generals Lee and Longstreet, but also to the many thousands of junior officers and men who were being urged forward uphill along the long, hot, dusty, and congested pike on which infantry, artillery, and wagon trains vied for the right of way.

Confederate Traffic Jam

That single road approach through Cashtown pass to the Gettysburg battlefield had a significant effect on Confederate fortunes. Just one conveniently located parallel highway would have been worth a couple of divisions to General Lee. As it was, he waited too long to start his army forward. The fortunes of war paved the way for the Union army, close to defeat on the afternoon of the first day, to dig its claws into Cemetery Ridge and hang on until nightfall, when the corps of Sickles and Slocum ar-

155

rived on the field to help redress the numerical balance
of power.

General Lee, mounted on Traveller, had left Chambersburg in company with Longstreet on June 30. He
bivouacked that night at Greenwood, 10 miles east of
Chambersburg and about half way between that town
and Cashtown. He was still anxiously waiting for some

MAJOR GENERAL RICHARD H. ANDERSON, C.S.A.
Commanding a division in Hill's corps.

word from Stuart, but was by that time fully convinced
that he had to get his army east of the Blue Ridge to
meet Meade, of whose strength and detailed dispositions
he was still unaware.

Early on the morning of July 1 the last division of Hill's
corps, Anderson's, filed past Greenwood. Soon thereafter
Lee mounted and rode along with Longstreet at the head
of the latter's corps, which had been ordered to follow

Anderson's division to Cashtown. Coming to a road junction a short distance ahead, they ran into Johnson's division of Ewell's corps which was cutting into the main pike from another dirt road that angled in from the northwest. This division, responding to Lee's first order of June 29 to return to Chambersburg, had come down the Carlisle Pike towards Chambersburg. On the road Johnson received Lee's message shifting the objective to Cashtown, whereupon he changed direction at Green Village, a few miles below Shippensburg, passed through Scotland and cut into the Chambersburg-Gettysburg Road near Greenwood. So there he was, blocking the only road to Cashtown. On Lee's order Longstreet halted his own corps to give Johnson the right of way, not knowing that behind that division were trailing the complete wagon trains of both Johnson and Rodes. Including Johnson's infantry and artillery, the column covered a good fifteen miles, so Longstreet's corps settled down for a wait that must have consumed at least six hours.

Lee Rides to the Sound of Guns

Impatient to get forward and learn what was happening east of the mountain, Lee and Longstreet, with their respective staffs, rode on past Johnson's marching men. As their horses climbed the western slope of the Blue Ridge, they met the occasional rumble of artillery fire and, after crossing the crest, the unmistakable sound of heavier firing. Leaving Longstreet to "hasten" the march of his corps, Lee spurred forward alone and after a fast ride met A. P. Hill at Cashtown. The latter, a sick man, knew little except that Heth's division had advanced on Gettysburg. Anderson was then sent for but he knew no more than Hill, so Lee galloped on again towards the front, never before having been so completely blanketed, in the presence of the enemy, by the traditional fog of war.

As a direct result of the aforementioned road jam, McLaws' division of Longstreet's corps failed to reach Marsh Creek, four miles west of Gettysburg, until a little after dark on July 1, while Hood's division, following McLaws, arrived in the same area about midnight. Longstreet's third division, commanded by General Pickett, remained at Chambersburg to guard the army trains.

Longstreet has written that his artillery was not able to hit the road from Greenwood until 2 A.M. on July 2, but there is some question as to the exactness of his memory on that point.

Imboden's cavalry, having covered the arrival of the cavalry brigades of Jones and Robertson from the Shenandoah Valley, was ordered to move from Mercersburg to Chambersburg to relieve Pickett's understrength division. The latter was then to proceed to Gettysburg. As it turned out, Imboden's brigade entered Chambersburg on Wednesday afternoon, July 1, and was thus available for a more active cavalry mission had Lee chosen to assign one.

A Contrast in Leadership

If there were any doubt that the Battle of Gettysburg started as a meeting engagement on the grand scale, it would quickly be dissipated by a study of the actions and orders of the respective army commanders during July 1, the first of the three days' battle. We have followed Lee on his ride from Chambersburg to the battlefield, which he reached in the early afternoon of July 1, in ample time to have decisively denied Cemetery Ridge to the Union army as a permanent resting place, had Ewell shown the aggressive qualities that Lee expected. Let us now visit Meade at his Taneytown command post and examine the means that he took to pierce the fog of war sufficiently to place his army in an effective posture of defense.

Meade had conferred at length with both Reynolds and Hancock, in whose loyalty and able generalship he had the fullest confidence, and to whom he had outlined his plans, such as they were at the time. Both were told that he could not make up his mind whether to attack Lee or ⌐cupy a defensive position until he had more information as to Lee's intentions and the extent of the concentration of his army.

To Reynolds' command Meade had committed three corps; two of these, the First and Eleventh, had been moved up to Gettysburg on the morning of July 1, in support of Buford's cavalry division, which had borne the brunt of the Confederate pressure from the direction of Cashtown during the early fighting. Reynolds' death before noon had created a quasi-vacuum in command that resulted in a welter of confusion and crosscurrents at the corps level, which was not fully overcome until Meade himself arrived on Cemetery Hill shortly before midnight. By this time the fighting of the first day had ended; the officers and men of the fighting and marching divisions were snatching what sleep they could manage in the short time available to them.

The sharp contrast in the attitudes of mind of the opposing army commanders is clearly evident in their physical and mental reflexes on that first day. The offensive-minded Lee was in the saddle at daybreak, supervising in person the march of Hill's and Longstreet's corps, urging them forward, and galloping past the toiling columns to see for himself what was happening at the front and to put himself in a position to influence events on the ground. Meade on the other hand, obsessed with the idea of fight-

ing defensively, sat immobile in his headquarters at Taneytown thirteen long miles away from Gettysburg. With him
were his Chief of Staff and most of the other members of
the staff. His several corps commanders, on and en route
to the battlefield, acted largely on their own initiative;
but did very well indeed under the circumstances, with
some inadvertent aid at the hands of the Confederates.

Meade Finally Takes Control

It was almost noon of July 1 before Meade received
the first news of the opening engagement west of Gettysburg. One of Reynolds' aides had been sent post-haste with
the news when Reynolds and Buford first met about 10
o'clock at the Lutheran Seminary, about the time the
First Corps was rushing in to relieve Buford's dismounted
cavalry. The essence of Reynolds' message was that the
enemy was advancing in strong force and might well seize
the Gettysburg heights before Reynolds could do so, but
that he would contest the advance "inch by inch" and "if
driven into the town, I will barricade the streets and
hold them back as long as possible."

Shortly after the Reynolds' message was received Meade
had the Buford dispatch to Pleasonton (quoted in full on
page 135) and about one o'clock received further news of
Reynolds' death. The logical man to succeed Reynolds,
General Hancock, was close at hand. Within a few minutes he was given written orders from Meade to turn over
the command of his Second Corps to Gibbon, proceed to
Gettysburg, take over the First, Eleventh, and Third Corps
and "if you think the ground and position there a better
one to fight a battle under existing circumstances, you
will so advise the General and he will order all his troops
up."

During the next few hours, as other news filtered back

from the front, Meade became convinced that Lee was concentrating his entire army at Gettysburg. Having reached that accurate conclusion, and without waiting for a positive recommendation from Hancock, Meade mentally discarded the Pipe Creek directive and at 4:30 P.M. sent word to Sykes' Fifth and Slocum's Twelfth Corps, at Hanover and Littlestown respectively, to move to Gettys-

MAJOR GENERAL GEORGE SYKES
Commanding the Fifth Corps.

burg, at the same time notifying Sedgwick to move his Sixth Corps from Manchester to Taneytown.

By 6 P.M. Meade had finally begun to cerebrate, sending a message to Hancock that Gettysburg seemed to be the inevitable battlefield, and that "if we can get up our people and attack with our whole force tomorrow, we ought to defeat the force the enemy has." At 7 P.M. fur-

ther orders were sent to Sykes' Fifth Corps to speed up its
march; to the Second Corps to move up from Taneytown;
and to the Sixth Corps to proceed directly by forced
marches to Gettysburg, 35 miles distant, with the significant comment that "we shall be largely outnumbered without your presence." That statement was in fact a substantial exaggeration, since Meade credited Lee with some
20,000 men in excess of his actual strength. But it had
become traditional for Federal army commanders, for
reasons best known to themselves, to overestimate the Confederate strength.

About 10 P.M., accompanied by his artillery chief,
General Hunt, and the rest of his staff, Meade started
on horseback for the front. It was pitch dark, and the road
was crowded with foot soldiers and artillery. One stop
only did he make, to confer with General Gibbon, commanding the Second Corps, which by that time had arrived within a few miles of Gettysburg. It was after midnight when Meade rode up to Cemetery Hill and took over
command from Slocum, who then rejoined his own corps.

Once on the ground, Meade took hold vigorously, made
a personal reconnaissance of the Ridge position, conferred
with his several corps commanders on the ground, and
ordered certain readjustments in the line. By 9 A.M.
July 2 he had six of his seven infantry corps (Sedgwick
being still on the road) skillfully disposed for defense along
the "fish hook."

Battlefield Control

Disturbing lack of positive information had plagued
both Lee and Meade during the early hours of July 1.
As the concentration of the two armies progressed with the
successive arrival on the field of new divisions from all
points of the compass, however, the picture began to be-

come clearer to both commanders. By early afternoon Lee was on Seminary Ridge in person, in time to see his troops drive the Federals back to Cemetery Hill. On the other side, Meade was still operating by remote control from his command post at Taneytown, thirteen miles from the battlefield, from which point he did not stir until two hours before midnight.

In contrast to present day techniques, and in retrospect, Civil War battles seem almost primitive insofar as communications, firepower, and battlefield control are concerned. The principles of war, however, were the same in 1863, when the exercise of troop leadership, skill in maneuver, logistical know-how, maintenance of morale among the men in the ranks, and all the other imponderables of warfare were just as important and, when effectively utilized by experienced and capable generals, just as rewarding as in today's atomic age.

The manner in which an army commander employs the means at his command, before, during, and after a battle, affords the measure of his generalship. The Confederate army was led by one of the finest gentlemen and ablest generals that this or any other country has ever produced. The Union army was commanded by a comparative newcomer who, it is true, had proven himself as a division commander and briefly as a corps commander, but who had yet to demonstrate his capacity to handle a large army with a sizable cavalry contingent attached. He was of course relatively unfamiliar with this army, the control of which was .thrown into his lap while on the march, virtually in the face of a confident, invading enemy of supposedly equal strength.

Lee had at Gettysburg only four corps commanders to deal with—Longstreet, Ewell, A. P. Hill, and J. E. B. Stuart; since Stuart was elsewhere, really only three, two of whom, Ewell and Hill, were new and as yet not blooded in corps command.

Meade had eight corps commanders in his army, Reynolds, Hancock, Sickles, Sykes, Sedgwick, Howard, Slocum, and Pleasonton. He would probably have been better off with half that number if someone had had the foresight to have reorganized the Army of the Potomac into a more

MAJOR GENERAL HENRY W. SLOCUM
Commanding the Twelfth Corps.

compact, more easily controlled type of fighting machine. Not the "Grand Divisions" of earlier, unhappy days, but something akin to them, such as the temporary three-corps wing that Reynolds commanded until his death in the early hours of the battle.

Meade's precautionary Pipe Creek retirement order, which, incidentally, never reached General Reynolds, had caused some misunderstanding, and in fact was almost disastrously interpreted by General Slocum, commanding the Twelfth Corps. Slocum's reluctance to assume the responsibility of commanding the fight on the afternoon of July 1, at Gettysburg, despite the fact that he was senior corps commander after Reynolds' death, is somewhat difficult to understand. General Howard stated in his official report that on three separate occasions during the afternoon he had sent messages to Slocum at Two Taverns, less than five miles from Gettysburg, appealing for support. The third messenger reached Slocum about 4:30 P.M. on the Baltimore pike, about one mile from Gettysburg, at which time Slocum sent back a message that he had already sent a division to the right and would send another to the left as requested but "that he did not wish to come up in person to the front and take the responsibility of the fight." Slocum afterwards stated that "it was against the wish of the commanding general to bring on a general engagement at that point" (apparently referring to the alternative position selected in the Pipe Creek order).

Despite his reluctance, when Slocum reached Cemetery Hill about 7 P.M. and discovered the true situation, he accepted the command that Hancock turned over to him. Hancock then rode back to Taneytown to confer with General Meade.

Troop Dispositions at Close of First Day

By midnight of the first day, with the two armies partially concentrated, the buildup had developed in such a way that the Confederate line occupied the terrain on and in prolongation of Seminary Ridge to the west, bending around through the town of Gettysburg and on to the east across Rock Creek in the direction of Culp's Hill. Thus it formed a curving line initially over three and ultimately about five miles in length, with sufficient cover in the woods and the town to prevent detailed observation of their movements from the Union side.

The Union line, in the form of the historic "fish hook," was initially somewhat shorter and practically ideal for defense, due to the character of the wood-covered ridge, the open fields towards the enemy main line, the rocky hills, and the useful road net leading south and east from the fish hook; and also because it gave Meade the advantage of interior lines that immeasurably simplified his problem of shifting reserves on short order to meet enemy thrusts against any part of the line.

With the Federal bow-shaped line presenting its convex side to the Confederates, its chord, when the entire length of the position was finally occupied, was not more than three miles as the crow flies from Meade's extreme right flank to his left; while Lee, the concave face of whose line was towards the Union position, had about nine miles to cover in the transmission of messages from the extreme of one flank to the other.

Comparative Strengths

At the close of the first day, with darkness covering the field of battle, Lee still held the advantage of numbers, but his superiority was diminishing and during the night disappeared entirely. By 6 A.M. on the second day, the Army of the Potomac had been reinforced by over 25,000 fighting men, giving Meade a decided edge in numerical strength, in addition to which the flexibility of control afforded by his position magnified the effect of his numerical superiority.

Hancock's Second Corps and Sykes' Fifth Corps were now up, together with the reserve artillery. The only absentees were Sedgwick's Sixth Corps and the two cavalry divisions of Gregg and Kilpatrick. The Sixth Corps, more

than 15,000 men, making a forced march from Manchester, thirty-five miles distant, trudged the roads all that
night. With a short rest the following morning this corps
reached Gettysburg about mid-afternoon July 2, when it
became the army reserve east and in rear of the Round
Tops.

Pickett's division of Longstreet's corps remained at
Chambersburg awaiting relief by Imboden's cavalry; Law's
brigade of Hood's division had not yet reached the field,
and Stuart's cavalry was still absent. Otherwise the Army
of Northern Virginia was now fully assembled and in the
positions ordered, the cavalry brigades of Jones and
Robertson having reached the Chambersburg area.

Effect on Gettysburg Civilians

A civilian eyewitness within Gettysburg has described
the situation as it looked to those who were caught between and among the fighting armies the first day of the
battle. Professor J. Howard Wert, a Pennsylvania historian, recalled the scene as follows:

> During the fighting of the afternoon in the suburbs
> of the town a few of the inhabitants had withdrawn
> to the rear. Those who remained were obliged to
> spend much of the following days in their cellars
> whilst storms of lead and iron were hurtling over
> them.
>
> In many cases, they did this on very limited rations,
> for no magician, by his magic "presto, change," caused
> anything to disappear more quickly than the unin-
> vited guests from "Dixie" disposed of all available
> food, after they came swarming into the town. Rapid
> marching to reach the battlefield and hours of fighting
> had given them excellent appetites.
>
> Those citizens were not alone in their cellars. Many
> officers and men of the Eleventh Corps, when hard
> pressed by the foe during the retreat, had leaped

HOUSE NEAR CEMETERY HILL

Heavy fighting occurred here during Confederate attacks on Cemetery Hill. Note bullet holes in the fence. This house stood on Baltimore Street where a side street now goes to the high school.

through an open cellar door or a back yard gate into any place of concealment that appeared to hold forth some promise of escape.

A systematic search of the houses of the town was made by the Confederates and many of these men were captured. Still a goodly number were successfully concealed by the citizens until the Federal troops again entered Gettysburg. Amongst those who thus escaped was General Alex. Schimmelfennig who had fought under Louis Kossuth for Hungarian independence and was now a brigade commander in Howard's corps. Severely wounded in the battle of July 1st, he was assisted into the town by some of his men and successfully concealed by citizens.

Owing to the fact that Gettysburg lies in a valley, as compared with the ridges on either side, the town itself received comparatively little damage during the furious engagements of the two following days when great hostile armies were arrayed against each other on either side and storms of artillery missiles were flying directly over the town. A few houses, in the southwestern suburbs, which were partly in the path of the third day's cannonading, were badly shattered by shells, whilst buildings all over the town were marked by many musket balls.

This was especially the case in the southern part of Baltimore street adjacent to the Cemetery. The houses here were occupied by sharpshooters of the two armies in close proximity to each other. Between these men in blue and gray there was a continuous exchange, day and night, of deadly leaden messengers. Every shutter or external door in the vicinity was pierced with from ten to twenty bullet holes; whilst citizens, when at length able to leave their cellars, in some cases found dead men in their parlors or bedrooms.

Night on the Battlefield

A battlefield when the carnage has ceased is a hideous spectacle. When night falls upon it, it seems to take on redoubled horror.

That night of July 1st was a sad night in Gettysburg. The gloom of the citizens, their terror and alarm was in vivid contrast to their exultation when Buford's stalwart troopers had ridden into the town the day before, and their rejoicings when the Confederate prisoners of the morning had been marched through the streets (Archer's troops).

All the town, except the extreme southern suburb near the Cemetery, in possession of the men in gray! On every street dead men trodden under foot; and barricades hastily constructed of carts, paving stones, demolished fences, and furniture taken from adjoining homes!

The Theological Seminary, on the ridge west of Gettysburg, full of wounded; Pennsylvania College, on the very verge of the Eleventh Corps' disastrous field, full of wounded; every warehouse and every school house full of wounded; all the churches filled with moaning men; every public hall a hospital; men shot, and torn, and riddled out of all semblance of humanity in every private house!

A Union chaplain, attending to the sufferers was shot dead on the steps of Christ's church on Chambersburg street, and citizens were wounded on the streets whilst carrying bandages to the hospital.

CONFEDERATE SOLDIERS PREPARING SUPPER

CHAPTER 14

THE PAUSE BETWEEN BATTLES

GENERAL Lee and his chief lieutenant, Lieutenant General James Longstreet, were far apart in their military thinking—both strategic and tactical—prior to and during the course of the invasion and the culminating Battle of Gettysburg. At no time during those historically decisive days of June and July, 1863, was there anything but a superficial meeting of minds between the two, concerning lines of action to be pursued.

Longstreet Favors the Defensive

Longstreet was opposed to the invasion in the first place, believing that the cause of the Confederacy would be better served by reinforcing the western armies, under the direct command of Lee, with the object of defeating Grant and relieving Vicksburg. When those views were rejected, he had urged Lee to adhere to the strategic defensive in the course of his march into Pennsylvania, and, recalling Fredericksburg, to lure the Army of the Potomac into another attack against a position of Lee's own choosing, and thus to allow Hooker, then in command of the Union army, to shatter it in a repeat performance.

Lee was more offensive-minded. While he had listened politely to his "old war-horse," he was not impressed with Longstreet's theory. The latter was fully assured in his own mind, however, that Lee, while refusing to adopt the plan for a *strategic* defensive, had in fact accepted Longstreet's conception of the *tactical* defensive. He held to that assurance all through the battles at Gettysburg, with complete and almost casual disregard of Lee's actions and direct orders to the contrary.

Such misunderstanding, if it can be called only that, was more than an imponderable; it became a concrete and quite possibly *the* decisive factor in the outcome of the battle. The Gettysburg story is not complete without recording the historic exchange of views between Lee and Longstreet on the afternoon of the first day, and the certain impact, on the tactical developments of July 2 and 3, of the diametrically opposed thinking of the two generals.

As Longstreet with his staff rode along the Chambersburg Pike through Cashtown towards the sound of firing, his trained eye had appraised the tactical possibilities of the terrain west of Gettysburg. He reconstructed the broad outlines, based on the positions of the large number of dead and wounded soldiers of both armies, of the clash that morning between Heth's infantry and Buford's cavalry.

It was late afternoon of July 1 when he crossed the last low ridge, saw the houses of Gettysburg off to the east,

THE HOLLOW SQUARE IN THE CIVIL WAR

This formation, illustrated by Union troops, was employed by the Confederates on the first day of Gettysburg. Late in the afternoon Buford was ordered to cover Doubleday's withdrawal in the Cemetery Hill area. Buford formed his cavalry as if to charge, which would have been a desperate attempt. The Confederates immediately commenced forming hollow squares to repel his expected assault. This gave sufficient delay so that the remmants of Doubleday's First Corps were enabled to escape.

and joined Lee on Seminary Ridge. From this slight eminence Lee had for sometime been observing the Federals retreating across the shallow valley to Cemetery Hill.

The exact words used by Lee and Longstreet at this initial meeting on the battlefield have been variously reported by historians, who agree generally as to their substance. Lee remarked that they seemed to have run into Meade's main body, that something must have happened to Stuart, and that he had sent word to Ewell "to seize that hill south of town (Cemetery Hill) if practicable." He added further that he had not intended to fight at Gettysburg, but could not withdraw without impairing the morale of his men, and that "if Meade is there tomorrow I will attack him."

Longstreet's opinion as to the wisdom of adhering to the tactical defensive had not changed, and Lee's comments seemed to fall on deaf ears. Whether or not Ewell should succeed in driving the Federals off the hill, Longstreet pressed his argument that the thing to do was to move around Meade's left flank, place Lee's army between Meade and Washington, and duplicate Fredericksburg by forcing Meade to attack. Lee reacted impatiently to what he must have regarded as Longstreet's obstinacy, and repeated that if Ewell didn't move "those people" tonight, he would attack them next day.

Thus perversely does the fate of battles hinge on a turn of the wheel. Here was Longstreet, Lee's most experienced corps commander, proposing in effect that Lee move into the very position for defense (the Big Pipe Creek area), the occupancy of which had so obsessed Meade's mind until a few hours before; while Meade, himself planning a defensive battle, had preempted the Longstreet thesis and was getting set to do a Fredericksburg in reverse by encouraging the Confederates to pound themselves to death against the hard anvil of Cemetery Ridge and the Round Tops.

Considering what actually happened on the last two days of the battle, Longstreet's plan, had Lee adopted it, might have resulted in a Confederate victory. But at the time neither Lee nor Longstreet could possibly know, in Stuart's absence, the extent of the Federal concentration, nor the exact location of those elements of Meade's army which had not yet arrived on the field. An interesting war game could be developed by simulating Longstreet's proposed flank march at daybreak of July 2. There would have been meeting engagements all over the place, southeast of Gettysburg. No one can say with any assurance who would have come out on top.

A pertinent commentary may be found in a conversation between Ewell and Meade several years after the war.

Meade, in answer to Ewell's question, stated flatly that if Ewell had pushed his advantage and attacked Cemetery Hill during the afternoon of the first day (as Lee had directed him to do, "if practicable") he would unquestionably have driven the disorganized Federals off the hill, which in turn would have uncovered the rest of Cemetery Ridge and changed the entire complexion of the Federal buildup. While Meade did not actually say so, the implication was plain that the Pipe Creek order would have immediately been invoked and Meade's army put into reverse under extremely adverse circumstances.

Lee, however, was giving the orders and his corps commanders were expected to carry them out loyally and to the best of their ability. How these subordinate commanders responded left much to be desired, although there is something to be said on both sides. In retrospect, it is clear that at Gettysburg Lee fought his worst battle. He failed to outline a comprehensive or concise plan of action, issued his orders in oral and fragmentary form, and made no visible effort to coordinate the operations of the three corps. As read, the orders sound more like conversational suggestions, leaving to Ewell and Longstreet, particularly, an excess of discretionary authority, in the exercise of which Lee's hastily conceived and inadequately transmitted battle plans lost whatever cohesiveness they may have had in his own mind.

The Situation on the Night of July 1

At the end of the first day the Federals had lost the town of Gettysburg—while Lee had firm possession of the Chambersburg and Hagerstown roads to the west, thus securing his line of communications and supply through the South Mountain passes and the Cumberland Valley. The Chambersburg Pike was the corps dividing line, with

A. P. Hill to the south and Ewell to the north and east. The Confederates occupied a horseshoe position with the open end facing south, which controlled all the road spokes of the wheel of which Gettysburg was the hub, except the Emmitsburg, Taneytown, and Baltimore Pikes. Seminary Ridge was manned by Hill's men southwardly to a point opposite Cemetery Hill, and "no man's land" was therefore only a few hundred acres of open ground south of Gettysburg and between the two ridges, although of course the opposing armies were likewise in contact east of the town in the area of Culp's Hill.

CEMETERY HILL GATE, WITH EARTHWORKS USED BY FEDERALS

Near this gate to the Gettysburg town cemetery there stood during the battle this sign: "All persons found using firearms in these grounds will be prosecuted with the utmost rigor of the law." Many a soldier must have smiled grimly at these words, for this gateway became the key of the Federal line, the very center of the cruelest use of firearms yet seen on this continent. On the first day Reynolds saw the value of Cemetery Hill in case of a retreat. Howard posted his reserves here, and Hancock greatly strengthened the position. On this eminence where thousands were buried, was dedicated the soldiers' National Cemetery. Baltimore Pike runs in front of the gate.

Lee Decides to Attack Early on July 2

Lee's own determination to follow up the advantage which the Confederates had gained on the first day was never in question. Aggressive action to keep the Federals off balance, and then defeat them in detail before Meade's concentration could be fully achieved, was for Lee the approved solution to a logical military estimate of the situation. Everything he said and did on the eve of and during the morning of the second day confirmed his intention to launch an attack as early as practicable on the morning of July 2. He planned to make the main effort with Ewell's corps against the Union right flank.

And it was certainly possible to have done so at least four hours before Longstreet finally gave his corps the signal to advance, late in the afternoon. The trouble lay in the fact that Longstreet and Ewell each interpreted the Lee plan in a different manner than intended by Lee. For that the blame must rest chiefly on the latter, because of his failure to convert his decision into either clean-cut missions to the several corps or definite attack orders. There is no record of Lee having summoned his three corps commanders to receive definite orders simultaneously at his headquarters on the Chambersburg Road, near Seminary Ridge, a central point that was within a few minutes hand-gallop of all three corps commanders. On the contrary, Lee spent the morning of July 2 thinking over the implementing details of his attack plan, waiting impatiently for word from Stuart and for the arrival of the last of his infantry divisions, and in successive but separate conversations with Longstreet and Ewell at various points of the compass. In retrospect the Confederates would have profited greatly by a Command conference between Lee, Longstreet, Ewell and Hill.

Ewell Operates in a Mental Vacuum

On the evening of the first day's battle, after Ewell had failed to exploit the early Confederate success by seizing Culp's Hill and making Cemetery Hill, the northern anchor of the Federal position, untenable, Lee rode over to Ewell's headquarters on the northern edge of Gettysburg to discuss the plans for the next day.

The power of decision seemed utterly to have left that corps commander. Johnson's division had lately arrived and all elements of the corps were on hand. Nevertheless Early and Rodes took the lead away from Ewell in arguing against a renewal of the principal effort from that direction, on the ground that the Federals had been greatly reinforced, had made their position too strong to take, and that losses from the July 1 fighting and the exhausted condition of their own troops made such an attack a hazardous gamble. Ewell himself had little to say except to concur in the views of his division commanders. Lee, whose own feelings of frustrated disappointment can easily be imagined, reluctantly proceeded to revamp his own plan by informing Ewell that the attack would instead be made by Longstreet against Meade's left or southern flank, with Ewell launching a concurrent attack from the north when he should hear Longstreet's guns open.

Longstreet's Stalling Tactics

Ex post facto writers of the anti-Longstreet faith have condemned that general unmercifully on the premise that he nullified all chance for a Confederate victory by willful disobedience of specific orders from Lee "to attack with his corps at daylight on July 2." Direct evidence is lacking to support that view, and it does Longstreet an injustice in the face of Lee's own vacillation in reaching a decision

on the form and character of the attack. Whether Longstreet, in the exercise of the discretion invariably allowed
by Lee, made victory impossible by his slowness in launching his attack is another matter. His own version, written
after the war, stated:

> On the night of the 1st I left General Lee without
> any orders. On the morning of the 2nd, I went to his
> headquarters at daylight and renewed my views
> against making an attack. He seemed resolved, how-
> ever, and we discussed the probable results. About
> sunrise General Lee sent Colonel Venable of his staff
> to General Ewell's headquarters, ordering him to
> make a reconnaissance of the ground in his front,
> with a view to making the main attack on his left.
> A short time afterward he followed Colonel Venable
> in person. He returned about 9:00 o'clock and in-
> formed me that it would not do to have Ewell open
> the attack. He finally determined that I should make
> the main attack on the extreme right. It was fully
> 11:00 o'clock when General Lee arrived at this con-
> clusion and ordered the movement.

But Longstreet does not explain why it took him fully
five hours *after* 11:00 A.M., or until 4:00 P.M. to move
the two divisions of his corps the few miles intervening
from their bivouac west of Seminary Ridge to the jumpoff
position assigned them on the Emmitsburg road.

All evidence shows clearly that Longstreet was strongly
opposed to the attack as planned and ordered by Lee, and
that he made every effort to change the latter's mind by
argument, by delay in insisting on waiting for the arrival
of Law's brigade of Hood's division, and by childish ex-
cuses of one sort or another. His preoccupation with his
own proposed plan of action to outflank Meade by moving
to the south of Round Top and setting up a defensive line
there was such that he seemed blind to the fact that Lee's

CONFEDERATE ARTILLERY IN BIVOUAC

mind had been made up to attack up the Emmitsburg Road with the object of rolling up the Federal line from south to north. Longstreet was in that frame of mind that led him to be hypercritical of everything Lee said or did with respect to the projected attack, including the early staff reconnaissance that Lee had initiated to ascertain the Federal strength and dispositions along the Ridge; the character and direction of the approach march to get his troops into position for the attack; the development for the attack; and even the direction of the attack itself.

It does appear that Longstreet had some justification for his dissatisfaction with the way the situation was developing, in that Lee, at variance with his usual custom, pretty much took out of Longstreet's hands the preparatory moves leading up to the actual attack, even to the extent of ignoring the customary command channels by himself tracing on McLaw's map the exact position astride the Emmitsburg road where Lee wished him to place his division for the attack.

It was unheard of to bypass a corps commander and give instructions directly to a division commander, and it added fuel to the flames of discontent that were already consuming the usually placid Longstreet. First the repudiation of his own cherished plan; then a reconnaissance by one of Lee's staff officers that proved to be completely inadequate but upon the accuracy of which Lee based his tactical decisions for Longstreet's corps; next Lee's designation of that same staff officer, a mere captain, to lead Longstreet's troops into position; and finally the crowning humiliation of ignoring Longstreet's presence and giving direct attack orders to one of his subordinates. All this was too much for Longstreet, who sulked like a spoiled child, revealing by his actions and side remarks his innermost thoughts which in modern terms might be paraphrased as "O. K., you old so-and-so; it's your baby and if that's the way you insist on playing it, go to it, but I'm against the whole business and I won't lift a finger to make your plan work the way you think it should."

Right or wrong, it *was* Lee's baby and there are some who think Longstreet should have been summarily relieved from command, as a result of his attitude, then and there. The patient Lee was sorely tried, but kept his temper hour after hour while Longstreet temporized. Finally that patience was used up and Lee gave Longstreet peremptory and unequivocal oral orders to launch the attack without further delay.

The Battle Area of July 2-3

There is a road leading due west from the Peach Orchard that crosses in succession the Emmitsburg Road and Seminary Ridge and then, after passing Pitzer School House and Willoughby Run, continues on until it ultimately joins the Hagerstown Road. This road was destined to receive additional historical recognition ninety-two years later when Dwight David Eisenhower, President of the United States, bought the farms that lay between Willoughby Run and Seminary Ridge, including Pitzer Woods and Biesecker Woods—farms across which ran the road from Peach Orchard—in preparation for the day when a great soldier and statesman could browse at leisure on the very terrain where Longstreet's two divisions marched and countermarched in that inefficiently conducted approach march to the battle on the afternoon of July 2, 1863.

The fighting on July 1 had been fluidly characteristic of meeting engagements, with plenty of give and take, rapid shifting of position by smaller troop elements, hair-trigger decisions and movements by brigades and regiments without even the knowledge of the higher commanders, let alone the opportunity for them to influence the action.

The battle as joined was both unplanned and premature as to time and place, for Lee and Meade alike. The strategic job of concentration and troop disposition for the main event had greater significance than the tactical footwork and hasty exchange of blows by the contestants in the first round.

By the time darkness had ended the July 1 engagements, there was no further uncertainty. All hands knew that the Army of the Potomac and the Army of Northern Virginia were irrevocably committed to a major fight to the death. This would occur in a comparatively small area that from the character of the terrain would allow less room for maneuver than that to which both armies had been accustomed in Virginia.

History records few if any military campaigns in which

CEMETERY RIDGE, LOOKING SOUTH.

View from the vicinity of Bloody Angle, facing toward the Round Tops.
The bearded civilian in the foreground is Paul Philippoteaux, who painted
the famous Gettysburg Cyclorama.

so many soldiers have fought it out in such a small cockpit—within so short a span of time. Except for the cavalry
fight east of the Gettysburg area on July 3, the main battles
of July 2-3 were fought to the bitter end on a rectangular
field of only a few square miles, which lies due south of
the town of Gettysburg.

A brief description of the "stadium" will serve to orient
the reader for the battles of the second and third days.
From Gettysburg three roads ran south, designated from
east to west the Baltimore, Taneytown, and Emmitsburg
Roads. The first named angled off to the southeast shortly
after emerging from Gettysburg and passing Culp's Hill
within the Federal lines; the second headed due south,
crossing Cemetery Hill and skirting the base of the Round
Tops on the east. Both of these roads served Meade's

DEVIL'S DEN, LOOKING WEST ACROSS PLUM RUN

army well throughout the Gettysburg campaign, and were of vital strategic and logistic importance to him. The Emmitsburg Road ran for a short distance along the western base of Cemetery Hill and then swung in a south-westerly direction diagonally across the battle amphi-theater until it crossed Seminary Ridge opposite the Round Tops, as though to demonstrate its neutrality in the frat-ricidal contest about to take place in its bailiwick.

From Ziegler's Grove near the western base of Cemetery Hill, south to the base of Round Top, the Federally-oc-cupied Cemetery Ridge dominated the terrain to the west along its length of about 2¼ miles. The Ridge for some hundreds of yards was open and in full view of the Con-federates on Seminary Ridge, which paralleled Cemetery Ridge at a distance of slightly less than a mile across a shallow valley covered by fields of wheat, corn, and other crops. At the southern extremity of the line the Round Tops rose to successive elevations of nearly 700 feet for Little Round Top and about 750 feet for Big Round Top, both rugged hills covered with large boulders and thick woods and connected by a 500-yard saddle. Big Round Top was entirely too steep and rocky for horse artillery to surmount. Rifle fire for mutual and interlocking support was ineffective at any distance from either hill; despite that tactical disadvantage, physical occupation of both was essential to control of Cemetery Ridge by the Federals.

About halfway between Cemetery Hill and Round Top, at what was then known as George Weikert's farm, Ceme-

THE LITTLE ROUND TOP AREA
As Geary's scouts saw the terrain early on the morning of July 2.

tery Ridge merged into a large area of rocks, hills, and woods, stretching for about 400 yards toward Plum Run. This stream ran along the western base of the Round Tops and where the ridge disappeared into low, marshy ground that reached to the base of Little Round Top.

About 500 yards due west of Little Round Top stood a bold, rocky height, steep on its eastern side and extending as a ridge to the west. This was Devil's Den, somewhat lower than Little Round Top, and composed of gigantic rocks with innumerable crevices that afforded ideal positions for sharpshooters.

The Taneytown and Emmitsburg Roads were linked by a crossroad that skirted the northern base of Devil's Den. From there it led past a wood on the north and a wheat field on the south until it reached the Peach Orchard at the edge of the Emmitsburg Road about 1,000 yards west of Devil's Den and less than a half-mile from the Confederate position on Seminary Ridge.

Looking across the valley of death, from little Round Top.

VIEW FROM THE POSITION OF HAZLETT'S BATTERY ON LITTLE ROUND TOP

CHAPTER 15

THE SECOND DAY

A S THE rapidly marching Federal corps reached the battlefield during the night of July 1 and the morning of July 2, they were successively assigned positions along the "fish hook" in prolongation, to right and left, of the initial positions taken by the First and Eleventh Corps following their retreat on the afternoon of July 1.

Meade Extends the Defensive Position

The Twelfth Corps was assigned a sector on the right of First Corps to include Culp's Hill. However, the first division of that corps to arrive, Geary's, had reached the battlefield at 4:30 P.M. on the 1st. Hancock, who was then acting for Meade on the ground, directed Geary to extend the line to the left of the First Corps along Cemetery Ridge and to occupy Little Round Top which Hancock saw

187

dominated the ridge and the roads on both sides of it. When A. S. Williams, with the other division of the Twelfth Corps arrived, he was placed on the north as intended; but this resulted in the corps being split. Meade planned to move Geary over to the right to occupy Culp's Hill on July 2, as soon as Geary could be relieved on Little Round Top by Sickles' troops. Geary actually made this move, as will be related later, but in so doing left Little Round Top unguarded.

Hancock's Second Corps, which came up shortly after daylight on July 2, was placed on the ridge to the left of the First Corps. On the left of Hancock was placed Sickles' Third Corps (less French's division, at Harper's Ferry), as far as Round Top. The Fifth Corps was in reserve, with its trains near Granite Schoolhouse Lane which connects the Baltimore Pike with the Taneytown Road. The Sixth Corps did not arrive from Manchester until the afternoon of July 2. Buford's cavalry division was guarding the left flank near Round Top, with Kilpatrick and Gregg maneuvering their respective divisions well out on the right flank towards Hanover and Westminster.

Having failed to take advantage of his golden opportunity to seize Culp's Hill on the afternoon of July 1, Ewell toyed with the idea of attacking that eminence on July 2. About daylight his reconnaissance parties (from Johnson's division) advanced on Culp's Hill but found the Federals in possession. Ewell decided to wait a bit longer and let Longstreet carry the burden.

Meade, seeing that Ewell did not follow up his reconnaissance or "demonstration," directed Slocum to prepare to attack Ewell with the Fifth and Twelfth Corps as soon as the Sixth Corps should arrive. Both Slocum and Warren advised strongly against the projected attack because of the unfavorable character of the ground, so Meade dropped the idea and reverted to his previous plan of waiting for Lee to further reveal his intentions.

Lull Before the Storm

The morning of July 2 was spent by both armies in improving their positions, fitting newly arrived units into their allotted slots, making small but unimportant passes at one another, bringing up artillery ammunition, and attending to the dead and wounded.

The rank and file of course did only what they were required to do, performing the multitude of housekeeping chores which from time immemorial have occupied soldiers when not actually engaged in battle. Thursday, July 2, was sultry and cloudy with occasional drizzles of rain after a clear moonlit night. As many men as could passed the time stretched out on the ground or propped against convenient trees.

They knew that the fighting of the first day would be resumed sooner or later. Many improved the time by writing letters to loved ones, quietly discussing the impending battle, or exchanging stories on their individual and unit experiences of the day before. The old-timers naturally spent their leisure time in catching naps or resting, having learned from other campaigns that stored-up energy can be money in the bank on occasions when war ignores the fact that nights were made for rest and sleep.

Skirmishers were moderately active off and on during the morning, with short but spirited exchanges of rifle fire between opposing pickets. The Confederates were observed from the Federal position to be extending their right on Seminary Ridge, a mile away, and it was chiefly the activity of their scouts which provoked the rifle fire that occasionally broke the stillness of the morning. The

ON THE SKIRMISH LINE

men in gray had been instructed to feel out the enemy to determine the length and compactness of his line and the location of his left flank, especially the latter.

Both armies were fully assembled by midmorning except for the Federal Sixth Corps, Pickett's Confederate division, Law's brigade of Longstreet's corps, and of course the peripatetic Jeb Stuart. Meade's strength now exceeded Lee's by a small, infantry-artillery margin. But the initiative remained with Lee, who was prepared to exercise it. Meade, having made up his mind to fight a defensive battle, applied himself to the task of making his position as strong as possible.

Meade's Orders to Sickles

On the evening of July 1 Meade had ordered Sickles to relieve Geary's division on Little Round Top by occupying that position so that Geary might rejoin his own Twelfth Corps. The orders were oral and not nearly as explicit as they should have been. Meade neglected to make a personal reconnaissance on the left at daylight the next morning, possibly because his mind was centered on the north end of the line where he anticipated a repetition of the pressure of the first day against Cemetery Hill and Culp's Hill. In this thinking he accurately estimated Lee's intentions, which in due course were thwarted by Ewell's unwillingness to undertake the job.

However, when the Second Corps came up shortly after daylight on July 2, and was placed to the left of the First Corps, Meade personally repeated his instructions to Sickles to extend his command "from the left of the Second Corps over the ground held by Geary." Geary knew that he was to be relieved by Sickles in order to rejoin Slocum, and Sickles had precise orders to relieve Geary, but as so often happens when adequate staff work is lacking, the plans and orders of the commanding general were not carried out as intended.

It seemed to be the custom in 1863 to leave the order writing to the top echelon of command. But from regimental up to and including corps commanders, oral and in most cases extremely fragmentary orders were the rule. Hence majors and captains on staff duty could and did foul up many a situation for an entire division by transmitting—perhaps inexactly—a hurriedly phrased remark of a corps commander such as "Tell Smith to come up immediately," or "Put your brigade on the left and guide on Jones."

Be that as it may, Sickles didn't think much of the position assigned his corps, because it was on low ground. He greatly preferred a line about a half mile to the west, on higher ground along the Emmitsburg Road, with the left at Sherfy's Peach Orchard.

Meade's Superior Battle Headquarters

Meantime Meade had moved his headquarters up from Taneytown to a small, whitewashed, unpretentious farmhouse just off the Taneytown Road. It stood in a defiladed area almost due east and but a few hundred yards in rear

MEADE'S HEADQUARTERS ON THE TANEYTOWN ROAD
General Meade arrived at Cemetery Hill at 1 AM July 2, and after daylight established his headquarters in the farmhouse shown. The building was struck by several shells during the cannonade on July 3.

of what is now called the "high water mark" or "bloody angle" on Cemetery Ridge, where Hancock's Second Corps was posted. The term defiladed area is used here in a relative sense only, because the building, with its stone-floored, grape-arbored patio on the south side, was protected only from direct observation by Cemetery Hill and Ridge. Spent rifle balls and unspent artillery missiles could and did strike the house, forcing Meade on the third day to transfer his headquarters to a quieter spot further east on a small hill which Slocum had selected for his corps command post.

This was an ideal spot for quick and easy contact with all parts of the Federal line and the reserve elements. Messengers to and from the ammunition and supply trains had relatively safe and easy access to their destinations; and Meade was able to direct personally, or at least under his own eyes, the rapid shift of brigades and divisions, both infantry and artillery, in the giant game of chess in which on July 2 and 3 he maneuvered his troops so successfully.

Sickles, riding over there to see Meade, requested permission to move his corps forward, urging the general to come and see for himself. Instead Meade told General Hunt, his Chief of Artillery, to return with Sickles and look over the terrain. But Hunt gave Sickles neither a yes nor a no decision. He agreed that the desired position had a better field of fire, and if strongly occupied was generally more desirable from the standpoint of the Third Corps. Despite Sickles' urging, Hunt refused to authorize him to occupy the new position without Meade's specific approval.

Hunt estimated that Meade could only thus extend his line by using the Fifth Corps, which was in reserve pending the arrival of the Sixth. This was a calculated risk that Meade was not prepared to take, although as it turned out, Longstreet's delay until 4 P.M. in attacking the Federal left made it in retrospect perfectly feasible, had the advanced line been occupied in the morning. Not being psychic, Meade could hardly have been expected to read Longstreet's mind and therefore can not be blamed for withholding approval of Sickles' request.

Round Tops Left Unoccupied

Geary's division of Slocum's corps, as previously noted, held the left to and including Little Round Top during the night of July 1. Slocum's orders to Geary to move to Culp's Hill may or may not have specified that the move was to follow relief by Sickles' corps. Sickles was purposely slow in assigning his troops to the position. Geary, becoming impatient at the delay, on his own responsibility withdrew his division from the ridge and rejoined Slocum. He

explained later in extenuation that he had sent a staff
officer to Sickles to guide his troops but found Sickles apparently undecided or at least vague as to just when he
would effect the relief. Thus the Round Tops were left
unoccupied, except for a small signal detachment until—
as will be described later—General Warren discovered the
absence of troops on that key position.

MAJOR GENERAL DANIEL E. SICKLES
Commanding the Third Corps.

Sickles' Corps Advances to Emmitsburg Road

About noon the cavalry and the signal station on Little
Round Top began to send in reports that the Confederates
were massing in large force opposite Round Top and the
left of the Third Corps. Sickles thereupon sent Colonel
Berdan with two regiments on reconnaissance to ascertain
the Confederate strength in the woods west of the Emmits-

burg Road. Berdan found out right quickly that the Southerners were there in large numbers that were rapidly growing larger. Soon thereafter Sickles took the bull by the horns, and without authority moved his entire corps forward to the new line.

Shortly after 1 P.M. the movement commenced, practically in parade formation and with colors flying. The officers of Hancock's corps on Sickles' right stared in mystification and concern, first because they thought the entire line of the army must have been ordered forward and the orders had failed to reach the Second Corps, and secondly because Sickles' move meant that their own left flank was thus left nakedly exposed.

Frank Aretas Haskell, who was an aide to General Gibbon of Hancock's Second Corps, described the forward movement of Sickles' corps in a letter to his brother, written shortly after the battle. The following excerpt* from this letter gives the picture vividly:

> It was magnificent to see those ten or twelve thousand men—they were good men—with their batteries, and some squadrons of cavalry upon the left flank, all in battle order, in several lines, with flags streaming, sweep steadily down the slope, across the valley, and up the next ascent, toward their destined position! From our position we could see it all. In advance Sickles pushed forward his heavy line of skirmishers, who drove back those of the enemy, across the Emmetsburg road, and thus cleared the way for the main body. The Third Corps now became the absorbing object of interest for all eyes. The Second Corps took arms, and the 1st Division of this corps was ordered to be in readiness to support the Third Corps, should circumstances render support necessary. As the Third

---

* Frank Aretas Haskell, *The Battle of Gettysburg*, Harvard Classics, New York, P. F. Collier & Son, 1910.

Corps was the extreme left of our line, as it advanced,
if the enemy was assembling to the west of Round
Top with a view to turn our left, as we had heard,
there would be nothing between the left flank of the
Corps and the enemy, and the enemy would be square
upon its flank by the time it had attained the road.
So when this advance line came near the Emmetsburg
road, and we saw the squadrons of cavalry mentioned,
come dashing back from their position as flankers, and
the smoke of some guns, and we heard the reports
away to Sickles' left, anxiety became an element in
our interest in these movements. The enemy opened
slowly at first, and from long range; but he was square
upon Sickles' left flank. General Caldwell was ordered
at once to put his Division—the 1st of the Second
Corps, as mentioned—in motion, and to take post in
the woods at the left slope of Round Top, in such a
manner as to resist the enemy should he attempt to
come around Sickles' left and gain his rear. The Division moved as ordered, and disappeared from view in
the woods, toward the point indicated at between
two and three o'clock P.M., and the reserve brigade—
the First, Col. Heath temporarily commanding—of
the Second Division, was therefore moved up and occupied the position vacated by the Third Division.
About the same time the Fifth Corps could be seen
marching by the flank from its position on the Baltimore Pike, and in the opening of the woods heading
for the same locality where the 1st Division of the
Second Corps had gone. The Sixth Corps had now
come up and was halted on the Baltimore Pike. So
the plot thickened. As the enemy opened upon Sickles
with his batteries, some five or six in all, I suppose,
firing slowly, Sickles with as many replied, and with
more spirit. The artillery fire became quite animated,
soon; but the enemy was forced to withdraw his guns
farther and farther away, and ours advanced upon
him. It was not long before the cannonade ceased
altogether, the enemy having retired out of range,

and Sickles, having temporarily halted his command, pending this, moved forward again to the position he desired, or nearly that.

The departure of Buford's Cavalry was one of the unexplained occurrences of the second day. While it is true that his men were tired after their strenuous work of July first, cavalry on the flank south of Gettysburg was absolutely indispensable—a gold mine for Meade in the absence of Stuart on the Confederate side. It is quite likely that Meade had given Pleasonton, his cavalry commander, general instructions which covered the contingency of a reversal and withdrawal of the army to the south. Pleasonton has stated that on the afternoon of July 2, "General Meade gave me the order to get what cavalry and artillery I could as soon as possible and take up a position in the rear to cover the retreat of the army from Gettysburg." It would be helpful in solving the riddle if it were known whether orders had been sent to Merritt at Mechanicstown (Thurmont) to relieve Buford, or if the instructions were garbled and Pleasonton pulled Buford out prematurely without providing a replacement. Whatever happened, Sickles' forward move uncovered the left flank of the Army of the Potomac and there was no cavalry there to provide the necessary protection. It is of course always easy to criticize after the event, and the paucity of written orders, even scribbled instructions on field message blanks or the back of an old envelope, affords a wonderful opportunity for ex post facto explanations.

Meade's Council of War

Meantime, what was General Meade doing? He was holding a council of war.

Meade had a liking for councils of war, at least in the early days following his sudden elevation to army com-

mand, possibly because he had been catapulted into the
top echelon at a time when he personally felt that either
Reynolds or Hancock had stronger claims to the promotion. He may have reasoned that, at that stage, it was
diplomatically wise to consult his corps commanders and
invite their best judgment on the course to be pursued,
or it could have been that he needed and wanted reas-
surance that he was following the right course. Councils
of war had never been militarily fashionable, or even
sound—at least under that name—but they were considered
by some commanders the thing to do during the Civil
War, particularly by those generals who weren't too confident of their own judgment.

About 3 P.M. Meade had summoned his corps commanders to the Leister House, his small, frame command
post on the Taneytown Road, for a council of war. Sickles
asked to be excused for the reason that his corps was in
direct contact with the enemy and he was greatly concerned about his left flank. The request was disapproved,
but by the time Sickles reached Meade's command post,
rifle and artillery fire could be heard to the west. Meade
met Sickles at the door, told him to return at once to his
front, broke up the council, and followed Sickles.

Meade Again Takes Control

In the few minutes that elapsed before Sickles and
Meade successively reached the new Third Corps position
along the Emmitsburg Road, Confederate artillery fire
had increased in volume and enemy infantry was observed
moving out from the woods of Seminary Ridge to the
south. Sickles' offer to return his line to Cemetery Ridge
was countered by Meade's comment that it was too late,
he must fight it out where he was, and he, Meade, would
move troops at once to support him. All credit to Meade

for a prompt and soldierly decision to make the best of a bad bargain. And Meade was as good as his word. Watching the battle closely, he saw immediately that Sickles must be withdrawn or supported. The former was too risky, so Meade promptly ordered Sykes' Fifth Corps, in reserve where Rock Creek crosses the Baltimore Pike, into line on Hancock's left to restore the original continuity of the defensive position on Cemetery Ridge.

Nor did Meade stop there. He also sent for Caldwell's division of Hancock's Second Corps, a division from Slocum's Twelfth Corps in the vicinity of Culp's Hill, and later for additional troops from Sedgwick's Sixth Corps, recently arrived from Manchester as the newly designated Army Reserve.

Viewed objectively, Meade deserved to win the game July 2. Thrown off balance initially by Sickles' action, and despite his own failure to make certain that the cavalry was still protecting the army left flank (which it was not), he reacted constructively and decisively to correct the errors insofar as it was within his power, even though in so doing he weakened his right wing and committed a portion of his newly constituted Army Reserve. It was sound procedure, despite the risk that Ewell might exploit the opportunity thus offered him on Meade's right (which Ewell again failed to do), and it paid off by giving the Federals numerical superiority at the point of impact. Without Meade's prompt action in shifting his troops there might well not have been a "third day."

The Confederate Attack

As described in the previous chapter, General Lee had planned to attack the left of the Federal army on July 2. The attack, first ordered for daylight, was postponed until 11 A.M. But as the hours passed and Longstreet's attack failed to materialize, Lee became increasingly impatient. The orders had been clear enough, they just weren't being executed.

Lee's plan of attack, simply expressed in his report of the battle, was this:

> It was determined to make the principal attack upon the enemy's left, and endeavor to gain a position from which it was thought that our artillery could be brought to bear with effect. Longstreet was directed to place the divisions of McLaws and Hood on the right of Hill, partially enveloping the enemy's left, which he was to drive in.
>
> General Hill was ordered to threaten the enemy's center to prevent reinforcements being drawn to either wing, and cooperate with his right division in Longstreet's attack.
>
> General Ewell was instructed to make a simultaneous demonstration upon the enemy's right, to be converted into a real attack should opportunity offer.

With Pickett still on the road from Chambersburg, Law's brigade having finally arrived from New Guilford, Longstreet had only two of his three divisions available. Since he objected to "fighting with one boot off," he kept whittling and taking catnaps and generally stalling in the hope that Pickett would reach the field before Lee should force the issue and demand action forthwith.

Tacitly accepting Longstreet's delaying tactics, Lee reluctantly permitted him to wait for Law. Later, to replace Pickett, he attached Anderson's division of Hill's corps to Longstreet's command, with instructions to make a frontal attack in cooperation with the First Corps envelopment of the Federal left. The remainder of Hill's corps was to keep on its toes to exploit any advantage that might accrue to the Confederates from the planned joint attack by Longstreet and Ewell against the enemy left and right flanks.

Lee knew about Sickles' occupation of the Peach Orchard and Emmitsburg Road, because he pointed out to Longstreet personally the tactical importance of the Peach Orchard, suggesting that there was the major target against which the attack should be directed. But he was

MAJOR GENERAL JOHN B. HOOD, C.S.A.
Commanding a division in Longstreet's corps.

clearly uninformed of the fact that the Federal line extended to the south, in a salient to Devil's Den, or he would not have kept insisting that the Peach Orchard marked the left of the Federal line, or that Longstreet's attack "must be up the Emmitsburg Road" to roll up the Union line from south to north. Lee evidently believed Sickles' line to be a portion of the main Federal position, and apparently it didn't occur to Longstreet or

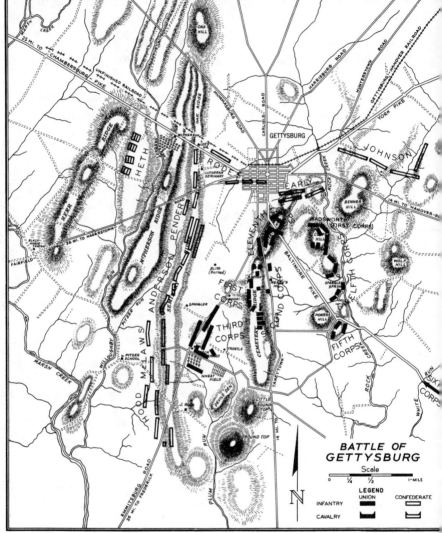

Map 11. THE SITUATION AT 3:30 PM, JULY 2

This map shows the Federal disposition after Sickles' had made his advance to the Emmi
burg, and before the attack of Hood and McLaws had developed.

anyone else on the Confederate side to send out reconnaissance parties during the early part of the afternoon
to learn first-hand the outline and strength of the position.

The divisions of Hood and McLaws, which were shifted
from the Seminary Ridge position to the south to make
the major effort, were not in position for the jumpoff until
4 P.M. In order to avoid observation from Round Top
they had been exhaustingly marched by a circuitous route
in the stifling heat, but finally reached their designated
position astride the Emmitsburg Road south of a line
drawn through the Peach Orchard. They found themselves moving north against an enemy in position and
directly in front of them, whereas they had been led to
believe that the hostile line faced to the west.

As soon as he discovered the true situation General
Hood sent repeated messages and staff officers to Longstreet urging that he be permitted to extend further to
the east and to circle Round Top in order to outflank
Meade's line on the left rear. But Longstreet was obdurate
and replied to each request simply that General Lee had
said to attack up the Emmitsburg Road.

As the massive Confederate artillery of sixty batteries
concentrated their fire on the key Federal hinge at the
Peach Orchard, and the infantry moved to close in for
the assault, Longstreet himself caught fire. He put aside
his personal pique over Lee's uncompromising attitude,
and jumped into the fight with the vigor and decisiveness
which always characterized him when the heat of battle
took hold of his soldierly mind and heart.

The afternoon was far gone, however—it was well after
four o'clock—his two divisions had been committed, and
it was too late for him to effectively coordinate their confused reactions. He did the best he could, but it was not
good enough. His earlier stalling now came back to

plague him, when, instead of attacking as a team, Hood and McLaws entered the fray disjointedly and successively, with the result that neither was able to attain other than local and inconclusive successes.

The Round Tops are Reoccupied

It was nip and tuck, considering the time and space factors, whether Hood's Texans would grab and hold the unoccupied Round Tops. These were the key to assured victory, though neither Meade nor Lee seem to have been aware of that fact, certainly not Lee.

It was at this stage that General Warren, Meade's Chief Engineer, established his secure niche in the hall of fame of American arms. After leaving Meade and Sickles on the latter's front, Warren rode over to Little Round Top to have a look. To his amazement he found it empty except for a handful of signal personnel who for some reason were packing up to pull out. Maybe they were just lonely. In any case Warren persuaded them to stay and continue to wave their flags as evidence to the enemy that the hill was occupied.

Warren's appreciation of topography and its tactical significance was of a high order. He realized at once the crisis that Confederate possession of Little Round Top would cause for Meade and the Army of the Potomac. From the commanding elevation that overlooks much of the battlefield he could see the Confederates like waves overlapping the Federals as Hood's men spread ever farther to the east toward the high ground on which he stood.

Warren lost no time in plugging the gap. By extreme good fortune Barnes' division of the Fifth Corps was seen advancing rapidly along the western base of Little Round Top to counterattack and neutralize the early Confederate

BRIGADIER GENERAL GOUVERNEUR K. WARREN AT LITTLE ROUND TOP

success in breaking Sickles' line and forcing the Third Corps back. In the name of the Commanding General, Warren detached Vincent's brigade and directed it to the crest of Little Round Top just in time to meet and repulse with the bayonet the extreme right regiment of Hood's division, which had already crossed the shoulder of Big Round Top and was moving rapidly to take Little Round Top and consolidate its gains.

In a letter written in 1872 General Warren adds color to his dramatic action in saving Little Round Top by stating that, when he arrived there and noted that it was the key to the whole position, and that the Confederates could assemble unseen in the woods west of the Emmitsburg Road, he directed a nearby battery commander to fire a single shot into the enemy woods. This was done and, according to Warren, the Confederate infantry naturally turned their heads in the direction of the shot. In so doing, their infantry gun barrels and bayonets reflected the sunlight, revealing that they were in line and already greatly outflanking the Federal position. Whereupon Warren immediately sent word to General Meade that Little Round Top was in danger, to send him a division at once. It was at that point that Meade summoned help from the Fifth Corps.

Peach Orchard and the Wheatfield

Frank Haskell's letter* describes graphically, from the Federal viewpoint, the fighting which occurred as the assault of Longstreet's corps got under way:

> It was now about five o'clock, and we shall soon see what Sickles gained by his move. First we hear more artillery firing upon Sickles' left—the enemy seems to be opening again, and as we watch the Rebel batteries seem to be advancing there. The cannonade is soon opened again, and with great spirit on both sides. The enemy's batteries press those of Sickles, and pound the shot upon them, and this time they in turn begin to retire to position nearer the infantry. The enemy seems to be fearfully in earnest this time. And what is more ominous than the thunder or the shot of his advancing guns, this time, in the intervals between his batteries, far to Sickles' left, appear the long lines and the columns of the Rebel infantry, now unmistakably moving out to the attack. The position of the Third Corps becomes at once one of great peril, and it is probable that its commander by this time began to realize his true situation. All was astir now on our crest. Generals and their staffs were galloping hither and thither—the men were all in their places, and you might have heard the rattle of ten thousand ramrods as they drove home and "thugged" upon the little globes and cones of lead. As the enemy was advancing upon Sickles'

* Frank Aretas Haskell, *op. cit.*

left flank, he commenced a change, or at least a partial one, of front, by swinging back his left and throwing forward his right, in order that his lines might be parallel to those of his adversary, his batteries meantime doing what they could to check the enemy's advance; but this movement was not completely executed before new Rebel batteries opened upon Sickles' right flank—his former front—and in the same quarter appeared the Rebel infantry also. Now came the dreadful battle picture, of which we for a time could be but spectators. Upon the front and right flank of Sickles came sweeping the infantry of Longstreet and Hill. Hitherto there had been skirmishing and artillery practice—now the battle began; for amid the heavier smoke and larger tongues of flame of the batteries, now began to appear the countless flashes, and the long fiery sheets of the muskets, and the rattle of the volleys mingles with the thunder of the guns. We see the long gray lines come sweeping down upon Sickles' front, and mix with the battle smoke; now the same colors emerge from the bushes and orchards upon his right, and envelope his flank in the confusion of the conflict.

THE TROSTLE HOUSE

Sickles' headquarters and the scene of heavy fighting on the afternoon of the second day. Sickles lost a leg here.

THE PEACH ORCHARD
Looking eastward across the Emmitsburg Road toward Round Top. From a
rare photo taken shortly after the Civil War.

Sickles' new line as formed made a perfect V, with the
point at the Peach Orchard. Humphrey's division was on
the right, extended some distance up the Emmitsburg
Road. Birney's division was on the left, partly on the Emmitsburg Road and then refused along a lane in a south-
easterly direction extending for nearly a mile from the
Peach Orchard to Devil's Den along the edge of the now
famous Wheatfield. The strength of the Third Corps was
about 12,000 men.

The Peach Orchard position—the forward point of
Sickles' salient—was an arrowhead pointed straight towards
and almost touching the heart of the Confederate line on
Seminary Ridge and about two-thirds of the distance
across country from Cemetery Ridge. The Orchard was
on the high point of the shallow valley between the two
armies, the angle of that point being formed by the inter-
section of the two ridges, one along the Emmitsburg
Road, the other leading east to Devil's Den. The country
south of a line drawn through Round Top, Devil's Den,
the Wheatfield, and Peach Orchard, was open, rolling,
and broken into numerous fields surrounded by stone and
rail fences.

The Confederate attack, as previously noted, was disjointed and largely uncontrolled. But the Southerners were fiery and aggressive and the conflagration spread rapidly from right to left as McLaw's brigades took up the fight after Hood became engaged. Successively the brigades of Wright, Perry, and Wilcox, of Anderson's division, initiated their frontal attack against Humphrey's position on the north end of the field.

Longstreet himself concentrated on the reduction of the Peach Orchard, which was the keystone of the advanced Federal line and the specific objective which Lee had directed to his attention and desired that he capture. The fighting in and around Sherfy's Peach Orchard was terrific and the losses on both sides correspondingly great. In spite of this, at the very heart of the position, right on the crest of the ridge, an 87-year old farmer, John Wentz, remained unharmed in the cellar of his small cottage all during the battle, while from the front yard a son whom he had not seen for twenty-four years served

THE STRUGGLE FOR DEVIL'S DEN

THE WHIRLPOOL

Scene of sanguinary fighting on the second day. A view of a portion of Trostle's pasture land, looking from the Emmitsburg Road toward the Round Tops. The Wheatfield is on the right, beyond the two prominent trees. From a rare photo taken soon after the war.

his gun of the Washington Battery of New Orleans when Longstreet finally broke the Union line and forced the Federals to fall back on Cemetery Ridge.

For almost four hours the battle raged at close range, up and down the line, over the Wheatfield, amid the rocks of Devil's Den, on the slopes of Little Round Top, and across the Emmitsburg Road between Seminary and Cemetery Ridges. The concurrent attack against the Federal right by Anderson's brigades was as lacking in coordination as was Longstreet's against the left, consequently was equally unproductive insofar as Lee's plans were concerned.

When the Peach Orchard was taken the center of gravity of the battle shifted to the Wheatfield. In this small cockpit many regiments from five different corps slugged it out, hour after hour, until the earth oozed blood and the brooks ran in crimson streams. In six successive attempts the Confederates captured the field and six times were driven back by vicious counterattacks. In this limited area the field was covered with dead and wounded of both armies—five hundred Confederate dead were found in the Wheatfield alone. It is doubtful if at any time or at any place in America has so much human blood been spilled in a comparable battle area, except possibly at Antietam. The Wheatfield has been aptly called the "whirlpool" of the battle, because of the manner in which regiments on both sides were seemingly sucked into its vortex. But it could with equal justification have been termed a quicksand, from the way in which it swallowed up regiment after regiment of Blue and Gray.

Seldom in the history of warfare have two forces engaged in a battle of such fluidity as characterized the fighting over the Wheatfield. Time after time one of the contestants would gain a tactical success only to find a fresh opponent springing up on flank or rear. Thus the success would be quickly wiped out only to find the new winner confronted with a similar embarrassment from still another direction.

The supporting frontal attack by Anderson's division, directed at Humphrey's segment of Sickles' line along the Emmitsburg Road from the Peach Orchard to a point near the Codori House, might have paid off had there been a more competent directing head. Only three of Anderson's five brigades became fully engaged. Although uncoordinated, those three brigades made a valiant effort. Wright succeeded in effecting a lodgment on Cemetery Ridge. Posey's brigade, slated to follow Wright on the left, failed to reach even the Emmitsburg Road, while Mahone's brigade did not move at all. Wright's was the only one which penetrated the Federal line on Cemetery Ridge, but he was unsupported, left high and dry. Of course he was soon ejected, as one might remove a thorn imbedded in his arm.

THE CHARGE OF ALEXANDER'S ARTILLERY PRESSING SICKLES' RETREAT

Confederate Command Ineffective

A. P. Hill does not seem to have been very active as a corps commander during the second day of the Battle of Gettysburg. Lee's own movements and actions in the late afternoon have not been recorded. Longstreet was busy from four o'clock on. But in retrospect Lee, Hill, and Ewell might just as well have been playing pinochle at Cashtown so far as any direct action on their part to influence the battle of the late afternoon was concerned.

Pickett's division of Longstreet's corps arrived from Chambersburg about the middle of the afternoon, but was not employed. Neither were two of Hill's divisions, which sat it out in the center of the Confederate line without lifting a finger to intervene.

What was Lee doing? Why didn't he throw one or more of the divisions under Pickett, Pender, and Heth into the battle? Meade was certainly moving his knights and bishops with considerable skill, checking Longstreet's aggressive maneuvers with effective countermeasures. But Lee, having laid down the overall plan, followed his usual procedure and left the details of the action to his corps commanders. It would therefore seem that Meade's leadership in contrast to Lee's clearly entitled the former

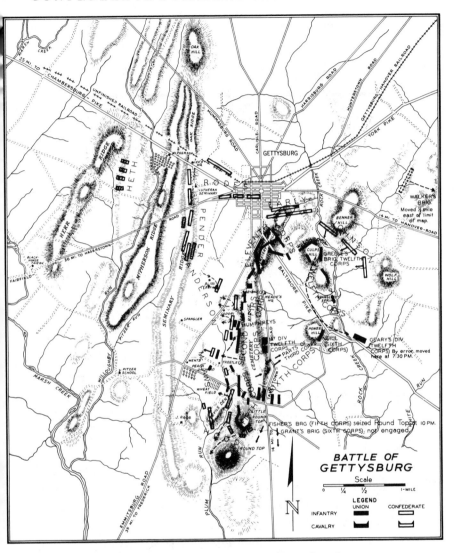

Map 12. THE SITUATION ABOUT 7:30 PM, JULY 2

The fighting in the Peach Orchard, the Wheatfield, and the Little Round Top area has ended. The Union line is now back along Cemetery Ridge — Round Tops, with the Confederates in close contact. Culp's Hill, held only by Greene's brigade, is soon to be attacked by Ewell, whose troops will drive Greene from his position on the southern slope. However the Confederates will be ejected on the following morning, thus losing a golden opportunity to outflank the entire Federal position.

HAND-TO-HAND FIGHT

Men of Rickett's Batteries F and G, 1st Pennsylvania Artillery, Fighting For Their Guns Near the Brow of Culp's Hill, on the Evening of the Second Day.

to a victory on points so far as the second round was concerned.

The Final Phase

The final phase of the day's operations proved to be an anticlimax, despite some tough fighting and a fair number of casualties. When he heard Longstreet's artillery open up about four o'clock, Ewell also commenced firing an artillery bombardment against Culp's Hill, preparatory to the planned infantry attack. To this the Federal artillery replied from Cemetery Hill with devastating effect. Several hours passed before Johnson's division advanced and seized the positions on Culp's Hill which had been vacated by The Twelfth Corps divisions of Geary and Ruger, sent to the aid of the Third Corps at the Peach Orchard. The remaining brigade of the Twelfth Corps, Greene's, fighting a magnificent defensive action, managed to hold out until reinforced by elements of the First and Eleventh Corps. The Confederate Johnson succeeded in reaching almost to the Baltimore Pike, but in the darkness of early evening failed to realize and exploit the advantage which he had gained. When daylight came, the Federal Twelfth Corps had been reconstituted and it was then too late.

When Johnson attacked Culp's Hill, Early drove for Cemetery Hill. Rodes was supposed to assist, but failed to make it, and this attack likewise miscarried. And thus ended the second day.

Losses

Both armies suffered heavily in killed and wounded. Meade's horse was shot out from under him, Sickles was

MAJOR GENERAL WILLIAM D. PENDER, C.S.A.
Commanding a division of Hill's corps. Mortally wounded the second day.

wounded and lost a leg, and Warren was slightly wounded. Among the brigade commanders killed were Weed, Willard, Zook, and Vincent of the Union Army, and Barksdale and Semmes of the Confederates. Division commander Pender was wounded and died a few days later. General Hood was severely wounded. Meade's official report stated that 65 percent of the Union casualties in the three-day battle occurred on the second day.

The Sickles Controversy

The Sickles controversy became a cause célèbre after the war, and a resume of the pros and cons is given here.

Major General Daniel E. Sickles, the only one of Meade's corps commanders who was not a professional soldier, had formerly been a Congressman representing New York State. He did not always think along the same well-charted military lines as those of his colleagues in the Army of the Potomac who had been trained and indoctrinated at West Point. There could be no doubt that he was a rugged individualist, and it is equally certain that he not only had plenty of self-confidence, but believed strongly in taking the law into his own hands on occasion, if in the opinion of Dan Sickles the situation demanded action. The historic example is the time when he shot

THE VALLEY OF DEATH

Between the Wheatfield and Little Round Top. An area of tragic memory for survivors of the fighting on the second day.

and killed Philip Barton Key, the son of Francis Scott Key, author of *The Star Spangled Banner,* for allegedly toying with the affections and honor of Sickles' wife, and was acquitted with the help of defense counsel Stanton, later the Secretary of War.

There is good reason to believe that Sickles lacked Meade's confidence, which is understandable in view of the miserable showing almost universally made in their military roles, in the early years of the war, by the ambitious politicians whom Lincoln was persuaded to clothe with the stars and authority of general officers. General Humphreys, a Regular commanding one of the divisions in Sickles' corps, was a favorite of Meade's and the man upon whom he relied to keep the Third Corps on an even keel.

On that background must be partly viewed the unilateral action which Sickles took on the early afternoon of the second day when, clearly in disobedience of orders, he vitiated Meade's tactical plan of passive defense along Cemetery Ridge, unhinged the Federal line on the left, exposed the vital anchor of the Round Tops to possible capture by the enemy, and created a wide gap on his own right and on the left of Hancock's Second Corps. To which Meade added the compounding error of shipping Buford's cavalry division off to Westminster without making certain of an immediate replacement from Kilpatrick's division. The result was that the Third Corps found itself lined up close to the enemy, parallel to but from half to three-quarters of a mile west of the main Federal line, with both flanks high in the air and correspondingly vulnerable.

In support of his action Sickles later pointed to Meade's vague and discretionary instructions on the posting of the Third Corps when they arrived from Emmitsburg; to

Geary's departure, without waiting to be relieved, from
Little Round Top, which had been occupied by two of
Geary's regiments the night of July 1-2; and to his, Sickles,
repeated urgings that Meade personally examine the
"more desirable" position that Sickles was so determined
to occupy. He further recounted General Hunt's concur-
rence in Sickles' recommendation, without mentioning

BRIGADIER GENERAL JOHN W. GEARY
Commanding a division in Slocum's corps. Later Governor of Pennsylvania.

Hunt's stated reservation, however, that the new line
would be too long for the Third Corps to hold effectively
by itself. Finally he used in self-justification Lincoln's
oblique approval of his actions when Sickles subsequently
applied for a Court of Inquiry and was dissuaded by the
President in these words:

> Sickles, they say you pushed your men out too
> near the enemy, and began the fight just as that

council (Meade's afternoon council of war) was about to meet, at three o'clock in the afternoon of the battle. I am afraid what they say is true, and God bless you for it. Don't ask us to order an inquest to relieve you from bringing on the battle of Gettysburg. History will set you all right and give everybody his just place, and there is glory enough to go all round.

Lincoln's appraisal of Sickles' action, written long after the battle, when there had been plenty of time to fit all the pieces of the picture together, reflected his dissatisfaction with Meade's cautious procedures, in contrast to which the Sickles move was on the bold, offensive side, and that was of course the prescription which the President had for a long time been urging on his generals.

Furthermore, on the asset side of Sickles' ledger, his action that day did in fact set in motion events which importantly affected the course of the three-day battle. His corps took the heaviest punishment from Longstreet's attack, being so badly shattered that it was never again reconstituted as a fighting team under the Third Corps designation. On the other hand the two Confederate divisions of Hood and McLaws, which Longstreet employed against Sickles that afternoon, likewise suffered heavy losses. They failed to achieve their objective of rolling up Meade's line, and found themselves at the end of the day locked in a position in the Devil's Den area from which Longstreet virtually refused to withdraw them July 3 for Lee's planned frontal attack on Meade's center.

It can therefore be argued, with considerable plausibility, that Sickles' action strongly influenced the course and possibly the final outcome of the battle. Technically he was entirely out of order in taking it upon himself to change position without Meade's express approval. In so doing he jeopardized both the commanding general's plan

of defense and the security of the Cemetery Ridge position. But he did succeed in blunting much of Lee's offensive strength. He so immobilized two-thirds of Longstreet's corps that the latter were relegated to a minor role
for the remainder of the battle; while Lee was forced to
draw additional divisions from A. P. Hill's corps to
strengthen Pickett for the final suicidal charge on the
afternoon of July 3.

Space does not permit further recapitulation of the ex
post facto viewpoints, but the account of General McLaws,
who commanded Longstreet's left division at the Peach
Orchard, affords a cool, dispassionate appraisal that is well
worth repeating.*

> But in the general results General Sickles might
> say that his corps, considered apart from the re-
> mainder of the army, was so posted that it not only
> occupied a strong position of itself, but one which,
> while inviting an attack, could be reinforced without
> the movement being known, as there was a dense
> wood in his rear; that in carrying that position against
> General Sickles and the strong reinforcements which
> were brought forward, that strong outwork as it were,
> Longstreet's forces exhausted themselves, and by the
> time the Confederate advance reached the main
> Federal line it was too scattered and had lost so many
> commanders and rank and file as to be unfit and un-
> able to make any further combined effort and was,
> in consequence, recalled from the most advanced posi-
> tion, as there was no support on hand from any other
> corps.
>
> In the sense I have last considered it, I suppose,
> General Sickles has argued that his position was the
> cause of victory, as events turned out.
>
> But before the crown of "victory" can be accorded

---

* *Philadelphia Weekly Press,* August 4, 1886.

to him we must discuss the chances and the strong probabilities of disaster which might have happened, not only to his corps, but to the Federal army, because of this advanced salient position, taken on his own responsibility, and then see if it would not have been more advantageous to his corps and the army if he had taken his position on the left extension of

MAJOR GENERAL LAFAYETTE McLAWS, C.S.A.
Commanding a division in Longstreet's corps.

the main line, occupying and fortifying the Round Tops.

If General Sickles had taken position on the extension of General Meade's main line occupying and fortifying Round Top and vicinity, certainly it would have been more difficult to carry Round Top by assault than it was when occupied for the first time in great haste by General Warren's orders, after the battle had commenced. And as it was not then seized by the Confederates, there could have been no apprehension felt by General Meade as to its capture had it been occupied as I have supposed—and as the Round Tops were natural fortresses and could have been made practically impregnable—the Confederates arriving there, and seeing the formidable preparations to receive them, would not, it is very probable, have made the attempt to take them. There would have been no need of a reserve force to aid in holding them.

Whereas General Sickles, instead of taking his place on the extension of the main line, which it would be natural for General Meade to suppose he had done, did, without special orders, take an advanced position forming a salient to the main line, and being there without orders and, as General Meade says, contrary to orders, of course no support was provided to maintain him in that salient position, unless General Meade had determined to make that his battleground. But he had no such intention, and as he was the commander-in-chief it reads strange to a Confederate that a subordinate should attempt to thwart the wishes of his chief.

Thus being in that salient position and "inviting" an attack, General Sickles was assaulted by two divisions of Longstreet's Corps and forced back to the main line, and if General Longstreet's advance had been supported, followed by even another division, I do not think there can be any doubt but that Round Top would have been occupied and held by the Confederates. Therefore, it would seem that, by occupying the salient position in the manner it was done without orders, a very great risk was run of losing the key to the battle-field.

That it was not lost was owing to the rapid concentration by General Meade of forces from other portions of the field, and one can imagine how astonished General Meade was when he found out how near he had been to losing Round Top, which he supposed, until then, had been occupied and fortified, but which had not been when his line was formed. The question may well be propounded here: By whose fault was this great catastrophe so near of accomplishment, and by whose exertions was it avoided?

If General Stuart, with his cavalry, had been with General Lee at Chambersburg—and he could have been if he had not gone within four miles of Washington in his travels—the whole of Longstreet's Corps, including Pickett's division, would have been up on the morning of the 2d of July, and the "supporting" division would have been present in the charge; but not only this, the advance would have been made early on the morning of the 2d of July, before Round Top was occupied!

If, when Longstreet's divisions of McLaws and Hood made their charge, General Ewell, who had been directed to cooperate, had so timed his advance on the right of the Federal army as to have struck General Meade's right when all but one brigade of the force stationed there had been withdrawn to resist Longstreet's assault, General Ewell could have carried the heights, and, advancing his whole corps, the Federal reserve being away, what then? If the Round Tops had been occupied and fortified there would have been no necessity of sending the reserve which had been posted there to aid in averting the danger to Round Top.

Thus the non-occupation and fortification of Round Top not only came near being the loss of this position, but it was a mere chance that it was not the cause of a very serious disaster on the right.

It would, therefore, appear that the arrangements of the troops made by General Meade, which contemplated the occupation of Round Top, were the best possible to meet all emergencies.

LEE'S HEADQUARTERS
General Lee used this old stone house, built in 1789, as his headquarters during a portion of the battle. This building, owned then by a Mrs. Thompson and today by the Larson family, stands on the north side of the Chambersburg Pike opposite the Seminary. It is now a museum.

CHAPTER 16

THE OPPOSING COMMANDERS REVIEW THE SITUATION

A T THE conclusion of the second day's battle, this was the situation. The Union army held its original defense position almost intact along the fish hook from Culp's Hill to Round Top inclusive, the exception being that Johnson occupied a portion of the Federal position on the east slope of Culp's Hill. The Confederate army had fought its way across the open fields between Seminary and Cemetery Ridges, was in possession of much of the Emmitsburg Road, the Peach Orchard position, part of Devil's Den, and held a precarious grip on the woods and rocks at the base of Big Round Top. On the other flank, Johnson had a toehold in rear of the Federal line; but there is no evidence to show that Ewell or anyone else was aware of the great opportunity thus offered to exploit what was actually a potentially critical breach of the Federal position.

Review of the Second Day's Action

As seen in retrospect the sanguinary battle of the second day had resolved itself into four successive phases. First, the belated but aggressive attempt by Longstreet's corps to outflank the Federal line opposite the Round Tops. Second, the repulse by the Federals, following General Warren's timely action in detaching troops from Sykes' corps to seize the unoccupied Little Round Top and deny it to Hood's division; this was coupled with Meade's rapid shift of divisions to threatened points. Third, the unco-ordinated and virtually undirected as well as belated frontal attack by a portion of Hill's Confederate corps on their left against Sickles' right on the Emmitsburg Road, which was partially successful but indecisive because unsupported. Fourth, Ewell's late and ineffectual attack against the Federal right on Culp's Hill, after Longstreet's flanking effort had failed.

The Confederate Attitude

The day had closed with the Confederates still confident of success but far less cocky than after they had chased the Federals through Gettysburg on the afternoon of the first day, cheerfully boasting to the townspeople of what they were going to do to the Yanks come morning.

General Lee, clearly disappointed that the Federals had not dropped into his lap like ripe cherries, put up a bolder front than he must have felt. He expressed confidence to members of his staff that the victory would be theirs next morning. His feeling was that, despite the heavy losses that the Confederates were less able to afford than their opponents, his army had driven the enemy from their position along the Emmitsburg Road, that Longstreet was now breathing down their necks at close range, and that a final strong attack the following day would break Meade's line and again crown the Army of Northern Virginia with the resounding victory to which it had grown accustomed.

Lee had first attacked Meade's line on the right, then on the left, and Meade was still holding fast on his chosen position. Lee figured that his adversary's center must have been weakened to support his left, which was partly true, but he failed to give sufficient weight to the possibility that Meade would recall divisions from his left and solidly

THE MAIN BATTLEFIELD ON JULY 2-3

Looking northwest and north from Little Round Top. Trostle's is in the mid-distance at the extreme left. Codori's barn, rebuilt after the battle, is in the center over the woods. To the right are Cemetery Hill and Culp's Hill. From an early photo taken before the monuments were erected.

restore the entire line of the fish hook. Nor did Lee know that Sedgwick's powerful corps had come up and given Meade a tremendous increase in the number of fighting men at his disposal.

Although his troops had won local successes, complete victory had eluded Lee in the attacks of July 1 and 2. Nevertheless he still held the initiative and, of even greater significance, the will to fight. The morale of his army had not suffered appreciably, and a substantial number of his divisions had either not been engaged at all on the second day or had not been seriously hurt. Reinforcements had arrived with Pickett's division, Stuart's cavalry of three brigades, and the four cavalry brigades commanded by Robertson, Jones, Imboden, and Jenkins. In Lee's estimation these manpower additions were sufficient to make up for the losses of the second day.

It is reasonable to believe that Lee could have defeated Meade and driven him from the field of Gettysburg at any time of his own choosing during the twenty-four hour period between 3 P.M. July 1 and 3 P.M. July 2, had Longstreet, Ewell, and Hill reacted individually and unitedly as a team in response to Lee's wishes and in accordance with his plans. But Meade was given all the time he needed to bring up and dispose his forces. Despite the Sickles' episode, when Longstreet at long last launched his attack, about 4 P.M., the last of Meade's corps, Sedgwick's 15,000 men, had arrived and the cards were fully stacked against Lee.

However he may have estimated the tactical situation, Lee decided to attack Meade's center the third day, confident that it was his weakest point and could be pierced. Now that Jeb Stuart had arrived with his cavalry, Lee was eager to wind up the business by a frontal attack that would split Meade asunder. Meantime the cavalry, circling to the north and east would get in Meade's rear, complete his discomfiture, and then gather up the pieces.

There occurred that evening an incident which—again in retrospect—was an omen of what was to transpire on the third and final day. Contrary to his usual custom, Longstreet neglected to ride over to Lee's headquarters

BRIGADIER GENERAL JOHN GIBBON
Commanding a division in Hancock's corps. Temporarily in command of the Second Corps.

to report and talk over plans, sending a written message instead. He remained overnight where he was, among his troops on the field west of Round Top, apparently still smarting over Lee's refusal to accept his cherished tactical plan of operations, while Lee in return contented himself with sending word to Longstreet that he must be prepared to resume the attack in the morning.

Meade Correctly Estimates Lee's Intentions

The fates had been kind to Meade, who at this point was thinking pretty straight. He divined Lee's plans for the third day and was so confident of what would happen that he told General Gibbon, commanding one of Hancock's divisions at the center of the line on Cemetery Ridge, that if Lee should attack next day it would be on his, Gibbon's, front. And to make certain that the Confederates would be given a hot reception he directed his Chief of Artillery to reshuffle his guns and mass them to bear heavily on the front of that portion of the line. The Army of the Potomac had fought well and its morale was up. The Northerners had gotten the breaks the second day and were confident in the security of their strong defensive position. They had stopped Lee almost in his tracks and were now ready for the best he might offer on his third try.

Meade's Council of War

When night had fallen, Meade summoned his corps commanders to a conference in the small farmhouse which served as his headquarters on the Taneytown Road. This meeting could have been made into one of the most picturesque and historic paintings of the war, had it been recorded by photography at the time or even sketched in rough outline for later reproduction on canvas.

All the corps commanders except the wounded Sickles were present, and in addition General Butterfield, Meade's Chief of Staff, General Warren, his Chief Engineer, and two other general officers, Williams of the Twelfth Corps and Gibbon of the Second. Outside the small conference room there must have been a gathering of the generals' aides-de-camp, because First Lieutenant Frank Haskell,

Gibbon's aide, sensing the historic nature of the gathering, has given us in his famous letter* to his brother a vivid description of the participants, quoted herewith:

> Meade is a tall, spare man, with full beard, which with his hair, originally brown, is quite thickly sprinkled with gray—has a Romanish face, very large

MAJOR GENERAL JOHN SEDGWICK
Commanding the Sixth Corps.

> nose, and a white, large forehead, prominent and wide over the eyes, which are full and large, and quick in their movements, and he wears spectacles. His fibres are all of the long and sinewy kind. His habitual personal appearance is quite careless, and it would be rather difficult to make him look well dressed.
>
> Sedgwick is quite a heavy man, short, thick-set and muscular, with florid complexion, dark, calm,

---

* Haskell, *op. cit.*

straight-looking eyes, with full, heavyish features, which, with his eyes, have plenty of animation when he is aroused. He has a magnificent profile, well cut, with the nose and forehead forming almost a straight line, curly, short, chestnut hair and full beard, cut short, with a little gray in it. He dresses carelessly, but can look magnificently when he is well dressed. Like Meade, he looks and is, honest and modest. You might see at once, why his men, because they love him, call him "Uncle John," not to his face, of course, but among themselves.

Slocum is small, rather spare, with black, straight hair and beard, which latter is unshaven and thin, large, full, quick, black eyes, white skin, sharp nose, wide cheek bones, and hollow cheeks and small chin. His movements are quick and angular, and he dresses with a sufficient degree of elegance.

Howard is medium in size, has nothing marked about him, is the youngest of them all, I think—has lost an arm in the war, has straight brown hair and beard, shaves his short upper lip, over which his nose slants down, dim blue eyes, and on the whole, appears a very pleasant, affable, well dressed little gentleman.

Hancock is the tallest and most shapely, and in many respects is the best looking officer of them all. His hair is very light brown, straight and moist, and always looks well, his beard is of the same color, of which he wears the moustache and a tuft upon the chin; complexion ruddy, features neither large nor small, but well cut, with full jaw and chin, compressed mouth, straight nose, full, deep blue eyes, and a very mobile, emotional countenance. He always dresses remarkably well, and his manner is dignified, gentlemanly and commanding. I think if he were in citizens' clothes, and should give commands in the army to those who did not know him, he would be likely to be obeyed at once, and without any question as to his right to command.

Sykes is a small, rather thin man, well dressed and gentlemanly, brown hair and beard, which he wears full, with a red, pinched, rough-looking skin, feeble blue eyes, long nose, with the general air of one who is weary and a little ill-natured.

Newton is a well-sized, shapely, muscular, well dressed man, with brown hair, with a very ruddy,

MAJOR GENERAL JOHN NEWTON
Temporarily in command of the First Corps.

clean-shaved, full face, blue eyes, blunt, round features, walks very erect, curbs in his chin, and has somewhat of that smart sort of swagger that people are apt to suppose characterizes soldiers.

Pleasonton is quite a nice little dandy, with brown hair and beard, a straw hat with a little jockey rim, which he cocks upon one side of his head, with an unsteady eye, that looks slyly at you and then dodges.

Gibbon, the youngest of them all, save Howard, is about the same size as Slocum, Howard, Sykes and Pleasonton, and there are none of these who will weigh one hundred and fifty pounds. He is compactly made, neither spare nor corpulent, with ruddy complexion, chestnut brown hair, with a clean-shaved face, except his moustache, which is decidedly reddish in color, medium-sized, well-shaped head, sharp, moderately-jutting brow, deep blue, calm eyes, sharp, slightly aquiline nose, compressed mouth, full jaws and chin, with an air of calm firmness in his manner. He always looks well dressed.

I suppose Howard is about thirty-five and Meade about forty-five years of age; the rest are between these ages, but not many under forty. As they come to the council now, there is the appearance of fatigue about them, which is not customary, but is only due to the hard labors of the past few days. They all wear clothes of dark blue, some have top boots and some not, and except the two-starred straps upon the shoulders of all save Gibbon, who has but one star, there was scarcely a piece of regulation uniform about them all. They wore their swords, of various patterns, but no sashes, the Army hat, but with the crown pinched into all sorts of shapes and the rim slouched down and shorn of all its ornaments but the gilt band —except Sykes who wore a blue cap, and Pleasonton with his straw hat with broad black band. Then the mean little room where they met,—its only furniture consisted of a large, wide bed in one corner, a small pine table in the center, upon which was a wooden pail of water, with a tin cup for drinking, and a candle, stuck to the table by putting the end in tallow melted down from the wick, and five or six straight-backed rush-bottomed chairs.

The Generals came in—some sat, some kept walking or standing, two lounged upon the bed, some were constantly smoking cigars. And thus disposed, they deliberated whether the army should fall back from its present position to one in rear which it was said was stronger, should attack the enemy on the morrow, wherever he could be found, or should stand there upon the horse-shoe crest, still on the defensive, and await the further movements of the enemy.

As to what transpired in the council room, the fullest account is that of General Gibbon, a participant, which was originally published in 1887, in the Philadelphia Weekly Press, and condensed in *Battles and Leaders of the Civil War*. This was General Gibbon's account:

Soon after all firing had ceased a staff-officer from army headquarters met General Hancock and myself and summoned us both to General Meade's headquarters, where a council was to be held. We at once proceeded there, and soon after our arrival all the corps commanders were assembled in the little front room of the Liester House—Newton, who had been assigned to the command of the First Corps over Doubleday, his senior; Hancock, Second; Birney, Third; Sykes, Fifth; Sedgwick, who had arrived during the day with the Sixth, after a long march from Manchester; Howard, Eleventh; and Slocum, Twelfth, besides General Meade, General Butterfield, chief of staff; Warren, chief of engineers; A. S. Williams, Twelfth Corps, and myself, Second. It will be seen that two corps were doubly represented, the Second by Hancock and myself, and the Twelfth by Slocum and Williams. These twelve were all assembled in a large room not more than ten or twelve feet square, with a bed in one corner, a small table on one side, and a chair or two. Of course all could not sit down; some did, some lounged on the bed, and some stood up, while Warren, tired out and suffering from a wound in the neck, where a piece of shell had struck him, lay down in the corner of the room and went sound asleep, and I don't think heard any of the proceedings.

The discussion was at first very informal and in the shape of conversation, during which each one made comments on the fight and told what he knew of the condition of affairs. In the course of this discussion Newton expressed the opinion that "this was no place to fight a battle in." General Newton was an officer of engineers (since chief-engineer of the army), and was rated by me, and I suppose most others, very highly as a soldier. The assertion, therefore, coming from such a source, rather startled me, and I eagerly asked what his objections to the position were. The objections he stated, as I recollect them, related to some minor details of the line, of which I knew nothing except so far as my own front was concerned, and with those I was satisfied; but the prevailing impression seemed to be that the place for the battle had been in a measure selected for us. Here we are; now what is the best thing to do? It soon became evident that everybody was in favor of remaining where we were and giving battle there. General Meade himself said very little, except now and then to make some comment, but I cannot recall that he expressed any decided opinion upon any point, preferring apparently to listen to the conversation. After the discussion had lasted some time, Butterfield suggested that it would, perhaps, be well to formulate the question to be asked, and General Meade assenting he took a piece of paper, on which he had been making some memoranda, and wrote down a question; when he had done he read it off and formally proposed it to the council.

I had never been a member of a council of war before (nor have I been since) and did not feel very confident I was properly a member of this one; but I had engaged in the discussion, and found myself (Warren being asleep) the junior member in it. By the custom of war the junior member votes first, as on courts-martial; and Butterfield read off his question, the substance of which was, "Should the army

remain in its present position or take up some other?"
he addressed himself first to me for an answer. To say
"Stay and fight" was to ignore the objections made
by General Newton, and I therefore answered somewhat in this way: "Remain here, and make such cor-
rection in our position as may be deemed necessary,
but take no step which even looks like retreat." The
question was put to each member and his answer
taken down, and when it came to Newton, who was
the first in rank, he voted in pretty much the same
way as I did, and we had some playful sparring as
to whether he agreed with me or I with him; the rest
voted to remain.

The next question written by Butterfield was,
"Should the army attack or wait the attack of the
enemy?" I voted not to attack, and all the others
voted substantially the same way; and on the third
question, "How long shall we wait?" I voted, "Until
Lee moved." The answers to this last question showed
the only material variation in the opinion of the
members.

When the voting was over General Meade said
quietly, but decidedly, "Such then is the decision;"
and certainly he said nothing which produced a doubt
in my mind as to his being perfectly in accord with
the members of the council.

In 1881 (eighteen years after the battle) I was
shown in Philadelphia, by General Meade's Son
(Colonel George Meade), a paper found amongst
General Meade's effects after his death. It was folded,
and on the outside of one end was written, in his well-
known handwriting, in ink, "Minutes of Council,
July 2d, '63." On opening it, the following was found
written in pencil in a handwriting (General Daniel
Butterfield's) unknown to me:

Minutes of Council, July 2d, 1863.
Page 1, Questions asked:

1. Under existing circumstances is it advisable for

this army to remain in its present position, or to retire to another nearer its base of supplies?

2. It being determined to remain in present position, shall the army attack or wait the attack of the enemy?

3. If we wait attack, how long?

Page 2, Replies.

Gibbon: 1. Correct position of the army, but would not retreat. 2. In no condition to attack, in his opinion. 3. Until he moves.

Williams: 1. Stay. 2. Wait attack. 3 One day.

Birney: Same as General Williams.

Sykes: " " "

Newton: 1. Correct position of the army, but would not retreat. 2. By all means not attack. 3. If we wait it will give them a chance to cut our line.

Page 3.

Howard: 1. Remain. 2. Wait until 4 P.M. tomorrow. 3. If don't attack, attack them.

Hancock: 1. Rectify position without moving so as to give up field. 2. Not attack unless our communications are cut. 3. Can't wait long; can't be idle.

Sedgwick: 1. Remain. (2.) and wait attack. (3.) At least one day.

Slocum: Stay and fight it out.

(On the back, or first page of the sheet):

Slocum stay and fight it out. Newton thinks it a bad position; Hancock puzzled about practicability of retiring; thinks by holding on inviting to mass forces and attack. Howard favor of not retiring. Birney don't know. Third Corps used up and not in good condition to fight. Sedgwick doubtful whether we ought to attack. Effective strength about 9000, 12,500, 9000, 6000, 8500, 6000, 7000. Total, 58,000.

(Endorsement:)

Minutes of Council, held Thursday, P.M., July 2d, 1863. D.B., M.G., C. of S. (Daniel Butterfield, Major-General, Chief of Staff).

The memoranda at the bottom of the paper were doubtless made while the discussion was going on, and the numbers at the foot refer probably to the effective strength of each corps.[1]

Several times during the sitting of the council reports were brought to General Meade, and now and then we could hear heavy firing going on over on the right of our line. I took occasion before leaving to say to General Meade that his staff-officer had regularly summoned me as a corps commander to the council, although I had some doubts about being present. He answered, pleasantly, "That is all right. I wanted you here."

Before I left the house Meade made a remark to me which surprised me a good deal, especially when I look back upon the occurrence of the next day. By a reference to the votes in council it will be seen that the majority of the members were in favor of acting on the defensive and awaiting the action of Lee. In referring to the matter, just as the council broke up, Meade said to me, "If Lee attacks to-morrow, it will be in your front." I asked him why he thought so, and he replied, "Because he has made attacks on both our flanks and failed, and if he concludes to try it again it will be on our center." I expressed the hope that he would, and told General Meade, with confidence, that if he did we would defeat him.

---

[1] A careful study of the original suggests that these notes "at the bottom" (on the back) were made before the questions were formulated.

Editors.

CONFEDERATE SKIRMISHERS AT THE FOOT OF CULP'S HILL

CHAPTER 17

LEE REGROUPS FOR THE SUPREME EFFORT

THE Army of the Potomac used the night of July 2 to good advantage in strengthening its defenses. The Round Tops were made virtually impregnable, and artillery was wheeled up to provide powerful bands of cross-fire from Little Round Top and Cemetery Hill across the open space between the contestants west of Cemetery Ridge.

Culp's Hill Remains Critical

The dangerous crack in the Federal line on the eastern and southeastern slopes of Culp's Hill, which reached almost to the Baltimore Pike, was marked down to receive the Twelfth Corps' attention as soon as daylight should permit a resumption of the fighting. All of Slocum's regiments which had been shifted to the support of the Third Corps on the afternoon of July 2 had now been returned to him, with the addition of Shaler's brigade of the Sixth

Corps, and Lockwood's Independent Brigade, attached to assure ample strength for Slocum to dislodge the enemy.

Johnson's Confederate division was equally determined to exploit its advantageous position, widen the entering wedge and place itself squarely on the rear of the Federal right center. If this attempt should prove successful it would have the effect of clamping a neck hold on the Federal body. But because of the difficult character of the ground, Johnson had been unable to bring his artillery

SPANGLER'S SPRING, EAST OF CULP'S HILL

UNION TROOPS COUNTERATTACKING ON CULP'S HILL AT 10 AM JULY 3
This was the 29th Pennsylvania, part of Geary's division, Twelfth Corps.

with him and was thus at a marked disadvantage compared to Slocum.

Slocum's men had been thoroughly disgusted when they returned from the left. They were tired, hungry, and ready to move back into their intrenchments on Culp's Hill for a good rest and some hot food—only to find their snug breastworks swarming with enemy troops. They were forced to bide their time until morning, and to catch such sleep as they might on the open ground along the Baltimore Road and in the adjacent meadows. Some were not too annoyed, however, to mingle pleasantly with the interlopers at nearby Spangler's Spring, within a few yards of the Union right flank in one direction and the Confederate left flank in the other. Naturally enough the spring was the object of visits by thirsty soldiers from both lines during the night.

Slocum Restores Culp's Hill

With Johnson and Slocum poised for action as soon
as it should become light enough to see clearly, the battle
on the right was promptly joined. Stonewall Jackson's old
brigade led off the attack, meeting Geary's division head-

BRIGADIER GENERAL GEORGE S. GREENE

Commanding the Third Brigade, Geary's division. When Geary moved to Little
Round Top early on July 2, Greene's brigade was left to hold Culp's Hill. It
resisted strong Confederate attacks during the day, being driven off finally
late in the evening.

on. Almost immediately the fighting spread all along
Slocum's front. Time and again the Confederates hurled
themselves against the determined Federals. The fight
raged for hours until about 10 o'clock, when a countercharge by the Federals slowly forced Johnson's men out
of the breastworks they had seized in the previous day's
fighting.

As the Confederates stubbornly withdrew and came under the fire of the Federal batteries they were assailed by repeated charges of grape and canister and mercilessly cut down until the dead covered their path of retreat in the front of Geary's division.

It was in this engagement that Maryland opposed Maryland, with one regiment in Johnson's Confederate division pitted against three from Slocum's corps. In the early days of the war each had been recruited from the same part of the border State and by a quirk of fate they met on Culp's Hill to fight grimly in mortal combat, brother against brother, and neighbor against neighbor.

The name of Culp was a common one in the Gettysburg of 1863. Young Wesley Culp was born there, but had gone south as a youth, only to return as a member of Virginia's "Stonewall Brigade." On July 2, with the Confederates occupying the town, Culp seized the opportunity to visit his two sisters and promised them he would be back again. But he never returned, because Wesley Culp the next day became one of the "unknown soldiers" on Culp's Hill.

For seven hours, from four to eleven in the morning, the fierce fighting continued, with what must have been a tremendous expenditure of ammunition, because it ruined one of the finest oak forests in that area. For decades this forest had been Gettysburg's favorite picnic grounds, but it was shot to death that morning, some trees having close to two hundred musket balls imbedded in their trunks. After the battle, those trees that were not cut down for transfer, in sections, to various historical societies of the New England states, crumbled into dust in a few years and for half a century at least that particular "plateau of death" remained a hillside of desolation.

Meade's council of war the night of July 2 had con-

DAMAGED GROVE ON CULP'S HILL

Photographer Brady is seated amid the battered trees. The possession of the southern slope of Culp's Hill by Johnson's division at nightfall on July 2 was one of the factors which influenced Lee to renew the general assault the next day. However, Ewell, who did not fully appreciate the critical value of the hill, allowed his troops to be driven from it the next morning.

firmed his defensive plan, so all the Federals had to do was sit tight, keep on the alert, and wait for the inevitable Confederate attack which Meade anticipated would be launched against his center, and in preparation for which he moved up all available artillery from General Hunt's Reserve.

Lee and Longstreet Still at Cross Purposes

Across the way, on Seminary Ridge, Lee figured that Meade had weakened his line at the center, in order to hold Ewell back on the Federal right and to pin Longstreet down on his left, after the latter had pushed virtually into the vestibule of the Round Tops and was keeping one large boot in the door overnight.

Furthermore Lee reasoned that he now had Pickett's division and Stuart's cavalry; scarcely more than half of his infantry had done any serious fighting on the second day; while the penetration of Cemetery Ridge by Wright's brigade, which failed to split the Federal line only because it had been unsupported by the rest of Anderson's division, had convinced him of the practicability of a frontal attack. The attack which he planned for July 3 was to drive in Meade's center with Longstreet's corps, while Ewell would continue his efforts to take over Culp's Hill, and the cavalry was to circle around Gettysburg to the north, place itself squarely on the Federal rear, and turn the anticipated Confederate breach of the Federal line into a rout.

Full of fight and confidence, Lee rode out early to Longstreet's field headquarters southwest of Round Top to discuss the details and to give him final instructions for the attack. Still at cross purposes with his commanding general, Longstreet hastened to tell Lee that his scouts had been out all night and "you still have an excellent opportunity to move around to the right of Meade's army and maneuver him to attack us." Pointing to Cemetery Ridge Lee replied, "The enemy is there and I am going to strike him." Still Longstreet persisted, unwilling to yield to Lee's judgment, even going to the extent of stating that it couldn't be done. His exact words, as he reported them himself after the war were: "General, I have been a soldier all my life. I have been with soldiers in couples, by squads, companies, regiments, divisions and armies, and should know as well as anyone what soldiers can do. It is my opinion that no fifteen thousand men ever arrayed for battle can take that position."

General Lee quickly brought the discussion to an end by inviting Longstreet to ride around with him while he explained the attack plan in detail. General Alexander, Longstreet's Chief of Corps Artillery, was to mass his guns to concentrate their fire on Cemetery Hill with a view to putting the enemy guns out of action, to demoralize the infantry, and pave the way for Longstreet, with Pickett's division as the spearhead, to crash through the center and roll up the Federal line in both directions.

It seemed to Lee to be a good plan, but he neglected to inquire as to the amount of artillery ammunition available. Neither Longstreet nor himself had checked that important detail or, if Longstreet had done so he failed to mention it to Lee. As it developed later, the oversight

SCENE IN A UNION FIELD HOSPITAL

was a serious one and had a notable effect on the outcome of the fight.

Battery after battery was wheeled into position, from the Peach Orchard northward along the Emmitsburg Road as far as the Codori House; along Seminary Ridge, partly concealed by the woods along the crest; and around the ridge to the Harrisburg Road—possibly one hundred and twenty guns all together.

In a final effort to change Lee's mind, Longstreet informed him that he could not expect the divisions of Hood and McLaws to participate in the attack because they were in close contact with superior Federal forces, and if they should be pulled out and shifted to a new line of departure for the attack against Meade's center, the Federals would naturally move out to occupy the vacated position and thus be on Longstreet's flank and rear.

Lee Compromises

Confronted with Longstreet's continued unwillingness to carry out the attack as conceived, what Lee should have done was to replace him then and there. Instead he once more compromised what he regarded as the better plan and allowed Longstreet to keep Hood and McLaws where they were. In their place he assigned Heth's division and two brigades of Pender's, both from A. P. Hill's corps, thus giving Longstreet about the same number of men he would have had were he to employ only the First Corps.

As this change necessitated some troop reshuffling, Lee sent word to Ewell that Longstreet's attack would be delayed until 10 A.M. Meantime, although Lee did not know it, Johnson was already being mauled on the north flank and was in no shape to disengage even if the word

had reached him that Longstreet would not attack as
early as planned. Once more, as on the first and second
days, the carefully conceived plans of General Lee were
to be thwarted by an almost complete lack of coordination by his three corps commanders on the several areas
of the battlefield. Once again, through his own failure to
issue clean-cut, succinct battle orders to his army, through
the three key men who must perforce execute them, and
for the success of which it was essential that they work
together as a team, Lee for the third successive day contributed to the justly earned historic appraisal of Gettysburg as his worst-fought battle.

Even after his last-minute agreement to change the
composition of the attacking force and to bring two-thirds
of Hill's corps into the planned assault under Longstreet's
command, Lee labored under the mistaken notion that
the attack would be launched at 10 A.M. He may have
thought that his separate orders to Longstreet, Hill, Ewell,
and Stuart were adequate to effect a synchronized effort
between them. But in the later execution of the plan it
became crystal clear that, if indeed the battle plans had
been carefully explained, somewhere down the line
through corps, divisions, and brigades, the picture of what
was specifically expected of the lower echelons was somewhat fuzzy. Nor could it be expected that elements of two
different corps, hastily merged into a single attack echelon just before the jumpoff, would function as smoothly
as an already integrated group of divisions that had fought
together as a team and knew each other's capabilities and
limitations. And finally, in command of the attack was a
general, Longstreet, who was opposed to the plan, reluctant to carry it out, and convinced that it was doomed in
advance to fail. Certainly the fates were less than kind to
General Lee that day.

Confederate Plan of Attack

The Confederate battle plan was simple in conception. Eleven brigades, about fifteen thousand men, under Longstreet, would attack frontally the Union center, while the remainder of Hill's corps would support the left and the divisions of Hood and McLaws would keep the Federals occupied on the right. Ewell was to threaten the Federal right rear and Stuart would exploit the breakthrough.

Pickett's division of three brigades, Heth's division of four brigades under Pettigrew, two of Pender's brigades under Trimble, and Wilcox's and Perry's brigades made up the assault echelon. They would advance in two echelons, the leading wave of six brigades covering about a mile of front, from Peach Orchard on the right to the hollow road just south of Gettysburg on the left. The second wave, two hundred yards in rear of the first, included four brigades, while Wilcox's was echeloned to the right rear of the second line to protect the flank against a possible oblique counterattack during the advance.

Lee indicated the objective as a clump of trees on the crest of Cemetery Ridge several hundred yards northeast of the Codori House, located on the Emmitsburg Road. From this it followed that the attack must be a converging one that would require the infantry on the flanks of the long line to make a change of direction as they neared the enemy ridge.

Assault Troops Prepare to Jump Off

The assault troops were placed under cover of the woods on Seminary Ridge and only their officers were permitted to move up to the crest to examine the terrain over which they would soon lead their men. Most of the

CONFEDERATE TROOPS WAITING TO ATTACK

officers could see clearly the strong post-and-plank fences which lined the Emmitsburg Road on both sides, and could also note other fences that crisscrossed the fields over which they would advance. The sharp-eyed among them, looking further eastward to the Federal defense line on the military crest of Cemetery Ridge, observed a post-and-rail fence which ran north and south and behind which it was possible to catch glimpses of a stone wall, two and one-half to three feet high, that had been built up from loose boulders that were readily at hand to the industrious boys in blue.

Fifty Confederate regiments lay waiting in the stifling heat of midday for the signal to form up for the attack. Nineteen of them were Virginians, fifteen were from North Carolina, seven from Alabama, and three each from Mississippi, Florida, and Tennessee. While they waited, and the artillery gunners stood poised to fire their cannon, General Longstreet paced up and down in an agony of conflicting emotions, knowing in his heart that the die was cast but hoping desperately that some miracle might occur to lift from his shoulders the heavy responsibility of sending those fifteen thousand men into what was certain death or dismemberment for a large proportion of them.

The signal was to be the firing of two guns, one after the other, from their position at the Peach Orchard, upon hearing which all the Confederate batteries would open fire simultaneously, concentrating on the Federal batteries in the area of the objective, and continuing the bombardment until the enemy guns were silenced and unable to inflict serious punishment on the advancing infantry. The latter were not to move until the artillery fire had done its work. Longstreet was assigned the responsibility of determining when that moment should arrive, at which time General Pickett, in command of the assault troops, would ride out to lead the charge.

Longstreet Unhappily Seeks to Pass the Buck

Everything was set. It was now past noon, and still Longstreet temporized. Unworthily he wrote a note to his artillery commander, Colonel Alexander: "If the artillery fire does not have the effect to drive off the enemy or greatly demoralize him, so as to make our effort pretty certain, I would prefer that you should not advise Pickett to make the charge. I shall rely a great deal upon your judgment to determine the matter and shall expect you to let General Pickett know when the moment offers."

It is an old army saying that "the buck is never passed upward," but Alexander deserved better of his corps commander than to have such a momentous "buck" as that one passed down to him. Alexander diplomatically responded by informing the General that he could scarcely be expected to accurately appraise the results of his artillery fire, since the enemy infantry was pretty well concealed; and if there was any alternative to the planned infantry charge, it had better be determined beforehand, and not after the artillery bombardment opened. Furthermore, Alexander stated, there was only enough artillery ammunition for this one effort, and if that didn't work there would be none left for a second try.

Concluding the exchange of written notes, Longstreet repeated his earlier message to Alexander in a slightly modified form, which in effect instructed him to advise Pickett when he, Alexander, thought the infantry attack would be warranted.

GROUND OVER WHICH PICKETT CHARGED
Shows Bloody Angle and High Water Mark. Codori House Visible to the Right.

CHAPTER 18

LONGSTREET NODS AND PICKETT ATTACKS

GENERALS Hancock and Gibbon were seated under a group of trees with members of their staffs enjoying an unusual repast of stewed chicken, which Gibbon's devoted colored servant had somehow managed to promote, when General Meade rode up, was invited to share the ancient fowl, and promptly accepted. A handy crackerbox was pressed into service for a seat, and the meal was well underway when two additional generals, Newton and Pleasonton, attracted no doubt by the pleasant aroma, sauntered up and were offered a fallen log as their place at the table.

About 12:30 the group finished their meal, wiped their several mouths with the backs of their hands, lit cigars and were, for a few precious moments at least, at such peace with the world as only a field soldier can experience after a satisfying replenishment of the inner man.

Meade soon hastened back to headquarters, Hancock started to dictate some routine orders to a field clerk, and

253

the rest wandered off or lolled on the ground while the fateful minutes ticked on.

Suddenly the world blew up in their faces!

The Artillery Duel

At 1 P.M. or a few minutes after, the two signal guns at the Peach Orchard signalled the opening of the Confederate bombardment. All along the two-mile line upon which were ranked more than one hundred and twenty pieces the guns belched forth 24-pound, 20-pound, 12-pound and 10-pound projectiles of solid shot and shells of various shapes.

Almost immediately over 80 Federal guns, from all along Cemetery Ridge, replied to the challenge with 20 and 10-pound Parrotts, 10-pound rifle ordnance, and 12-pound Napoleons. Together the combined and incessant roar of more than 200 guns was the greatest ever heard on the American continent, before or since.

Quickly the battlefield was covered with a pall of smoke through which the booming crash of the guns and the bursting shells afforded a scene that would have tested the powers of a John Milton to describe. Lieutenant Haskell, Gibbon's aide, compared the cannonading to second Bull Run, Antietam, and Fredericksburg, remarking that "at the early battles we thought that we had heard heavy cannonading; they were but holiday salutes compared to this. Besides the great ceaseless roar of the guns, which was but the background of the others, a million various minor sounds engaged the ear. The projectiles shriek long and sharp. They hiss, they scream, they growl, they sputter, all sounds of life and rage; and each has its different note, and all are discordant."

An interesting commentary on the terrific cannonade and the resulting vagaries of the sound effects appeared in

Hoke's *The Great Invasion of 1863* in the form of letters from several "witnesses" in the western part of Pennsylvania. These reports indicated that the sound of the bombardment was heard *one hundred and forty miles* from Gettysburg, while but few of the citizens in Chambersburg, only twenty-five miles away, heard it at all.

Author Hoke was so intrigued with the phenomenon that he communicated with the Smithsonian Institute in Washington and received a letter of explanation which in general attributed the event to the action, on the sound waves, of favorable winds in the upper atmosphere. In 1875 acoustic phenomena were imperfectly understood, and while the Smithsonian explanation is not necessarily wholly incorrect, it does not go far enough. The acoustics of cannon and projectiles have been studied mathematically and experimentally only beginning in 1917, and form the basis of present day systems of sound ranging used in all modern armies.

Sound waves, like light waves and radio waves, are subject to bending (refraction), reflection (echoes), and to various types of modulation. They cast "shadows," have "skip" distances, and even have been known to produce acoustical images or pseudo-sounds analogous to mirages. When a large gun is fired most of the sound rays normally are projected up into the air, and are continually refracted upward so that they never descend to where they are audible on the earth's surface. The sound of the gun which is heard at a distance comes from those rays which travel close to the earth. This sound bounces along from terrain irregularities, and is subject to distortion from other causes, so that it usually reaches the ear of the observer as a low, prolonged rumbling. This is noted also in the case of thunder produced by distant lightning.

It is possible, though very rare, because of an inversion

in the temperature gradient, the existence of exceedingly favorable winds aloft, and from other causes such as reflection or refraction from dense air strata at great altitudes, for a sound wave to be bent back to earth after it has traveled a considerable distance. Undoubtedly this is what occurred in the case cited by Hoke, although one would not expect a sound of lesser power than that produced by an atomic bomb to be heard at a distance of 140 miles. What is much more common, and this was noted during the Battle of Gaines Mill,* is that the sound of a terrific battle may be practically inaudible at a distance of as little as three miles.

The two divisions of Hancock's Second Corps, the Second and Third, which occupied the right center of the Federal line with some 6,000 men, held a defensive front of about 1,000 yards, including the clump of trees which Lee had indicated as the target for Pickett's charge. When the barrage opened, the Union infantry at once seized their arms and leaped to their assigned positions under cover behind the stone wall and in thickets, hugging the ground as closely as possible. As a result, and because the Confederate artillery had been advised that the reverse slope of Cemetery Ridge was the place to drop their shells, on the premise that the Federal infantry would naturally take shelter on the slope away from the enemy, the Blue infantry suffered little damage from the terrific bombardment. Far greater hurt was done to the supports, the medical services, the supply and ammunition dumps, and the artillery; horses, mules, and every other living thing which happened to be in the impact area were the victims which bore the brunt of the Confederate artillery fire.

---

* Battles and Leaders of the Civil War, Vol. II, p. 365.

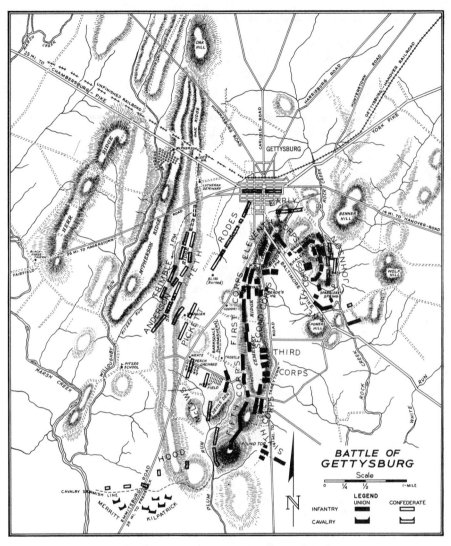

Map 13. The Situation About 3 pm, July 3

At 1 PM the cannonade commenced, signaling Lee's final effort at Gettysburg. About this time Pender's division moved south, under Trimble, to its jumpoff position. On the Federal side Meade ordered Robinson to move his division forward to a point from which he could counterattack in case Lee assaulted the Union lines, as expected, near the Cemetery. Robinson started this movement at the instant the artillery fire commenced, and his march was made through tremendous fire, yet with little loss. This shift, which anticipated the Confederate main blow, was one of the critical events which resulted in the repulse of the left portion of Longstreet's assault. This map shows the positions of all units just before Longstreet's assault (charge of Pickett et al) was launched.

For two solid hours, until 3 P.M., the heavy artillery duel continued, with scarcely a pause. Batteries destroyed or out of ammunition in the Federal lines were quickly replaced, but the artillery losses on both sides, guns, men, and animals, were severe. Meade's artillery commander, General Hunt, handled his guns with considerably greater skill and efficiency than did his opposite number, Con-

BRIGADIER GENERAL HENRY J. HUNT
Chief of Artillery, Army of the Potomac, Hunt's control of the Federal artillery played a vital part in the Union success on the third day.

federate General Pendleton. Without waiting for orders from General Meade, Hunt foresaw that a massive infantry attack was scheduled to follow the artillery preparation, and wisely ordered his guns to cease firing some ten or fifteen minutes ahead of the Confederate cease-fire. This action was misinterpreted by the Confederates to mean that they had been successful in silencing the Federal batteries, which was of course their main purpose. Shortly before Hunt ordered the Federal batteries to suspend firing, Alexander had sent a written message to General Pickett: "If you are coming at all, come at once, or I cannot give you proper support; the enemy's fire has not slackened at all; at least eighteen guns are still firing from the Cemetery district."

BRIGADIER GENERAL WILLIAM N. PENDLETON, C.S.A.
Chief of Artillery, Army of Northern Virginia.

Several minutes later the Federal artillery did slacken off and the Confederates observed a number of guns in the Cemetery moving out. Alexander thought this was the psychological moment and dashed off the final historic message: "For God's sake come quick; eighteen guns are gone; unless you advance quick, my ammunition won't let me support you properly."

"General, Shall I Advance?"

Pickett with the curly locks rode jauntily up to Longstreet, saluted, and said: "General, shall I advance?" Unable or unwilling to speak, Longstreet slightly inclined his head, whereupon Pickett wheeled his horse, galloped to the center of the line, and the Confederate mass started to move.

The battlefield was now strangely silent. As the long gray infantry lines emerged from the center of the woods on Seminary Ridge, every eye focused on the amazing picture. Some units marched with their rifles at the right shoulder; others carried them at the trail or in the position of a hunting piece. The lines marched as on parade, with colors flying, fifteen thousand men, and those in both armies who were temporary observers never forgot the sight.

On horseback, on the crest of Cemetery Ridge, General Gibbon, commanding the Second Division of the Second Corps, watched the impressive spectacle with his aide, as the Confederates corrected their alignment and moved eastward across the shallow valley. Haskell recorded his impressions:

> Every eye could see his legions, an overwhelming resistless tide of an ocean of armed men sweeping upon us! Regiment after regiment and brigade after brigade move from the woods and rapidly take their places in the lines forming the assault. * * * The red flags wave, and horsemen gallop up and down; the arms of eighteen thousand men (Ed. note: an over-estimate by 3000),—barrel and bayonet, gleam in the sun, a sloping forest of flashing steel. Right as they move, as with one soul, in perfect order, without impediment of ditch, or wall or stream, over ridge and slope, through orchard and meadow and cornfield, magnificent, grim, irresistible.

Union Guns Decimate Pickett's Troops

Responsive to General Hunt's strict instructions to his batteries, the Federal guns remained silent for a short space of time, while the gray masses moved steadily forward over half the distance to the Federal lines. About the time the forward line was approaching the Emmitsburg

MAJOR GENERAL GEORGE E. PICKETT, C.S.A.
Commanding a division in Longstreet's corps.

Road, Hunt's guns reopened. As the advance continued, and Pickett's men came closer and closer, the gunners changed from shell to shrapnel and then to canister, wreaking terrific havoc among the unwavering Confederate lines, which grimly closed ranks each time a shell found its mark. Federal artillery from Little Round Top, reinforcing the indirect frontal fire of the batteries along the Ridge, created a devastating effect in enfilading Pickett's advancing lines, while the Confederate guns remained silent, through fear of hitting their own men or because they were out of ammunition, or both.

THE CHARGE OF PICKETT, PETTIGREW, AND TRIMBLE

From a wartime sketch made from the Union position. In front of the artillery the Federal infantrymen are opening fire, from behind the stone wall, on the nearing Confederates. At the left is Stannard's brigade drawn up in close formation. In a few minutes it will move forward opposite Pickett's exposed right flank, wheel to the right, and enfilade Pickett at close range. Stannard commanded a brigade, never in battle previously, in the Third Division, Doubleday's First Corps. Their action here was vital in repelling the Confederate assault.

Gibbon, cool and collected, rode along the line cautioning the men to take their time, let the enemy come close, and then aim low—the age-old custom of the experienced soldier who knows that a bullet below the waist that disables one or both legs will stop a man more surely than an arm or shoulder wound that many times is merely superficial.

With the pounding that the courageous Confederates were now receiving from the Federal guns, it was not surprising that the parade formation should begin to give a little at the seams. When the time came to change direction in order to converge on the objective, the brigades of Wilcox and Perry on the right were slow to conform, with the result that a constantly widening gap appeared between the marching forces.

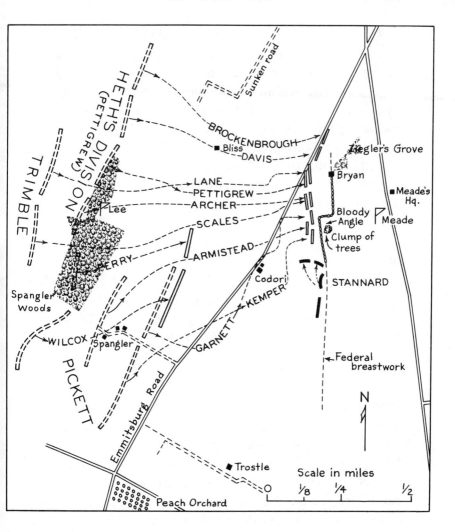

Map 14. The Assault of Pickett, Pettigrew, and Trimble

his map shows by broken lines and arrows the routes of the attacking brigades. The ositions which they reached in front of the Union lines—the High Water Mark of the onfederacy—are indicated. Note Stannard's Union brigade moving forward into the nterval on Pickett's right. Stannard, closely observed by Hancock, wheeled to the right, and s Pickett's ranks passed by "in review" poured a devastating fire into the Confederates at close range. This was another critical factor in Pickett's defeat.

Hancock Spots an Opening; Breaks Pickett's Right

General Hancock, quick to spot the opening, took immediate steps to exploit the opportunity by throwing the three Vermont regiments of Stannard's brigade into the gap. Although Hancock was wounded in this effort, the "Green Mountain" boys, nine months' men who had never before been under fire, dashed into the breach and poured a murderous flanking fire first northward into Kemper's brigade, and shortly afterwards in the opposite direction against Perry and Wilcox.

It was too much for Wilcox and Perry, first demoralized by artillery and now, completely blocked off from their comrades, being shot to pieces by the Vermonters. Wavering momentarily, the two Southern brigades, or rather what remained of them, were soon thoroughly bewildered, commenced to wander back towards their lines, and were no longer a factor in the battle.

The Confederates Keep Moving

Now the leading Confederate wave has broken down the fences, crossed the Emmitsburg Road, and moved steadily closer to the watching and waiting men of Gibbon's division. These latter, under brigade commanders Harrow, Webb, and Hall, represent six States—four Pennsylvania regiments, three each from New York and Massachusetts, and one each from Minnesota, Michigan, and Maine. Confidently and with commendable discipline they withheld their fire as instructed, although the temptation to open up must have been almost irresistible.

General Pickett, on his coal-black horse, followed closely behind his advancing lines and took position in the orchard of the Codori house, within musket range of the Federal position on the ridge. At that point he was posted

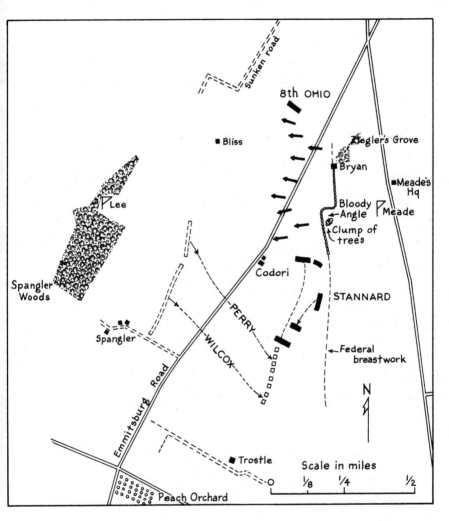

Map 15. The Advance of Perry and Wilcox, and the Ebb of the Tide

The brigades of Perry and Wilcox advanced in two stages, as shown on Maps 14 and 15. But this assault was not properly coordinated with that of Pickett, whose flank was thus exposed. This contributed to the Confederate defeat in detail, for the Union artillery and Stannard's infantry were able to concentrate their fire on these units and easily repulse them. This map also shows the broken fragments of Pickett's, Pettigrew's, and Trimble's divisions streaming back to their initial positions.

to exercise whatever control might remain to the commander of an attacking column under such conditions.

Pettigrew's Division is Chopped Up

Pettigrew's division, advancing on the left towards Hancock's right at Ziegler's Grove, was in trouble. A Federal regiment, which had been stationed in extended order west of the Emmitsburg Road, was wheeled at a right angle as the Confederates moved toward the ridge, to be greeted by a deadly flanking fire that badly shook Pettigrew's brigades. On they came, however, until every weapon of the Federal arsenal on that part of the front opened on them simultaneously. Human flesh and nerves simply couldn't stand such punishment. The Southern lines broke, the men ran for cover, and the dead and wounded covered the field.

Pickett's right had been broken and repulsed. Now the left had suffered a similar fate. Everything depended on the regiments in the center, and the support which Anderson's division in reserve was waiting to furnish.

It is the moment for the final charge and, despite already heavy losses, the Confederates are ready. They have passed over the level ground and are slowly dogtrotting uphill on the western slope of Cemetery Ridge, within a hundred yards or less of the stone wall, when Gibbon's officers give the word to the trigger-impatient men of the Second division. A blaze of rifle fire in the faces of the advancing Confederates crumples many of them, with but little seeming effect. Pausing only to lower their own muskets to return the fire, the momentum of their drive carries them up to the wall.

The destiny of the world may well have hung in the balance during the next five minutes, minutes in which the preservation of the Union, the downfall of the Confederacy, and the death of slavery were finally decided.

The High Water Mark

One hundred and fifty yelling men in gray pour over the wall, with General Armistead at the center, sword still raised with his hat on the point. The Federal guns at the "Angle" have fallen silent because those who had served them up to the last were now either dead or wounded. Webb's Union brigade panics and breaks for the rear. It is a tense moment. In short order the retreating Federals are stopped, turned back, and recover their nerve. Fresh batteries are rushed forward, unlimber and open fire within half a dozen yards of Armistead and his men, while the recovered infantrymen pour fire from all sides into the little island of Confederates. Armistead puts his hand on a captured Federal gun and is shot to death.

Wilcox, meanwhile, had not advanced, and, Pettigrew being routed, Pickett's division was left alone, but undaunted. Their fierce onset struck first upon Webb's brigade, which, posted behind a low stone wall, occupied Gibbon's front line. They broke this, and charged right among the batteries, where a fierce hand-to-hand struggle took place . . . Gibbon, as it chanced, was a little to the right, urging the regiments there to follow Pettigrew's routed troops, and was struck down. Webb's brigade fell back from the stone wall over which the assailants were surging, but only to the second line behind the crest. Gibbon had a little before sent Lieutenant Haskell to Meade with tidings that the enemy were upon him. He was returning, and had just reached the brow of the hill, when he met Webb's brigade falling back. Without waiting to find Gibbon, Haskell rode to the left, and ordered the whole division to the right to meet the advancing foe. At that critical moment the virtual command was exercised by this young lieutenant.

"There was one young man on my staff who has

been in every battle with me, and who did more than any one man to repulse that last assault at Gettysburg, and he did the part of a general there, yet he has been (April, 1864) only a first lieutenant until within a few weeks. I have now succeeded in getting the Governor of Wisconsin to appoint him to a colonelcy, and I have no doubt he will before long come before the Senate for a star."—Gibbon, in Com. Rep. ii, 445.—He never came before the Senate for a star; among the killed at Cold Harbor not two months later we read the name of the Gallant Colonel Franklin A. Haskell, 36th Wisconsin.*

Discouraged and bewildered, exhausted from their strenuous approach march and hand-to-hand fighting, and without visible support from their comrades on the other side of the wall, the temporarily victorious Confederates turn wearily to the west, back over the wall and down the hill. Armistead's little band of doughty fighters had been alone in their penetration of Meade's defense.

"The line to the right and left, as far as I could observe, seemed to melt away until there was little of it left," was the way in which Colonel Shepard of Tennessee, one of Trimble's brigade commanders, put it in his report. Longstreet had been right—Lee had asked the impossible of the men whom he thought to be invincible—the battle of Gettysburg was over.

A Cheer of Victory from the Union Lines

As the broken gray lines staggered back to Seminary Ridge, leaving over 7,000 of the attacking force dead or wounded, and many hundreds more as prisoners in the hands of the Federals, 40,000 men in blue stood massed

---

* Excerpts from *Harper's Pictorial History of the Great Rebellion,* Part Second, page 512. By Aldred H. Guernsey and Henry M. Alden. Harper & Bro., New York, 1868.

along the crest of Cemetery Ridge from the cemetery to Round Top, while cheer after cheer of victory rang out all along the line. These men were not to be denied, and understandably so. The cheers were not of exultation over a brave but fallen foe, but of elation over the first clean-cut victory, even though a defensive one, that the Army of the Potomac had won since the beginning of the war. That long-suffering, badly-generalled army had finally been given competent, intelligent leadership and it fought at Gettysburg that day better than it had ever fought before.

Monuments on Cemetery and Seminary Ridges now mark the positions from which the two army commanders observed the climactic clash of July 3. Lee watched from Seminary Ridge the advance and repulse from the very beginning, when Pickett's consolidated brigades first formed up under cover for the assault. Meade, who had been forced by the galling Confederate artillery fire to move

CEMETERY RIDGE AFTER PICKETT'S CHARGE

SIXTEEN YEARS AFTER PICKETT'S CHARGE

A view from the vicinity of Bloody Angle, looking north toward the Bryan house, seen through the trees. The wagon track is now Hancock Avenue, lined with numerous monuments. The two figures by the wall at the left are artist Philippoteaux and an assistant, evidently trying to inject some realism into their terrain study.

his command post to Power's Hill during the bombardment, rode up to the crest of Cemetery Ridge just in time to see his troops recover their equilibrium, counter-attack Armistead's penetration, and drive the unwelcome invaders from the Federal lines.

Longstreet was calm and collected as he watched the rise and fall of the Confederate fortunes. It was still his battle, and he moved promptly to rally the defeated foot soldiers and to reshuffle the artillery in preparation for the Federal counterattack which he was sure would follow hard on the heels of Meade's successful defense.

The divisions of Hood and McLaws, which had been firmly locked in position and kept busy by the Federal Fifth Corps on their front at Devil's Den and the Round Tops during Pickett's assault, were ordered to withdraw to the positions they had held before the fight on the second day, while Longstreet busied himself with such other details as were found necessary in tidying up the unfortunate reverse and to be ready for whatever the god of war might be preparing to dish out to his depleted corps.

"This was All My Fault!"

On another part of the field, Lee moved among the men and officers who had survived the attack, as they dragged weary bodies back to the relative security of Seminary Ridge. Riding up to where Pickett was reporting to Longstreet, Lee remarked: "This was all my fault, General Pickett. This has been my fight and the blame is mine. Your men did all men can do. The fault is entirely my own."

Fifteen thousand soldiers had headed east only a short hour before, full of fight and confident of victory. Scarcely more than half of them returned, sullen and exhausted,

BEHIND THE LINES

Part of the Cyclorama. This scene depicts the crude first aid and surgical treatment of the wounded during Pickett's charge. Actually this Union field hospital was on Rock Creek, to the east, but the artist moved it up to the immediate area of the fighting. He also used as his model the Thompson house, which actually stood west of Gettysburg.

but they returned at a walk, acting not in the least like men who had been defeated. This had been a new and unpleasant experience for them and they didn't like it. The spirit of the Army of Northern Virginia was anything but quenched and these men would have asked for nothing better than to have their old enemy try to come across and take *their* line.

CAVALRY ENGAGEMENT BETWEEN GREGG AND STUART EAST OF GETTYSBURG
ON THE THIRD DAY

CHAPTER 19

THE BATTLE ENDS WITH A CAVALRY FIGHT

KILPATRICK'S cavalry division of two brigades had been operating on Meade's right flank, in the direction of Hanover, on July 2, when new orders were received from Pleasonton to detach Custer's brigade for duty with Gregg. The remaining brigade under Kilpatrick's direction was to cover the army left in the vicinity of Round Top. The mixup that sent Buford's cavalry back to Westminster on the morning of the second day had finally been discovered at Meade's headquarters and the orders to Kilpatrick, belated as they were, meant that the Union army would again have a force of cavalry to protect its flank and give Longstreet's divisions a few extra headaches.

The two brigades which were to execute this mission were commanded respectively by Brig. Gen. Wesley Merritt and Brig. Gen. Elon J. Farnsworth. The latter, until a few days before Gettysburg a captain-aide on Pleasonton's staff, had, in company with Custer and Merritt, been jumped four grades for gallantry in the field and given his star in the latter days of June; but his formal commission had not yet been issued. Merritt's brigade, a part of Buford's division, had been on a special mission in the vicinity of Thurmont, Maryland, and only reached Gettysburg on July third.

Federal Cavalry on the South Flank

About noon of July 3 the two brigades took position near the Confederate artillery at the southern end of Seminary Ridge. When the artillery cannonade which preceded Pickett's charge had been underway for sometime, the Federal cavalry engaged the Confederate regiments on their front. For a time there was lively but inconclusive fighting between gray infantry and blue horsemen in the rear of Law's Confederate division, which was still in contact with the left of Meade's main line on the slopes of Round Top and in the Devil's Den area.

Kilpatrick's orders from Pleasonton were to press the Confederate right and to attack at the first opportunity. The young general, who had supreme confidence in the ability of his troopers to fight successfully over any kind of terrain, was eager to get into the battle.

Farnsworth's Fruitless Charge

At five o'clock in the afternoon, sometime after Pickett had been repulsed and returned to the Conferate lines on Seminary Ridge, Kilpatrick, who was under the impression or at least chose to believe that Meade was about to launch a major counterattack, ordered Farnsworth to send the first West Virginia regiment of his brigade to attack a Texas regiment on its front. Twice the West Virginians charged and twice were driven back with severe losses. Dissatisfied with the meager results, Kilpatrick directed General Farnsworth personally to lead a final charge in the hope of breaking the Confederate line.

With three hundred men in the attacking echelon Farnsworth gallantly led a hell-for-leather mounted attack which reminds one of the Charge of the Light Brigade at Balaklava in the Crimean War. As in the case of that suicidal charge of the British against the Russians, Farnsworth's attack was equally fruitless. The Federals galloped impetuously through the Confederate infantry, over rocks and fences, some half mile or more deep into hostile territory, circled around, and galloped back, gathering in about one hundred prisoners but suffering over sixty casualties, including General Farnsworth, who was killed on the return journey. It was a brief and thrilling performance, but in reality proved nothing. The participants always stoutly maintained, however, that it was a worthwhile effort that would have had an important effect on Union fortunes had Meade ordered the counterattack along the army front which Hancock had urged as he was borne from the field on a stretcher earlier in the afternoon.

Meade Decides not to Counterattack

Confident that the Confederate attack would not be repeated, Meade rode over to Round Top and from Sykes' corps on the left ordered out skirmish parties to test the strength and further intentions of the enemy on that front. It soon appeared that Lee's artillery was still very much in control of the situation on Seminary Ridge, decisively commanding the ground in the direction of the Federal line. Longstreet's divisions had been ordered back and were moving calmly to the west towards the Peach Orchard, as several Union brigades eased their way forward across the Wheatfield and through the woods on its fringe. A. P. Hill's line was still virtually intact to the north and it became apparent that the Confederates had the strength and will to give Meade a hot reception should he choose to follow up the repulse of Lee's forces with a serious counterattack.

Armies of the size that fought at Gettysburg do not switch over from the defensive to the offensive at the drop of a hat. Time is necessary to re-group, estimate the situation, make the major decisions, and issue the necessary orders, which must then percolate through the intermediate echelons of command and be absorbed and understood down the line if the component parts of the machine are to operate smoothly and effectively.

Meade had in reserve Sedgwick's large corps and a part of Sykes', the troops of which had done little fighting during the battle and could have been employed as a counter striking force. There were plenty of critics of Meade's timidity in failing to throw this available force at Lee's discomfited divisions in order to turn their repulse into a retreat. After-the-event strategists can always present evidence to support their contentions. It is true nevertheless that another, more audacious commander such as the late General Patton probably would not have "taken counsel of his fears," but would instead have promptly sent Sedgwick's corps tearing around Lee's right, and Patton-like have gotten away with it. There is no doubt that Meade had discussed the possibility with Hancock and perhaps others, but without formulating a definite plan or issuing precautionary oral orders, which suggests that he wasn't too sold on the idea himself.

But it was George Gordon Meade and not George S. Patton who was Army Commander that day. Meade, thinking and acting defensively for three solid days, was not quick enough on the mental trigger to exploit his success. Nor can it be forgotten that he had left the initiative to Lee from the very beginning. Some generals, like leopards, cannot change their spots on the spur of the moment.

At least four of Meade's corps commanders, Hancock, Doubleday, Howard, and Pleasonton, subsequently put themselves on record as having supported the idea of an immediate counterattack, but it remained for cavalryman Pleasonton to record the most positive, and it must be admitted, somewhat flamboyant account of his views. General Pleasonton wrote:

> From the suddenness of the repulse of the last charge on July 3d, it became necessary for General Meade to decide at once what to do. I rode up to him, and, after congratulating him on the splendid conduct of the army, I said: "General, I will give you half an hour to show yourself a great general. Order the army to advance, while I will take the cavalry and get in Lee's rear, and we will finish the campaign in a week." He replied: "How do you know Lee will not attack me again; we have done well enough." I replied that Lee had exhausted all his available men; that the cannonade of the last two days had exhausted his ammunition; he was far from his base of supplies; and by compelling him to keep his army together, they must soon surrender, for he was living on the country. To this the general did not reply, but asked me to ride up to Round Top with him; and, as we rode along the ridge for nearly a mile, the troops cheered him in a manner that plainly showed they expected the advance.

Meade's late afternoon reconnaissance to Round Top developed into quite a dramatic episode. Accompanied by General Pleasonton, his son, Major Meade, and several members of his staff, Meade rode out to the front of Cemetery Ridge. With his little cavalcade he galloped rapidly along the ridge to Little Round Top, accompanied by resounding cheers from the delighted Federals all along the way. As recounted by a writer in the Philadelphia *Weekly Press* of April 18, 1886:

> The effect upon the men was electrical. The enthusiastic cheers of the entire army greeted this appeal

to their enthusiasm; and the effect upon the dispirited Confederates is mentioned by Colonel Fremantle, of the British Guards, who accompanied General Longstreet during the campaign.

Anticlimactic Cavalry Fight

As the climax to the Gettysburg campaign was being reached between the ridges south of the town on the afternoon of the third day, a collateral phase of Lee's final

BRIGADIER GENERAL DAVID McM. GREGG
Commanding a cavalry division under Pleasonton.

attack plans was being played out about 2½ miles east of Gettysburg between the York and Hanover roads.

So much has been written about Pickett's charge and its dramatic role in featuring the high water mark of the rebellion that the cavalry fight behind the Federal line, which occurred about the same time as Pickett's charge was being driven home, was not only dwarfed by comparison, but has been correspondingly neglected by historians. Yet that spirited clash between four Confederate brigades under command of Major General J. E. B. Stuart and three Union brigades commanded by Brig. Gen. David McM. Gregg could have played an extremely significant part in the third day's activities.

As it happened, only two of the three brigades of Gregg's cavalry division were on hand to deter Stuart. While Kilpatrick's cavalry division had met the Confederate horsemen at Hanover several days before and hastened their northward trek toward York, Gregg's division had been following Stuart's march, nipping at his heels. The men and horses had had little rest.

General Lee's overall plan for the operations of the third day contemplated the penetration of the Federal center on Cemetery Ridge from the converging attack of the fifteen thousand men under Pickett. In order to exploit the anticipated breakthrough, Stuart's cavalry was assigned the mission of circling the Confederate left to the north around Gettysburg, coming in on Meade's rear at the psychological moment, and giving the Army of the Potomac the coup de grace.

Stuart's force consisted of the three brigades under Wade Hampton, Fitz Lee, and Chambliss, which had been proceeding north to the east of Meade's army, and Jenkins' brigade of mounted infantry, plus four batteries of artillery, a total of something over 6,000 men. Stuart had finally rejoined Lee at Gettysburg on the afternoon of July 2, with men and horses just about worn out, and it isn't likely that one night's rest had restored either to a fine edge for combat.

Moving to the north of Gettysburg and passing around Ewell's left to a point two miles east of Culp's Hill, Stuart's horsemen, about 2:30 P.M. and without opposi-

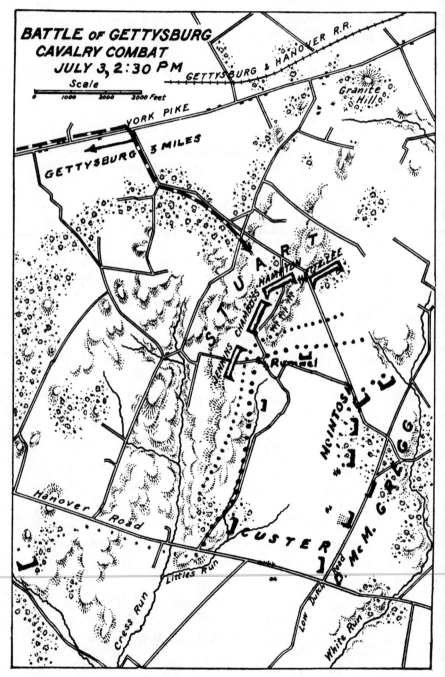

BATTLE of GETTYSBURG
CAVALRY COMBAT
JULY 3, 2:30 PM
Scale

0   1000   2000   3000 Feet

GETTYSBURG & HANOVER R.R.

Granite
Hill

YORK PIKE

GETTYSBURG 3 MILES

S T U A R T

HAMPTON

JENKINS CHAMBLISS

Rummel

McINTOSH

CUSTER

GREGG

D. McM.

Hanover   Road

Littles Run

Cress Run

Low Dutch Road

White Run

tion, took position along the elevated wooded region known locally as Cress Ridge, which runs north-south and from which they could command all the roads in the rear of Meade's line.

Half a mile to the east of Cress Ridge was another low ridge which was occupied by McIntosh's Federal brigade, and it was in the open fields between the two tree-covered ridges that the picturebook cavalry drama was enacted.

About the time Stuart showed up, McIntosh's Federal brigade was the only one nearby. Irvin Gregg's brigade was a short distance to the south, but was hastily brought up when a fight became imminent. George A. Custer's brigade, a part of Judson Kilpatrick's division, was on a temporary detached mission in the area but had received orders from Kilpatrick to rejoin him southwest of Round Top. Custer had started out in accordance with these orders when Gregg, seeing that a lively fight was in prospect, hastily pressed Custer's brigade into service. Always ready at the drop of a hat for anything that promised a fight, Custer was only too happy to oblige. With this addition to his depleted division, Gregg now had about 5,000 sabers and several artillery batteries to engage Stuart's somewhat superior strength, although Jenkins' mounted infantry through some mistake had only ten rounds of ammunition per man, a rather sketchy supply for a knock-down fight.

Map 16. THE CAVALRY FIGHT EAST OF GETTYSBURG OF JULY 3

Lee ordered Stuart to move out from the vicinity of Gettysburg and, simultaneously with Longstreet's main effort, drive hard for the Union rear. This sound plan failed because Gregg successfully intercepted Stuart in the area shown here. Stuart formed his brigades on Cress' Ridge. Then, after some preliminary action in which Gregg's dismounted units inflicted losses on the Confederates with their carbines, Stuart moved south across the pastures in a mounted attack. He was met headlong by Custer, whose brigade was then attached to Gregg. After a wild, confused melee Stuart withdrew, leaving the main Union position unmolested.

The engagement between the two cavalry forces started when dismounted skirmishers opened fire on one another in the vicinity of the Rummel House, which soon led to a buildup of larger bodies of dismounted men who joined the fire fight, while the field artillery contributed its share of destruction. This was not quite the conventional procedure for the Confederate cavalry, however, and it wasn't long before the horse squadrons were massed in preparation for the typical mounted charge so dear to southern hearts.

The combined brigades of Wade Hampton and Fitz Lee, formed in close columns of squadrons, sabers flashing in the sun, advanced in beautiful alignment. They were met by heavy artillery and rifle fire which caused great gaps in their line. On they came, despite losses, and it was at that stage that Custer, the "boy general," rode to the fame that was to end so disastrously not many years later on the Little Big Horn.

Custer's brigade, drawn up in close mounted column, was promptly ordered by Gregg to charge the oncoming Confederates. Placing himself at the head of his squadrons, Custer led them out to meet Hampton and Lee. As the two forces approached one another, each increased the gait to the trot and then to the gallop. Meeting head-on, the clash was so violent that many of the horses were turned end over end, carrying their riders to the ground with a crashing impact.* From then on the fight became something of a Donnybrook Fair, with charges and countercharges all over the field, creating enough excitement to satisfy the most ardent proponent of the cavalry charge as a method of gaining a decision.

Other elements of Gregg's division executed effective

---

* *Battles and Leaders,* p. 404.

flank attacks against the gray squadrons, during one of which the Confederate General Hampton was seriously slashed by a Federal saber. The surprising resistance of the Federal cavalry seemed to demoralize the Confederates. After a bit the two forces separated as though by tacit agreement and reestablished their lines with Stuart's men on the ridge from which they had started, while Gregg remained in possession of the battlefield. When darkness fell, Custer's brigade marched away in belated obedience to Kilpatrick's earlier order. Stuart's Confederates withdrew to the north and returned to Lee's Army west of Seminary Ridge. And thus ended the third and last day of the Battle of Gettysburg.

Heavy Casualties

The Gettysburg campaign had been without exception

MAJOR GENERAL ALFRED PLEASONTON AND BRIGADIER GENERAL GEORGE A. CUSTER
Photo taken three months after the Battle of Gettysburg.

the most terrible blood-letting ever witnessed on this continent. Of the approximately 170,000 officers and men engaged, more than 50,000, over 29 per cent, were either killed, wounded, missing, or taken prisoner.

The official records of the two armies listed the casualties as follows:

	Federal	Confederate	Total
Killed	3,072	2,592	5,664
Wounded	14,497	12,709	27,206
Missing or captured ..	5,434	5,000 plus *	10,434 plus
	23,003	20,301	43,304

* Prisoner of war records in the Adjutant General's office in Washington bear the names of 12,227 wounded and unwounded Confederates captured July 1-5. There is therefore good reason to believe that the official Confederate losses, as given above, were underestimated.

The heaviest losses were incurred in the Union retreat to Cemetery Ridge the first day, in the Sickles' debacle July 2, and in Pickett's charge on July 3.

More than 30 general officers on the field became casualties. On the Federal side, Reynolds, Farnsworth, Weed, and Zook were killed, as were Colonels Vincent, Willard, and Cross, brigade commanders who had not yet received their stars, while Hancock, Gibbon, Sickles, Barlow, Graham, Webb, Stannard, Smyth, Meredith, Paul, Butterfield, Hunt, Brooke, Barnes, and Warren were wounded.

Of the 50 odd Confederate generals who entered Pennsylvania for the invasion, six were killed or died of wounds: Armistead, Barksdale, Garnett, Pender, Semmes, and Pettigrew; ten were wounded: Hood, Hampton, Trimble, Robertson, Kemper, Jones, Heth, Scales, Jenkins, and Anderson; and three were captured, Archer and the wounded Trimble and Kemper.

In Pickett's charge alone, two of the three Confederate division commanders were wounded, while in Pickett's own division of about 4,800 men actually in the attack, two of the three brigade commanders were killed and the third wounded; twelve of the fifteen regimental commanders were killed and two wounded, while the only field officer who escaped unharmed was a lieutenant colonel who was acting regimental commander. In all nearly 60 per cent of Pickett's divisional strength, or about 2,800 men and officers, were either killed, wounded, missing, or captured.

THE RETURN TO VIRGINIA

CHAPTER 20

THE LONG ROAD BACK

THE Army of Northern Virginia remained on the field at Gettysburg all day Saturday, July 4, waiting, expecting, and even hoping for a Federal attack which would give the disgruntled Confederates an opportunity to gain some revenge by turning the tables. When Pickett's attack had failed to pierce Meade's center, and neither Ewell nor Longstreet had done much more than mark time on the north and south flanks the afternoon of the 3d, Lee gave up all hope of dislodging Meade from his strong position. He then turned his thoughts to the serious problem of extricating his army, collecting and transporting his wounded back to Virginia, and planning tactical dispositions for the various elements of the army in preparation for their withdrawal to and across the Potomac River.

Lee Withdraws

On the evening of July 3 Lee had recalled Ewell from his Culp's Hill—Gettysburg position, pulled Longstreet all the way back to Seminary Ridge, and established as a temporary defense a line from Peach Orchard to Oak Hill, west of Gettysburg, with directions to the troops to improve their time by intrenching and otherwise giving the enemy the impression that they had no immediate intention of moving.

The plan conceived by Lee for the return trip to Virginia, after being polished and reduced to writing, was officially issued to the army on the afternoon of July 4. Earlier oral instructions had been given to assemble all available ambulances and wagons, load the seriously wounded, and start the train as quickly as possible that day westward through the Cashtown pass and south through the Cumberland Valley via Greenwood and Hagerstown to Williamsport, a prospective journey of 40 miles. Imboden's cavalry brigade was given the task of convoying the wounded and most of the army supply trains to the Potomac in advance of the troops. Stuart was directed to send one of his brigades to hold the Cashtown pass and prevent Federal cavalry from getting through and blocking the slow-moving convoy before they could reach safety in Virginia.

The plan for the rest of the army was for Hill's corps to lead off by way of Fairfield, followed by the combined corps trains; then Longstreet's corps, with Ewell's divisions to bring up and cover the rear, while the otherwise unassigned cavalry brigades would proceed south by the Emmitsburg Road to protect the army left flank and cooperate with Ewell in preventing major attacks against its rear.

The daily strength returns for July 4 informed Lee that he had about 50,000 men fit for duty, including some of the less seriously wounded, who were attached as ambulatory cases to the ambulance train. Many of these men

were capable of using their rifles in an emergency, and
that is just what a lot of them did in helping to drive
off subsequent cavalry forays against the column.

Both artillery and rifle ammunition had been mostly
used up during the three days of Gettysburg. Lee faced
an almost superhuman task in successfully extricating his

CARRY ME BACK TO OLE VIRGINNY

many thousands of wounded, over 4,000 prisoners, and
immense trains, to say nothing of the danger facing his
infantry and artillery during their retrograde movement,
strung along as they must be on a single road in an un-
ending column. It was inevitable that Meade's cavalry
corps, understandingly exuberant over their noteworthy
contribution to the Federal success at Gettysburg, would

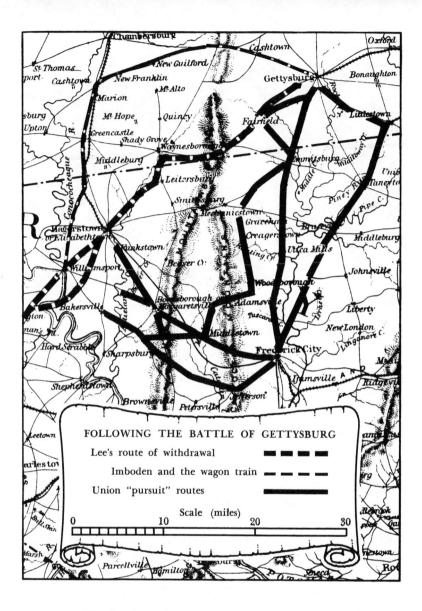

Map 17. Lee's Withdrawal and Meade's "Pursuit"

Note that the Union corps, moving by parallel routes, swung out to the east rather than follow the Confederates by the shorter routes through the mountain gaps. They moved so cautiously that they could not possibly have intercepted Lee north of the Potomac had not Lee been delayed by the high water in the river. The Federal cavalry acted boldly but were not supported.

IN THE WAKE OF BATTLE

Surgeon about to operate on a patient in a Union field hospital. He appears
to have donned white gloves for the occasion, and is assisted by several
spectators who, in lieu of anesthesia, are firmly holding the victim.

make strenuous efforts to impede the march and inflict
maximum losses on the retreating forces.

The Rains Descend

It started to rain about noon on Saturday, July 4.
During that day the torrential character of the downpour
caused the dirt roads to become running streams and
mud holes, to the intense suffering of the wounded who
were jolted and tossed about in the springless wagons
until many of them expressed a wish for death in preference to the continuous torture which they were forced
to undergo. As the column proceeded on its way, rain and
wind frequently so startled the animals that they would
try to run away and frequently would upset, spilling
wounded over the road. Imboden's strict orders were to
stop for nothing, so despite the apparent inhumanity of

the procedure, the column kept going and the wounded were left to shift for themselves.

Saturday night, when after a full day of inactivity no evidence had appeared to indicate that Meade planned to attack, the Army of Northern Virginia started its retirement down the Fairfield Road and thence westward through the mountain pass toward Hagerstown and Williamsport. By early Sunday morning the last of the Confederates had left Gettysburg. The Federal army found itself alone on the field.

All day Sunday the rain continued to fall as heavily as on the preceding day, making the roads almost impassable and adding immeasurably to the discomfort of the plodding Southern soldiers.

Meade Tarries at Gettysburg

When Meade had finally become convinced, late on the morning of July 5, that Lee was really retreating and not playing possum, he sent Irvin Gregg's cavalry brigade in pursuit on the Chambersburg Pike and started the infantry down the Fairfield Road, with Sedgwick's Sixth Corps in the lead. French's 7,000 troops at Frederick, which had not been engaged during the Gettysburg affair, had received orders from Meade July 4 to seize and hold the lower passes, to destroy the pontoon bridges over the Potomac in the Williamsport area, and to cause Lee's retreating forces as much damage as possible.

Early on Monday afternoon, July 6, Meade reported to Halleck that the army's movement "will be made at once on his flank via Middletown and South Mountain Pass"; and added—"I cannot delay to pick up the debris of the battlefield and request that all those arrangements may be made by the Departments. My Headquarters will be tonight at Cregerstown (a few miles southeast of Thurmont). Communication received from General Smith, in command of 3,000 men, on the march from Carlisle towards Cashtown. Field returns last evening gave me about 55,000 effectives in the ranks, exclusive of cavalry, baggage guards, ambulance attendants, etc. Every available reinforcement is required and should be sent to Frederick without delay."

Tuesday morning, July 7, the head of Lee's army and the trains under Imboden had reached the Hagerstown-Williamsport area, and the tail was rapidly closing up to the Potomac. Meade decided that he would direct General Couch, in command of the Department of the Susquehanna at Harrisburg, but under Meade's orders, to move down the Cumberland Valley "to threaten the enemy rear." Concurrently Meade had been informed by Halleck that reinforcements were on the way from Washington and he thereupon expressed to Halleck his desire that they be advanced to Harper's Ferry as soon as possible.

Shortly after passing Fairfield on the road to Hagerstown, Sedgwick reported to Meade that the Monterey Pass appeared to be strongly held, with a large force of the enemy on hand. Whereupon Meade halted the rest of the army and sent two corps to support the attack which Sedgwick had projected. Almost immediately, however, Meade changed his mind, decided it would take too long to dislodge the Confederates, and that he would therefore leave McIntosh's cavalry brigade and one of Sedgwick's to follow the enemy through the Fairfield Pass while the main body continued the march southward, but east of the mountains.

Federal Cavalry Harasses the Confederates

The blue cavalry divisions of Kilpatrick and Buford having moved on ahead of the Federal infantry, engaged in harassing attacks against Imboden's column in the mountainous country, damaging trains and capturing many prisoners, caissons and wagons, but the nearby presence of Confederate infantry and their willingness to pitch in to help the protecting cavalry, prevented any major attack from being driven home against the train column.

There was however one daring and wildly exciting attack against the Confederate main body as it wended its serpentine way through the mountains after entering the Monterey Pass of the Blue Ridge west of Fairfield. Huey's brigade of Gregg's cavalry division was attached to Kilpatrick's division. In the darkness the Federal cavalry was slipped in between the tail of Lee's trains and the head of Ewell's corps which followed as army rear guard.

The attack was made in the midst of a heavy thunderstorm about three o'clock in the morning. Charging down the road in the Stygian darkness lit up by lightning flashes, the fast-riding Federal cavalrymen caught up with the train at the small crossroads at Monterey and hit the surprised Confederates like a thunderbolt.

CONFEDERATE PRISONERS ON BALTIMORE PIKE AFTER THE BATTLE

One of the officers who was with the brigade in its wild ride, recorded his impressions:

> When we came up with the wagon-train, Federal and Confederate cavalry wagons, ambulances, drivers and mules became a confused mass of pursued and pursuing demons whose shouts and carbine shots, mingled with the lightning's red glare and thunder's crash, made it appear as if we were in the infernal regions. **Frequently a driver would be shot or leave his mule team, when the unrestrained animals would rush wildly down the narrow road, and in many instances the wagons with the mules attached would be found at daylight at the bottom of some deep ravine, crushed to pieces, with the mules dead or dying. **The result of this brilliant maneuver was the capture of a large number of wagons, ambulances and mules, with fifteen hundred prisoners. The brigade reached the foot of the mountain about daylight; leaving the Baltimore pike where it turns towards Waynesboro, the column moved on to Smithsburg, Maryland, where the wagons and ambulances were burned, and the command rested at this place during the day.

The greatest destruction occurred between Rouzerville and Leitersburg, where many of the Confederate wagon trains were burned up. Kilpatrick officially reported the almost complete destruction of the trains of Ewell's corps, capture of 1,360 prisoners and a large number of horses and mules, with a loss of but 5 killed, 10 wounded, and 28 missing.

The Potomac at Flood Stage

On Monday the 6th, Longstreet's corps, which had been given the head of the column that day, reached Hagerstown in the late afternoon. The ambulance train had by this time arrived at Williamsport with the wounded, only to find that their pontoon bridges over the Potomac had been destroyed by French's Federals. The river, rising rapidly from the heavy rains of the past three days, had become unfordable and the door of retreat slammed shut on the Confederate army. The river was now at flood stage and it was certain that a week or so must elapse before the waters would recede to fording depth.

BRIGADIER GENERAL JOHN D. IMBODEN, C.S.A.
Commanding a cavalry brigade.

Lee's engineers immediately laid out a defensive line covering an arc of about five miles from the Downsville area north around Williamsport to the Conococheague Creek, both flanks resting on water, and there Lee prepared to meet Meade's expected attack.

Imboden Protects the Trains

Rarely in Civil War days does one find an officer who combines soldierly qualities with a flair for adequately describing historic events. John D. Imboden, Brigadier General, C.S.A., was one of the exceptions. His firsthand account of the march of the ambulance train, which his brigade protected, is a colorful story of the way in which the difficult mission assigned him was executed. The dangers that were encountered and successfully overcome; the dramatic last-ditch defense at Williamsport, with their backs to the raging Potomac, while two Federal cavalry divisions strove mightily to overcome and capture the whole entourage; and finally the dangerous expedient of transporting the thousands of wounded* and Federal prisoners across the river, a few at a time by rope-ferry, as the Army of the Potomac came slowly but inexorably closer—all of this is so vividly described by General Imboden in *Battles and Leaders of the Civil War,* that it is reprinted here almost in its entirety:

> During the Gettysburg campaign, my command—an independent brigade of cavalry—was engaged, by General Lee's confidential orders, in raids on the left flank of his advancing army, destroying railroad bridges and cutting the canal below Cumberland wherever I could—so that I did not reach the field till noon of the last day's battle. I reported direct to General Lee for orders, and was assigned a position to aid in repelling any cavalry demonstration on his rear. None of a serious character being made, my little force took no part in the battle, but were merely spectators of the scene, which transcended in grandeur any that I beheld in any other battle of the war.

---

* 8,000 to 10,000 walking wounded in addition to the thousands transported by ambulance and wagon.

When night closed the struggle, Lee's army was repulsed. We all knew that the day had gone against us, but the full extent of the disaster was only known in high quarters. The carnage of the day was generally understood to have been frightful, yet our army was not in retreat, and it was surmised in camp that with tomorrow's dawn would come a renewal of the struggle. All felt and appreciated the momentous consequences to the cause of Southern independence of final defeat or victory on that great field.

It was a warm summer's night; there were few camp-fires, and the weary soldiers were lying in groups on the luxuriant grass of the beautiful meadows, discussing the events of the day, speculating on the morrow, or watching that our horses did not straggle off while browsing. About 11 o'clock a horseman came to summon me to General Lee. I promptly mounted and, accompanied by Lieutenant George W. McPhail, an aide on my staff, and guided by the courier who brought the message, rode about two miles toward Gettysburg to where half a dozen small tents were pointed out, a little way from the roadside to our left, as General Lee's headquarters for the night. On inquiry I found that he was not there, but had gone to the headquarters of General A. P. Hill, about half a mile nearer to Gettysburg. When we reached the place indicated, a single flickering candle, visible from the road through the open front of a common wall-tent exposed to view Generals Lee and Hill seated on camp-stools with a map spread upon their knees. Dismounting, I approached on foot. After exchanging the ordinary salutations General Lee directed me to go back to his headquarters and wait for him. I did so, but he did not make his appearance until about 1 o'clock, when he came riding alone, at a slow walk, and evidently wrapped in profound thought.

When he arrived there was not even a sentinel on duty at his tent, and no one of his staff was awake. The moon was high in the clear sky and the silent scene was unusually vivid. As he approached and saw us lying on the grass under a tree, he spoke, reined in his jaded horse, and essayed to dismount. The effort to do so betrayed so much physical exhaustion that I hurriedly rose and stepped forward to assist him, but before I reached his side he had succeeded in alighting, and threw his arm across the saddle to rest, and fixing his eyes upon the ground leaned in silence and almost motionless upon his equally weary horse,—the two forming a striking and never-to-be-forgotten group. The moon shone full upon his massive features and revealed an expression of sadness that I had never before seen upon his face. Awed by his appearance I waited for him to speak until the silence became embarrassing, when, to break it and change the silent current of his thoughts, I ventured to remark, in a sympathetic tone, and in allusion to his great fatigue:

"General, this has been a hard day on you."

He looked up, and replied mournfully:

"Yes, it has been a sad, sad day to us," and immediately relapsed into his thoughtful mood and attitude. Being unwilling again to intrude upon his reflections, I said no more. After perhaps a minute or two, he suddenly straightened up to his full height, and turning to me with more animation and excitement of manner than I had ever seen in him before, for he was a man of wonderful equanimity, he said in a voice tremulous with emotion:

"I never saw troops behave more magnificently than Pickett's division of Virginians did today in that grand charge upon the enemy. And if they had been supported as they were to have been,—but, for some reason not yet fully explained to me, were not,—we would have held the position and the day would have been ours." After a moment's pause he added in a loud voice, in a tone almost of agony, "Too bad! Too bad! OH! TOO BAD!"

I shall never forget his language, his manner, and

his appearance of mental suffering. In a few moments all emotion was suppressed, and he spoke feelingly of several of his fallen trusted officers; among others of Brigadier-Generals Armistead, Garnett, and Kemper of Pickett's division. He invited me into his tent, and as soon as we were seated he remarked:

"We must now return to Virginia. As many of our poor wounded as possible must be taken home. I have sent for you, because your men and horses are fresh and in good condition, to guard and conduct our train back to Virginia. The duty will be arduous, responsible, and dangerous, for I am afraid you will be harassed by the enemy's cavalry. How many men have you?"

"About 2100 effective present, and all well mounted, including McClanahan's six-gun battery of horse artillery."

"I can spare you as much artillery as you require," he said, "but no other troops, as I shall need all I have to return safely by a different and shorter route than yours. The batteries are generally short of ammunition, but you will probably meet a supply I have ordered from Winchester to Williamsport. Nearly all the transportation and the care of all the wounded will be intrusted to you. You will recross the mountain by the Chambersburg road, and then proceed to Williamsport by any route you deem best, and without a halt till you reach the river. Rest there long enough to feed your animals; then ford the river, and do not halt again till you reach Winchester, where I will again communicate with you."

* * * * *

Shortly after noon of the 4th the very windows of heaven seemed to have opened. The rain fell in blinding sheets; the meadows were soon overflowed, and fences gave way before the raging streams. During the storm, wagons, ambulances, and artillery carriages by hundreds—nay, by thousands—were assem-

CONFEDERATE WAGONTRAIN IN THE RETREAT FROM GETTYSBURG

bling in the fields along the road from Gettysburg
to Cashtown, in one confused and apparently inex-
tricable mass. As the afternoon wore on there was no
abatement in the storm. Canvas was no protection
against its fury, and the wounded men lying upon
the naked boards of the wagon-bodies were drenched.
Horses and mules were blinded and maddened by
the wind and water, and became almost unmanage-
able. The deafening roar of the mingled sounds of
heaven and earth all around us made it almost impossible to communicate orders, and equally difficult
to execute them.

About 4 P.M. the head of the column was put in
motion near Cashtown, and began the ascent of the
mountain in the direction of Chambersburg. I remained at Cashtown giving directions and putting
in detachments of guns and troops at what I estimated
to be intervals of a quarter or a third of a mile. It

was found from the position of the head of the column west of the mountain at dawn of the 5th—the hour at which Young's cavalry and Hart's battery began the ascent of the mountain near Cashtown—that the entire column was seventeen miles long when drawn out on the road and put in motion.

*   *   *   *   *

After dark I set out from Cashtown to gain the head of the column during the night. My orders had been peremptory that there should be no halt for any cause whatever. If an accident should happen to any vehicle, it was immediately to be put out of the road and abandoned. The column moved rapidly, considering the rough roads and the darkness, and from almost every wagon for many miles issued heart-rending wails of agony. For four hours I hurried forward on my way to the front, and in all that time I was never out of hearing of the groans and cries of the wounded and dying. Scarcely one in a hundred had received adequate surgical aid, owing to the demands on the hard-working surgeons from still worse cases that had to be left behind. Many of the wounded in the wagons had been without food for thirty-six hours. Their torn and bloody clothing, matted and hardened, was rasping the tender, inflamed, and still oozing wounds. Very few of the wagons had even a layer of straw in them, and all were without springs. The road was rough and rocky from the heavy washings of the preceding day. The jolting was enough to have killed strong men, if long exposed to it. From nearly every wagon as the teams trotted on, urged by whip and shout, came such cries and shrieks as these:

"O God! Why can't I die?"

"My God! will no one have mercy and kill me?"

"Stop! Oh! for God's sake, stop just for one minute; take me out and leave me to die on the roadside."

"I am dying! I am dying! My poor wife, my dear
children, what will become of you?"

* * * * *

During this one night I realized more of the hor-
rors of war than I had in all the two preceding years.

And yet in the darkness was our safety, for no
enemy would dare attack where he could not distinguish friend from foe. We knew that when day
broke upon us we should be harassed by bands of
cavalry hanging on our flanks. Therefore our aim was
to go as far as possible under cover of the night. Instead of going through Chambersburg, I decided to
leave the main road near Fairfield after crossing the
mountains, and take "a near cut"* across the country to Greencastle, where daybreak on the morning
of the 5th of July found the head of our column.
We were now twelve or fifteen miles from the Potomac at Williamsport, our point of crossing into
Virginia.

Here our apprehended troubles began. After the
advance—the 18th Virginia Cavalry—had passed perhaps a mile beyond the town, the citizens to the number of thirty or forty attacked the train with axes.
cutting the spokes out of ten or a dozen wheels and
dropping the wagons in the streets. The moment I
heard of it I sent back a detachment of cavalry to
capture every citizen who had been engaged in this
work, and treat them as prisoners of war. This stopped
the trouble there, but the Union cavalry began to
swarm down upon us from the fields and cross-roads,
making their attacks in small bodies, and striking the
column where there were few or no guards, and thus
creating great confusion.

Our situation was frightful. We had probably ten
thousand animals and nearly all the wagons of General Lee's army under our charge, and all the

_____
* The "Pine Stump" Road through Walnut Bottom, New Guilford, and Marion.

wounded, to the number of several thousand, that could be brought from Gettysburg. Our supply of provisions consisted of a few wagon-loads of flour in my own brigade train, a small lot of fine fat cattle which I had collected in Pennsylvania on my way to Gettysburg, and some sugar and coffee procured in the same way at Mercersburg.

The town of Williamsport is located in the lower angle formed by the Potomac with Conococheague Creek. These streams inclose the town on two sides, and back of it about one mile there is a low range of hills that is crossed by four roads converging at the town. The first is the Greencastle road leading down the creek valley; next the Hagerstown road; then the Boonsboro' road; and lastly the River road.

Early on the morning of the 6th I received intelligence of the approach from Frederick of a large body of cavalry with three full batteries of six rifled guns. These were the divisions of Generals Buford and Kilpatrick, and Huey's brigade of Gregg's division, consisting, as I afterward learned, of 23 regiments of cavalry, and 18 guns, a total force of about 7000 men.

I immediately posted my guns on the hills that concealed the town, and dismounted my own command to support them—and ordered as many of the wagoners to be formed as could be armed with the guns of the wounded that we had brought from Gettysburg. In this I was greatly aided by Colonel J. L. Black of South Carolina, Captain J. F. Hart commanding a battery from the same State, Colonel William R. Aylett of Virginia, and other wounded officers. By noon about 700 wagoners were organized into companies of 100 each and officered by wounded line-officers and commissaries and quartermasters,—about 250 of these were given to Colonel Aylett on the right next the river,—about as many under Colonel Black on the left, and the residue were used as skirmishers. My own command proper was held well in hand in the center.

The enemy appeared in our front about half-past one o'clock on both the Hagerstown and Boonsboro' roads, and the fight began. Every man under my command understood that if we did not repulse the enemy we should all be captured and General Lee's army be ruined by the loss of its transportation, which at that period could not have been replaced in the Confederacy. The fight began with artillery on both sides. The firing from our side was very rapid, and seemed to make the enemy hesitate about advancing. In a half hour J. D. Moore's battery ran out of ammunition, but as an ordnance train had arrived from Winchester, two wagon-loads of ammunition were ferried across the river and run upon the field behind the guns, and the boxes tumbled out, to be broken open with axes. With this fresh supply our guns were all soon in full play again. As the enemy could not see the supports of our batteries from the hill-tops, I moved the whole line forward to his full view, in single ranks, to show a long front on the Hagerstown approach. My line passed our guns fifty or one hundred yards, where they were halted awhile, and then were withdrawn behind the hill-top again, slowly and steadily.

*   *   *   *   *

A bit later in the afternoon, as described in Imboden's account, a tough fire-fight developed in which five of the enemy cavalry regiments dismounted and attacked on foot. They were finally repulsed with two of his regiments, nobly aided by a number of wounded and volunteer artillerymen who managed to put themselves in a position to enfilade the Federal attacking line, into which they poured such a heavy fire that the Northerners gave way rapidly when the Confederate cavalry charged into them.

Night was now rapidly approaching, when a messenger from Fitzhugh Lee arrived to urge me to "hold my own," as he would be up in a half hour with three thousand fresh men. The news was sent along our whole line, and was received with a wild and exultant yell. We knew then that the field was won, and slowly pressed forward. Almost at the same moment we heard distant guns on the enemy's rear and right on the Hagerstown road. They were Stuart's who was approaching on that road, while Fitzhugh Lee was coming on the Greencastle road. That settled the contest. The enemy broke to the left and fled by the Boonsboro' road. It was too dark to follow. When General Fitzhugh Lee joined me with his staff on the field, one of the enemy's shells came near striking him. General Lee thought it came from Eshleman's battery, till, a moment later, he saw a blaze from its gun streaming away from us.

We captured about 125 of the enemy who failed to reach their horses. I could never ascertain the loss on either side. I estimated ours at about 125. The wagoners fought so well that this came to be known as "the wagoners' fight." Quite a number of them were killed in storming a farm from which sharp-shooters were rapidly picking off Eshleman's men and horses.

My whole force engaged, wagoners included, did not exceed three thousand men. The ruse practiced by showing a formidable line on the left, then with-drawing it to fight on the right, together with our numerous artillery, 23 guns, led to the belief that our force was much greater.

By extraordinary good fortune we had thus saved all of General Lee's trains. A bold charge at any time before sunset would have broken our feeble lines, and then we should all have fallen an easy prey to the Federals. The next day our army arrived from Gettysburg.

CONFEDERATE PRISONERS

CHAPTER 21

A LOST OPPORTUNITY TO END THE WAR

MEADE'S obvious reluctance to press the pursuit of the Confederate army, other than by means of harassing cavalry tactics, was at least consistent with the cautious manner in which he had directed the battle operations of the Army of the Potomac. From the day he assumed command, June 28, the initiative had been left entirely to Lee. Meade not only seemed content to have it that way, but vigorously defended all his own decisions and actions based thereon, as though the extent of his mission had been to protect Washington and Baltimore, and see to it only that the bold invader of northern soil should shake the dust of Pennsylvania from his feet.

Some generals play it safe, forgetting perhaps that war is far from being a safe enterprise. Others take calculated risks when large results are possible. The great Captains have been those who audaciously and aggressively discounted the odds, whether actual or imagined, and by their very boldness won important victories. Lee was that kind of general. Meade was not.

Meade's Cautious Pursuit

It was therefore in character that Meade, who made fewer mistakes at Gettysburg than Lee, and whose corps commanders functioned more effectively as a team than did Lee's, should set his sights lower than Lincoln had hoped. Meade, declining to push his luck, concluded that Lee's failure to overwhelm him, if not a resounding victory for Federal arms, was at least a successful defense. He argued that he had given the Confederate cause a powerful setback and forced Lee to return home with nothing but substantial booty and manpower losses to show for his much advertised invasion.

True enough, the Union army had lost heavily in killed, wounded, and prisoners. But so had the Confederates, and probably to an even greater extent if accurate statistics were available. Meade however could better afford those losses; when the battle of Gettysburg was over, his army still had an effective strength of something over 70,000 men, with reinforcements available from Frederick, from Harrisburg, and from Washington. Thus it seems reasonable to estimate that, for the pursuit, Meade had an aggregate strength of over 80,000 against Lee's 50,000. But even with that disparity in numbers, Lee still remained a mental hazard to his opponent.

The slow ponderous movements of the Army of the Potomac, commencing Sunday, July 5, two days after the conclusion of the battle, with Federal cavalry snapping at the heels and flanks of the sullenly retreating Confederate army, were suggestive of a clawed lion-tamer gingerly prodding at an escaped beast in an effort to nudge him back into his cage.

Lincoln Waits Hopefully for Good News

As a hopeful President paced back and forth in the White House, eagerly scanning the messages which from time to time came in from Gettysburg, his spirit was with the Army of the Potomac urging Meade on to pin Lee to the ground, exploit the Gettysburg success, and end the war by destroying the Army of Northern Virginia.

Lincoln's experience as a soldier had been limited to a short period of bloodless service in a long forgotten and misnamed "Black Hawk War." But his basic, common, backwoodsman's horsesense enabled him to distinguish the woods from the trees. It helped him to evolve during the Civil War a concept of military strategy that more often hit closer to the requirements of the situation than did those of his succession of army commanders prior to the time when the hard-hitting Grant took hold and began to win his bulldog victories. Lincoln saw more clearly than Meade the great opportunity which was offered the latter, but which Meade failed pathetically to grasp.

The experience of General Birney who succeeded Sickles in command of the Third Corps, was typical. Ordered on July 4 to send out a reconnaissance at daylight to ascertain the position of the enemy, he did so early Sunday morning, reported that the enemy were in full retreat, and requested permission to open with his rifle batteries on the enemy column as it crossed near his position on the Fairfield road. The reply from Meade was a written order to Birney to make no attack.

Again, in the neighborhood of Fairfield, General Sedgwick, acting under instructions from Meade not to bring on a general engagement, likewise played it safe. One of his division commanders, in testimony before the Committee of Congress on the conduct of the war, described the method of pursuit in vogue:

> On the 4th of July, it seemed evident enough that the enemy were retreating. How far they were gone, we could not see from the front. We could see but a comparatively small force from the position where I was. On Sunday, the 5th, the Sixth Corps moved in pursuit. As we moved, a small rear guard of the enemy retreated. We followed them, with this small rear guard of the enemy before us, up to Fairfield, in a gorge of the mountains. There we again waited for them to go on. There seemed to be no disposition to push this rear guard when we got up to Fairfield. A lieutenant from the enemy came into our lines and gave himself up. He was a Northern Union man, in service in one of the Georgia regiments; and, without being asked, he unhesitatingly told me, when I met him as he was being brought in, that he belonged to the artillery of the rear guard of the enemy, and that they had but two rounds of ammunition with the rear guard. But we waited there without receiving any orders to attack. It was a place where, as I informed General Sedgwick, we could easily attack the enemy with advantage. But no movement was made by us until the enemy went away. Then one brigade of my division, with some cavalry, was sent to follow on after them, while the remainder of the Sixth Corps moved to the left.

The march tables of the Army of the Potomac, from Sunday, July 5, to Sunday, July 12, afford eloquent testimony to the sluggishness with which Meade inched after Lee. The Confederate army took two days to travel the 34 miles from Gettysburg to Hagerstown, while the Federal columns used up eight days in following a longer route measuring approximately 70 miles. The timidity of the pursuit was such that an uninformed observer might well have come to the conclusion that a ferocious animal was waiting around the corner, crouched and ready to spring on the back of "the pursuer." In actuality, as Meade must have known or should have deduced, Lee was short of ammunition, loaded down with impedimenta, wounded, and prisoners, and was in no condition to resume the offensive. Had Meade pressed the pursuit vigorously, keeping his army concentrated and moving rapidly, and had he launched an organized attack within 48 hours of Lee's arrival in the Williamsport pocket and before the latter could effectively organize the position for defense, there was more than an even chance that he could have delivered a knockout blow before the Potomac subsided sufficiently to allow Lee to recross into Virginia.

Revealing evidence of Meade's state of mind at this stage is found in his dispatch to Halleck at Washington on the afternoon of July 6:

> Yesterday I sent General Sedgwick with the 6th Corps in pursuit of the enemy towards Fairfield and a brigade of cavalry towards Cashtown. General Sedgwick's report indicating a large force of the enemy in the mountains, I deemed it prudent to suspend the movement to Middletown until I could be certain the enemy were evacuating Cumberland Valley. I find great difficulty in getting reliable information, but from all I can learn I have reason to believe the enemy is retiring, very much crippled and hampered with his trains. Gen. Sedgwick reported that the Gap at Fairfield was very formidable and would enable a small force to hold my column in check for a long time. I have accordingly resumed the movement to Middletown, and I expect by tomorrow night to assemble the army in that vicinity. Supplies will be then forwarded, and as soon as possible I will cross South Mountain and proceed in search of the enemy.

Your dispatch requiring me to assume the general command of the forces in the field under Gen. Couch has been received. I know nothing of the position or strength of his command except the advance under Gen. Smith which I have ordered here and which I desire should furnish a necessary force to guard this place while the enemy is in the vicinity. A brigade of infantry and one of cavalry with two batteries will be left to watch the enemy at Fairfield and follow them whenever they vacate the Gap. I shall send general instructions to Gen. Couch to move down the Cumberland Valley as far as the enemy evacuated it and keep up communication with me but from all the information I can obtain I do not rely on any active cooperation in battle with this force. If I can get the Army of the Potomac in hand in the valley and the enemy have not crossed the river, I shall give him battle, trusting, should misfortune overtake me, that sufficient number of my force, in connection with what you have in Washington, would reach that place so as to render it secure.

Shades of Murat, of Napoleon, of Patton and McAuliffe!

"I find great difficulty in getting reliable information" —"As soon as possible I will cross South Mountain and proceed in search of the enemy"—"If I can get the Army of the Potomac in hand in the valley and the enemy have not crossed the river"—"should misfortune overtake me. . . ." The mind and heart of Robert E. Lee, defeated and in retreat, still clearly dominated the mental processes of George Gordon Meade.

It was Tuesday, July 7, before Meade moved his headquarters from Gettysburg to Frederick. On that day his seven corps had advanced to a position east of South Mountain and extending generally from Middletown (west of Frederick) to Thurmont. During the next four days, individual corps were sifted gradually through Turner's

Gap and Fox's Gap to the area of Boonsboro and Antietam Creek, where they were still a safe distance from the Williamsport area in which Lee was waiting to make his stand. Meade moved his headquarters west from Frederick to Middletown on July 8, to Turner's Gap July 9, and finally on Friday, July 10, to Beaver Creek north of Boonsboro, where it remained until Lee had recrossed the Potomac.

Union Army Reestablishes Contact

By Sunday July 12, most of the Army of the Potomac had reached Funkstown, several miles south of Hagerstown and about the same distance east of Lee's defense line around Williamsport. Reconnaissances were made and the seven corps were placed in position to launch an attack if and when one should be ordered. Apparently at this late date, Meade was still taking counsel of his fears and was apparently unwilling to bear the responsibility of making the decision alone. So again he called his corps commanders to a council of war, which convened on the evening of Sunday, July 12, and which included Generals Wadsworth, Hays, French, Sykes, Sedgwick, Howard, Slocum, and Pleasonton. Following a full discussion of the situation, a vote was taken on the expediency of attacking the enemy Monday morning. Howard, Wadsworth, and Pleasonton all voted to attack, but the others were opposed. Meade expressed an opinion in favor of attacking, but stated he would not do so against the opinion and advice of a majority of his corps commanders. And on that note the council ended. Some at least of the generals who voted in the negative had earlier been strongly in favor of a rapid advance on the heels of the enemy after Pickett's repulse on July 3, but now they felt that the opportunity had been lost and the conditions were unfavorable to an attack.

Did Meade Want Lee to Escape?

Many were the missed opportunities which a resourceful and aggressive army commander would have grasped had he been in Meade's position. It seemed as if Meade had shot his bolt at Gettysburg and had reached that mental state where what he wanted most was for Lee to recross the Potomac and spare him the necessity of another major battle. Whether he felt that way from July 4 on will never be known. He *did* send the Federal cavalry to harass Lee's retreating columns; he *had* told French to destroy their bridges; and on July 5 he *had* wired directions to Washington to ship his bridge trains to Harper's

RAILROAD TORN UP BY THE CONFEDERATES WITHDRAWING FROM PENNSYLVANIA
Note the telegraph wires on the ground.

Ferry; all of which moves could have been the prelude to an annihilation attack.

But action was not taken to place his cavalry in the Valley to actually block Lee's retreat. And he did instruct his corps commanders not to bring on a general engagement in the course of the withdrawal. Meade was informed by his train commander, General Benham, that the two pontoon bridges had reached Harper's Ferry by July 9, ready to be towed wherever they might be required on the Potomac. But that's the last that was heard about the bridge trains, which could have so effectively been used in transferring a portion of Meade's cavalry to the south side of the river, where they should easily have been able to prevent Lee from recrossing at Falling Waters and Williamsport. That of course would have made a major battle inevitable on the north side of the river, and affords one more bit of evidence that Meade wanted Lee to get across without a fight.

When Halleck received Meade's report on the negative vote cast by his council of war of July 12, he wired Meade the following day:

> Yours of 5:00 P.M. is received. You are strong enough to attack and defeat the enemy before he can effect a crossing. Act upon your own judgment and make your generals execute your orders. Call no council of war. It is proverbial that councils of war never fight. Reinforcements are pushed on as rapidly as possible. Do not let the enemy escape.

Lee Crosses Potomac Unhindered

Monday the 13th dawned rainy and misty, and little could be learned of the enemy's position. That night General Meade decided to attack the next morning and orders to that effect were issued. But it was on Monday the 13th that the Confederate pontoon bridge was restored at Fall-

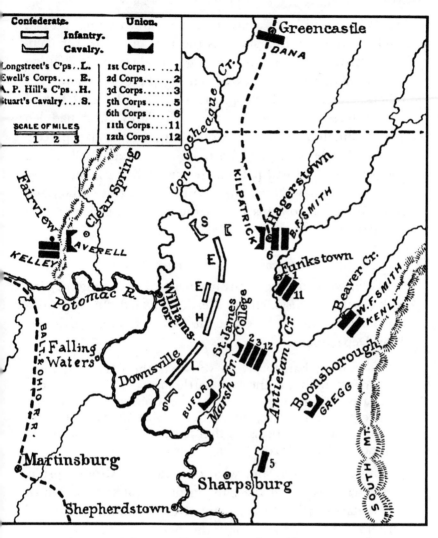

Map 18. THE SITUATION JULY 13

This map shows in broad outline the defensive position which Lee used to cover his crossings at Williamsport and Falling Waters. The Union corps came into position opposite Lee, but at a respectful distance. They showed more of a defensive than an offensive attitude. Nevertheless Meade, prodded from Washington, ordered an attack for the morning of the 14th. But it was too late; Lee late on the 13th crossed safely to the Virginia side. It will be noted that there are several Federal units participating in this situation which are not listed as being assigned to the Army of the Potomac. These are parts of the commands of Couch, French, and the Department of West Virginia which were ordered to support Meade.

ing Waters and Lee's army, by bridge and wading, crossed safely to the Virginia side. As the rear guard under General Pettigrew was approaching the bridge at Falling Waters Kilpatrick attacked, killing Pettigrew and 125 others, and taking 1,500 prisoners with a Federal loss of 105. Interestingly enough it was Pettigrew who had led the reconnaissance toward Gettysburg on the day preceding the battle, had played a part in the opening fight on the first day, and had participated in Pickett's great charge on the third day. Now, among the last to leave Maryland soil, he was to lose his life in the final struggle north of the Potomac.

Disappointment in Washington

When word of Lee's crossing reached Washington, Halleck's July 14 dispatch to Meade revealed the keen disappointment that was felt at the White House and in the War Department:

> I need hardly say to you that the escape of Lee's Army without another battle has created great dissatisfaction in the mind of the President and it will require an active, energetic pursuit on your part to remove the impression that it has not been sufficiently active heretofore.

This message was somewhat of a blow to Meade's pride, puncturing as it did the balloon of self-satisfaction which a few days earlier had prompted commendatory General Orders to the Army in the following language:

Headquarters, Army of the Potomac,
July 4, 1863.
General Orders, No. 68.

> The Commanding General, in behalf of the country, thanks the Army of the Potomac for the glorious result of the recent operations.

LEE'S FORCES RECROSSING THE POTOMAC

An enemy superior in numbers and flushed with the pride of a successful invasion, attempted to overcome and destroy this Army. Utterly baffled and defeated, he has now withdrawn from the contest. The privations and fatigue the Army has endured, and the heroic courage and gallantry it has displayed will be matters of history to be remembered.

Our task is not yet accomplished, and the Commanding General looks to the Army for greater efforts to drive from our soil every vestige of the presence of the invader.

It is right and proper that we should, on all suitable occasions, return our grateful thanks to the Almighty Disposer of events, that in the goodness of His providence He has thought fit to give victory to the cause of the just.

By Command of Major-General MEADE.

Official.

S. Williams,
Asst. Adjt. Gen.

It was the third paragraph of those orders which caused Lincoln to tear his hair in frustration. Was that all that Meade was going to do, "drive the invaders from our soil"!

Meade naturally regarded Halleck's dispatch as a censure. Somewhat reminiscent of Hooker's state of mind in late June, he suggested to Halleck that he would like to be relieved of command. Halleck took the request to Lincoln, who immediately sat down and composed a stinging letter to Meade, while Halleck sent off the following dispatch the same day:

> My telegram stating the disappointment of the President at the escape of Lee's Army was not intended as a censure, but as a stimulus to an active pursuit. It is not deemed a sufficient cause for your application to be relieved.

Meade considered the phrase "spur me on to an active pursuit" as more offensive than the original message, but he said no more about resigning.

This was what the frustrated Lincoln wrote out in longhand:

> Executive Mansion,
> Washington, July 14, 1863.
>
> Major-General Meade:
>
> I have just seen your dispatch to General Halleck, asking to be relieved of your command because of a supposed censure of mine. I am very, very grateful to you for the magnificent success you gave the cause of the country at Gettysburg; and I am sorry now to be the author of the slightest pain to you. But I was in such deep distress myself that I could not restrain some expression of it. I have been oppressed nearly ever since the battles at Gettysburg by what appeared to be evidences that yourself and General Couch and General Smith were not seeking a collision with the

enemy, but were trying to get him across the river
without another battle. What these evidences were,
if you please, I hope to tell you at some time when
we shall both feel better. The case, summarily stated,
is this: You fought and beat the enemy at Gettysburg,
and, of course, to say the least, his loss was as great
as yours. He retreated, and you did not, as it seemed
to me, pressingly pursue him; but a flood in the river
detained him till, by slow degrees, you were again
upon him. You had at least twenty thousand veteran
troops directly with you, and as many more raw ones
within supporting distance, all in addition to those
who fought with you at Gettysburg, while it was not
possible that he had received a single recruit, and yet
you stood and let the flood run down, bridges be
built, and the enemy move away at his leisure without attacking him. And Couch and Smith! The latter
left Carlisle in time, upon all ordinary calculation,
to have aided you in the last battle at Gettysburg, but
he did not arrive. At the end of more than ten days,
I believe twelve, under constant urging, he reached
Hagerstown from Carlisle, which is not an inch over
fifty-five miles, if so much, and Couch's movement
was very little different.

Again my dear general, I do not believe you appreciate the magnitude of the misfortune involved in
Lee's escape. He was within your easy grasp, and to
have closed upon him would, in connection with our
other late successes, have ended the war. As it is, the
war will be prolonged indefinitely. If you could not
safely attack Lee last Monday, how can you possibly
do so south of the river, when you can take with you
very few more than two thirds of the force you then
had in hand? It would be unreasonable to expect,
and I do not expect (that), you can now effect much.
Your golden opportunity is gone, and I am distressed
immeasurably because of it.

I beg you will not consider this a prosecution or
persecution of yourself. As you had learned that I was

dissatisfied, I have thought it best to kindly tell you why.

The following day the President, having cooled off somewhat, decided not to send the letter. Had he done so, on top of Halleck's critical telegram, Meade's name would almost inevitably have been added to the long list of dismissed army commanders. But Lincoln's sense of fairness and justness intervened, although he may have been partly influenced in his decision by the reflection that half a loaf was better than the breadless diet of military victories to which his generals had heretofore conditioned the country.

Presumably Lincoln and Halleck together decided that the Army of the Potomac, which had fought well at Gettysburg, scarcely deserved the implied reproach to their courage and fidelity that publication of the letter would have brought.

Although Meade was retained at the head of the Army of the Potomac until the end of the war, he never regained the full confidence of the War Department or the President. After Vicksburg, Lincoln called Grant in from the west, placed him in supreme command of all the Federal armies, and saw to it that Meade's defensive psychology should not again be permitted to come into play. The result was that Grant actually, although not in name, commanded the Army of the Potomac from then on, while Meade's role became largely an administrative one.

EPILOGUE

GETTYSBURG marked the climax of the Confederacy's supreme effort of the war. The Fourth of July, 1863 in retrospect was an Independence Day of vast historic significance, coupling as it did the capitulation of Vicksburg and the failure of Lee's invasion of the North, with all that those two important events were destined to mean for the preservation of the Union.

Viewed strictly as a military operation the battle could be termed a draw in that neither contestant was destroyed, there was no question of a surrender, and the casualties were comparable. Furthermore the ostensible winner, Meade, was sufficiently in shock, mentally if not physically, that he made no effort for at least forty-eight hours after the fighting was over to again risk tangling with his opponent, although the latter remained within sight and hearing until Sunday, July 5, and practically invited him to resume the battle.

From the strategic viewpoint, however, it was a stunning setback for the Confederacy. Gettysburg and Vicksburg together revived the Northern morale, drove the antiwar element underground, assured nonintervention on behalf of the Confederacy at the hands of England and France, and correspondingly brought home to the South the virtual hopelessness of winning.

The Confederate losses had been crippling but not mortal, and to that dubious extent Gettysburg was a Northern success. Meade himself never claimed it as a military victory, and the attitude of the Confederate rank and file, as they trudged wearily back to the Potomac and then to Virginia, was certainly not that of a defeated army.

The tactical fruits of the Gettysburg battle should however have fallen into the Federal lap, had Meade displayed the qualities of generalship to pluck them. Lincoln saw that clearly and was sorely disappointed at Meade's post-battle sluggishness. The opportunity to end the war in short order had been a golden one, in the President's view, but now it would have to run its course for two more long, weary, bloody years.

Lee and many of his generals were realistic enough to realize that their bold gamble had failed and that it was only a question of time until the doom of the Confederacy would be sealed. The Army of the Potomac had fought magnificently and, for a change, been led with professional competence, which was something new and foreboding.

The Almighty must have taken a direct hand in shaping the events which culminated in Gettysburg, either because He just couldn't trust the North to win the war by themselves or else on the premise that He had universal plans for later centuries which called for a united America, and developments by 1863 had failed to conform to His long-range program.

It has been said, more or less jocularly, that the Lord is on the side of the general with the most battalions, yet it doesn't always work out that way. Both Lee and Meade were God-fearing men, and the latter had more battalions. But Gettysburg was the first major battle that Lee lost in more than two years of war; it was historically his worst-fought battle, and on the record the Lord of Hosts seems to have shaped affairs so that the hopes of the Confederacy should be dashed at that small crossroads community.

Certainly the battles at Gettysburg were not planned

for that exact spot by either the North or the South. Lee's objective had been the York-Harrisburg area, where he would be in position to turn to his own advantage whatever strategic opportunity might present itself—a thrust at Baltimore, Washington, Philadelphia, or even New York. The stakes were high, and a mighty clash of arms somewhere, to determine who would sweep the chips from the table, was inevitable.

The defensive-minded Meade had his thoughts centered on a line along Big Pipe Creek, about 16 miles southeast of Gettysburg. Here he believed he could best protect Baltimore and Washington, in accordance with Stanton's directive of June 28, against an anticipated attack by Lee, when Lee should turn back from his advance toward the Susquehanna.

When the battle was joined by the armed clash a mile and a half west of Gettysburg on the morning of July 1, neither commander was ready for it nor desired to engage in a decisive test of arms on that day. Neither army had been concentrated—Lee was in the process of effecting his concentration, but Meade was still in a state of uncertainty as to where he would finally assemble his forces. As the picture unfolded, it became obvious that Gettysburg was the logical spot, forced by logistic circumstances. But ex post facto convictions that the convenient road net, of which the town was the center, or the parallel ridges which later gained such fame, were major tactical considerations that led either or both of the army commanders to select Gettysburg for the battle, are mere second sight.

Once committed, the three days of battle witnessed a massive slugging match between heavyweights. After the respective approach marches, which converged on Gettysburg from all points of the compass, there was a minimum of footwork and feinting, even by the cavalry. On the first day the contestants felt each other out without using their full strength; on the second, the aggressor sparred for openings, while the defender awkwardly but successively parried each blow; and on the third the challenger, boring in for the knockout blow, was thrown back with bloodied nose. At the end of the third round, both fighters were figuratively leaning on the ropes in their respective corners. While neither could claim a clean-cut victory, and the decision was awarded to the defender on points, that decision proved to be an inconclusive one because the challenger, although injured, was given a respite to recover and to take on his opponent again and again.

Why did Lee fail at Gettysburg? There can be no categorical answer, because a host of factors contributed to the final result and the weight given to each depends in turn upon other imponderables, ad infinitum. And therein may lie the principal reason why the battle of Gettysburg offers such a fascinating subject for study, for conversation, for far-ranging speculation and for delightful, friendly argument.

Historians even now do not fully agree on specifics. One will say that Meade won a tactical victory but threw away the strategic fruits by letting Lee escape with most of his booty, wounded, and prisoners, with all 241 guns, and with seven of Meade's own field pieces. Another will say that Meade won because he had more luck and made fewer mistakes than Lee. Still another may point out that Lee may have been the loser because, in the only Civil War battle fought on Pennsylvania soil, the Army of the Potomac was commanded by a Pennsylvanian; two of the corps commanders who played a prominent part in shaping the destiny of the battle, Reynolds and Hancock, were Pennsylvanians; and many of the units which fought in the forefront during critical phases of the battle were

Pennsylvania regiments, which displayed fanatic zeal in defending their home folks and native soil and thus swung the balance in favor of the Union forces. And so on.

There will always be honest differences of opinion regarding Lee's failure to win at Gettysburg. The answers to the *what, when, where,* and *how* of the battle can all be found in recorded facts. But the persistent search for the answer to the *why* is buried in a confusing combination of factors, no one of which can fairly be considered decisive in itself, although each was a constituent element in the end result. The various elements are presented herewith:

Lee's selection of Ewell and A. P. Hill, inexperienced and untried as leaders of large bodies of troops, for two of his three principal commanders, when he reorganized his army after the battle of Chancellorsville.

Hooker's reorganization of the Federal cavalry and its long overdue restoration to a combat role, with the result that the cavalry of the opposing armies were placed on a more equal footing.

Lee's discretionary orders to Stuart at the start of the invasion, under which Stuart guessed wrong, turned right instead of left when he bumped into Hancock's corps north of the Rappahannock, and from then on until the end of the second day of the battle of Gettysburg was out of touch with Lee's army, with all the disadvantage to the latter thus implied.

Lee's compounding failure to use the cavalry that was still available to him, despite the absence of Stuart and his three brigades.

Lee's overconfident belief that his men were invincible, plus his failure to coordinate the functioning of his three army corps on the field at Gettysburg, and the absence of clear-cut attack orders to the several elements of his command.

Ewell's failure to cerebrate under discretionary authority, which in turn caused him to forfeit the opportunity to take Cemetery Hill the afternoon of the first day and virtually to mark time for the remaining two days.

Longstreet's recalcitrant dragging of his feet all through the campaign.

Harmonious cooperation missing between the three corps commanders, Longstreet, Ewell and Hill, and a fateful lack of decision in the use of supporting troops during the battle.

Overextension of the Confederate line, resulting in insufficient depth for maximum offensive results, and loss of time in the transmission of messages and orders from one flank to the other.

The absence of Stonewall Jackson.

The Confederate errors of omission and commission were in certain instances caused or at least affected by positive or negative action on the part of the Federals, for better or worse. But since Lee did not achieve a victory as he so confidently expected, a more searching analysis to determine the reasons for his failure is naturally beamed in his direction. Conversely, since the shortcomings and errors on the Federal side, and there were plenty, did not lead to a defeat, nor even to prevent a quasi-victory, the impact of such errors as did occur was of temporary duration.

Certain it is that the Battle of Gettysburg has earned the reputation of being the best known battle of the Civil War. For many years military students assigned to general staff duty of foreign armies have crossed the oceans for a detailed study of all aspects of that campaign, as a part of their professional education. It may even be that Gettysburg deserves to join the ranks of Creasy's Fifteen Decisive Battles of the World; indeed it is already so classified by some military historians.

The phenomenal resurgence of interest shown in recent years by the people of the United States in all phases of the War between the States testifies to the enduring value of the stirring events of those historic days nearly 100 years ago.

Could it be that later wars, in which the grandsons and greatgrandsons of the boys in Blue and Gray gave their lives for their united country, have played a significant part in fulfilling the immortal words of Abraham Lincoln, on the field at Gettysburg:

> We here highly resolve that these dead shall not have died in vain—that this Nation, under God, shall have a new birth of freedom—and that government of the people, by the people, for the people, shall not perish from the earth.

THE GETTYSBURG ADDRESS

The Procession of Troops and Spectators Moving on Baltimore Street En Route to the Dedicatory Exercises on November 19, 1863. This View is on the Outskirts of Gettysburg, near the Cemetery Where President Lincoln Delivered the Gettysburg Address.

BIBLIOGRAPHY

BALLARD, COLIN R. *The Military Genius of Abraham Lincoln.* Cleveland: The World Publishing Co., 1952.

Battles and Leaders of the Civil War, Vol. III. Contributions by Union and Confederate Officers. New York: The Century Company, 1884.

BUCKERIDGE, J. O. *Lincoln's Choice (The Story of the Spencer Repeater).* Harrisburg: The Stackpole Company, 1956.

CATTON, BRUCE. *Glory Road.* Garden City: Doubleday & Co., 1952.

CREASY, SIR EDWARD S. *Decisive Battles of the World.* Harrisburg: Military Service Publishing Co., 1943.

FREEMAN, DOUGLAS SOUTHALL. *Lee's Lieutenants, Vol. III.* New York: Charles Scribner's Sons, 1944.

FREEMAN, DOUGLAS SOUTHALL. *R. E. Lee.* 4 vols. New York: Charles Scribner's Sons, 1935.

FREMANTLE, LT. COL. ARTHUR J. L., H. M. Coldstream Guards. *The Fremantle Diary* (on his three months in the southern states). Edited by Walter Lord. Boston: Little, Brown and Co., 1954.

GUERNSEY, ALFRED H. AND ALLEN, HENRY M. *Harper's Pictorial History of the Great Rebellion.* New York: Harper & Bro., 1868.

HASKELL, FRANK ARETAS. *The Battle of Gettysburg.* New York: P. F. Collier & Son, The Harvard Classics, 1910.

History of Franklin County, Pennsylvania, Chicago: 1887.

HOKE, JACOB. *Gettysburg, The Great Invasion of 1863.* Dayton, Ohio: 1887.

JACOBS, M. *Notes on the Rebel Invasion and the Battle of Gettysburg.* Philadelphia: Lippincott, 1864.

MEADE, GEORGE GORDON. *With Meade at Gettysburg.* Philadelphia: Winston Co., 1930.

MIERS, EARL S. AND BROWN, RICHARD A. *Gettysburg.* New Brunswick: Rutgers University Press, 1948.

PRATT, FLETCHER. *Eleven Generals.* New York: Wm. Sloane Associates, 1949.

Scott, James K. P. *The Story of the Battles at Gettysburg.* Harrisburg: The Telegraph Press, 1927.

Steele, Matthew Forney. *American Campaigns.* 2 volumes. Washington: War Department Document No. 324.

Street, James. *The Civil War.* New York: Dial Press, 1953.

Thomason, John W. Jr. *Jeb Stuart.* New York: Charles Scribner's Sons, 1934.

War of the Rebellion: Official Records of the Union and Confederate Armies. Government Printing Office: 1882-1900.

Williams, Ben Ames. *House Divided.* Boston: Houghton Mifflin, 1947.

Williams, Kenneth P. *Lincoln Finds a General,* Vol. II. New York: The MacMillan Company, 1949.

Williams, T. Harry. *Lincoln and His Generals.* New York: Alfred A. Knopf, 1952.

INDEX